FOR ORGANS, PIANOS & ELECTRONIC KEYBOARDS

23

E-Z PLAY® TODAY

FIRST 50 SONGS
YOU SHOULD PLAY ON KEYBOARD

T0069365

ISBN 978-1-4950-9520-7

7777 W. BLUEMOUND RD. P.O. BOX 13819 MILWAUKEE, WI 53213

Visit Hal Leonard Online at
www.halleonard.com

CONTENTS

And So It Goes

Registration 10
Rhythm: Waltz or None

Words and Music by
Billy Joel

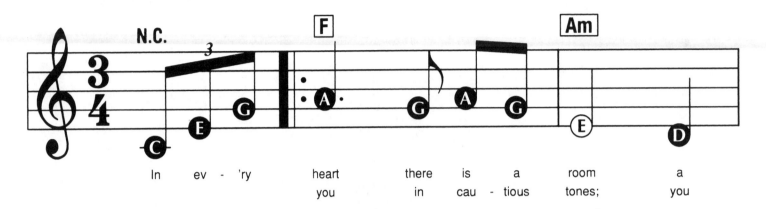

In ev - 'ry heart there is a room a
you in cau - tious tones; you

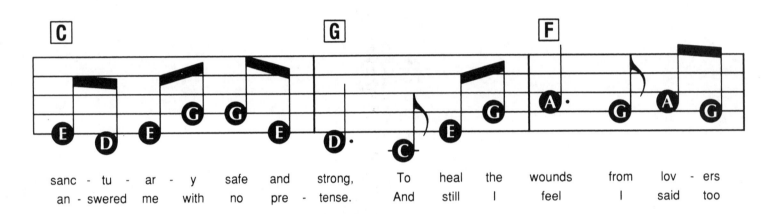

sanc - tu - ar - y safe and strong, To heal the wounds from lov - ers
an - swered me with no pre - tense. And still I feel I said too

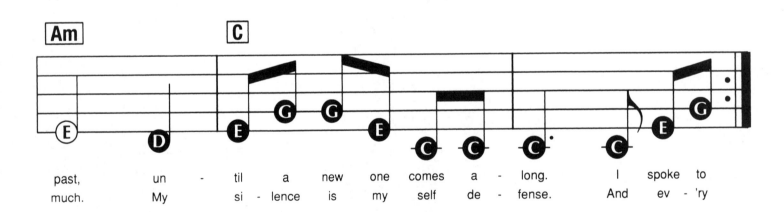

past, un - til a new one comes a - long. I spoke to
much. My si - lence is my self de - fense. And ev - 'ry

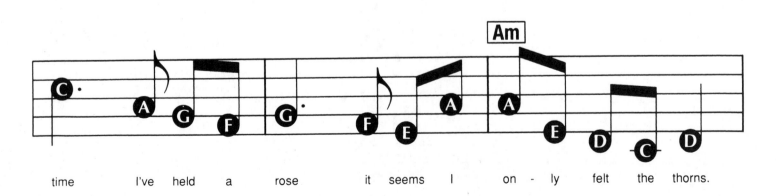

time I've held a rose it seems I on - ly felt the thorns.

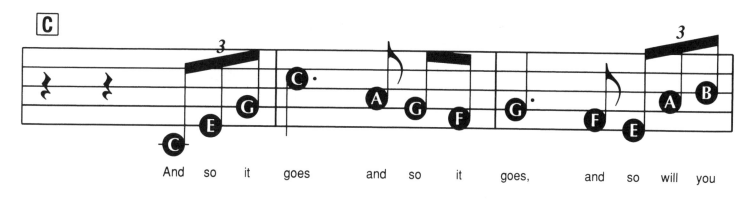

And so it goes and so it goes, and so will you

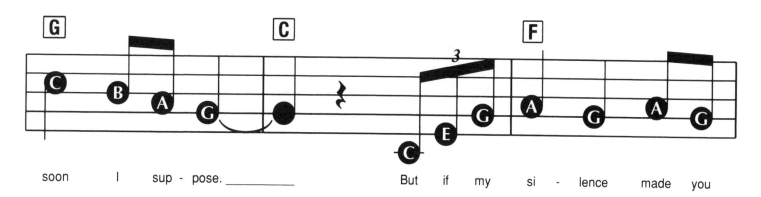

soon I sup - pose. _____ But if my si - lence made you

leave, then that would be my worst mis - take so I will

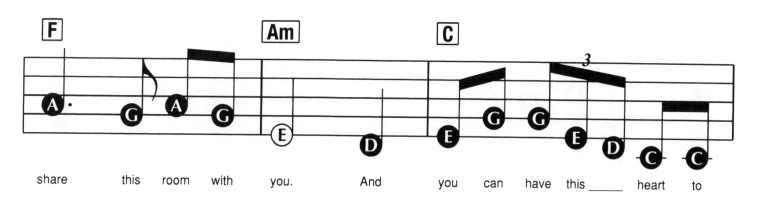

share this room with you. And you can have this ____ heart to

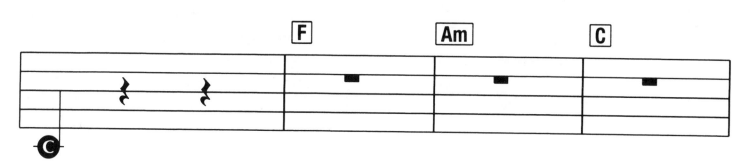

break.

6

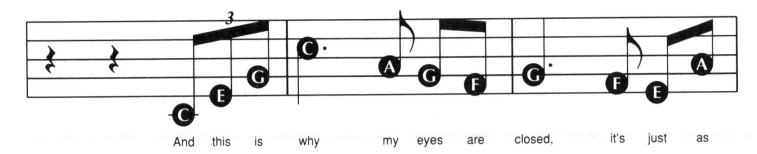

And this is why my eyes are closed, it's just as

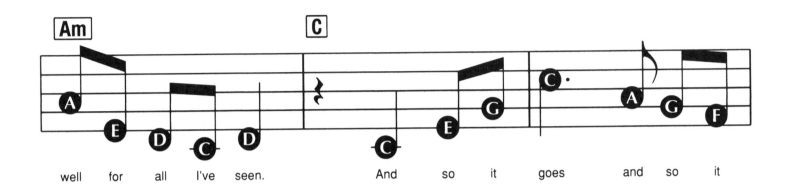

well for all I've seen. And so it goes and so it

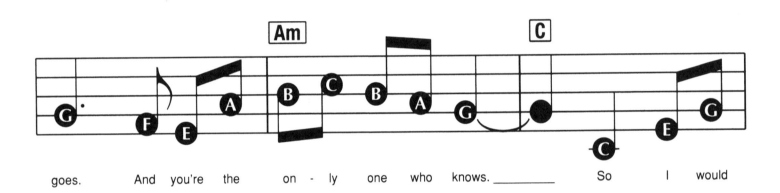

goes. And you're the on - ly one who knows. _____ So I would

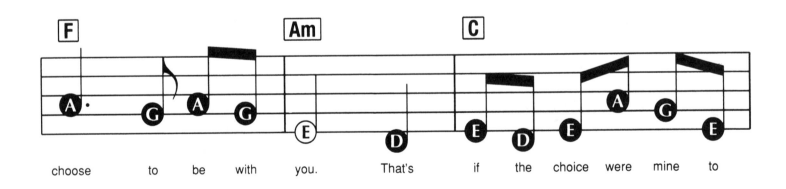

choose to be with you. That's if the choice were mine to

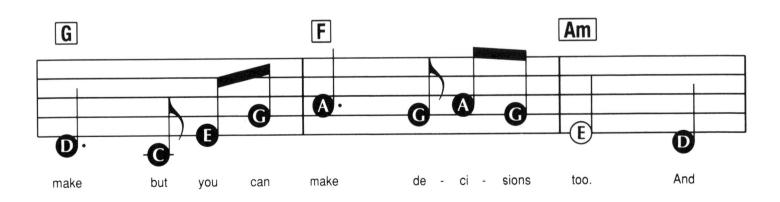

make but you can make de - ci - sions too. And

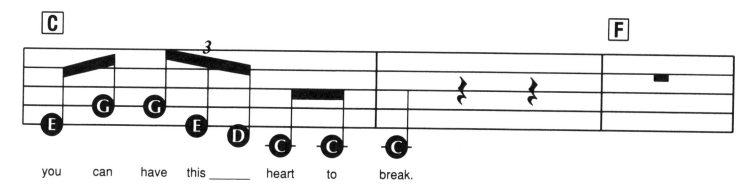

you can have this _____ heart to break.

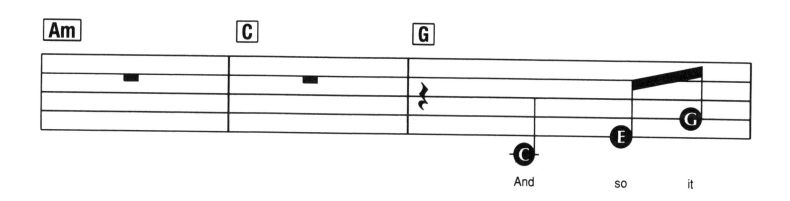

And so it

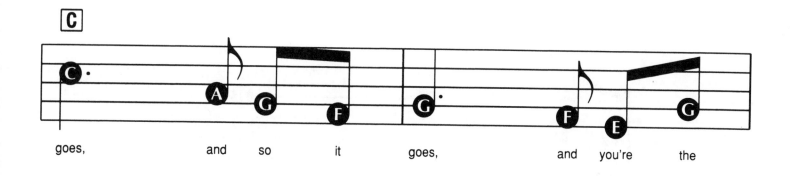

goes, and so it goes, and you're the

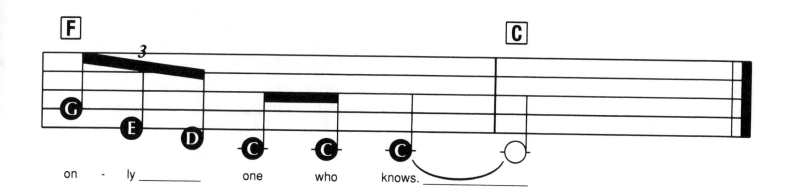

on - ly _____ one who knows. _____

Angela
Theme from the Paramount Television Series TAXI

Registration 1
Rhythm: 8-Beat

By Bob James

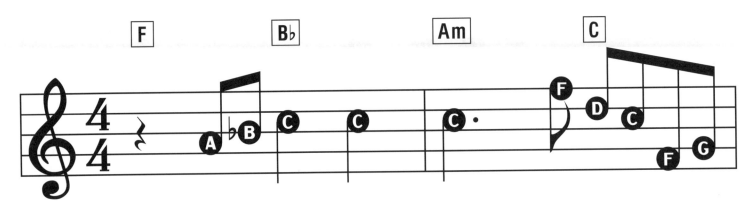

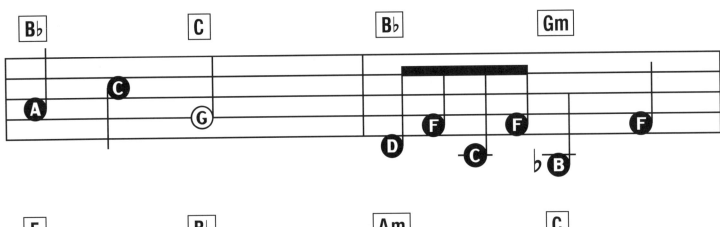

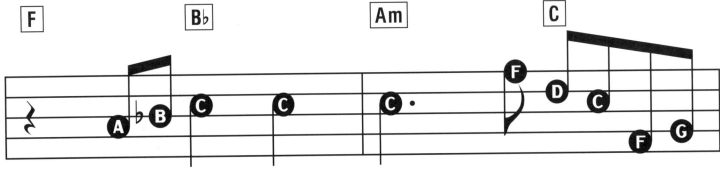

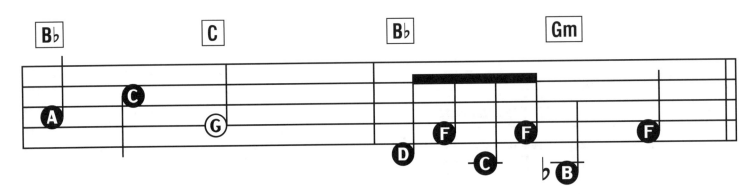

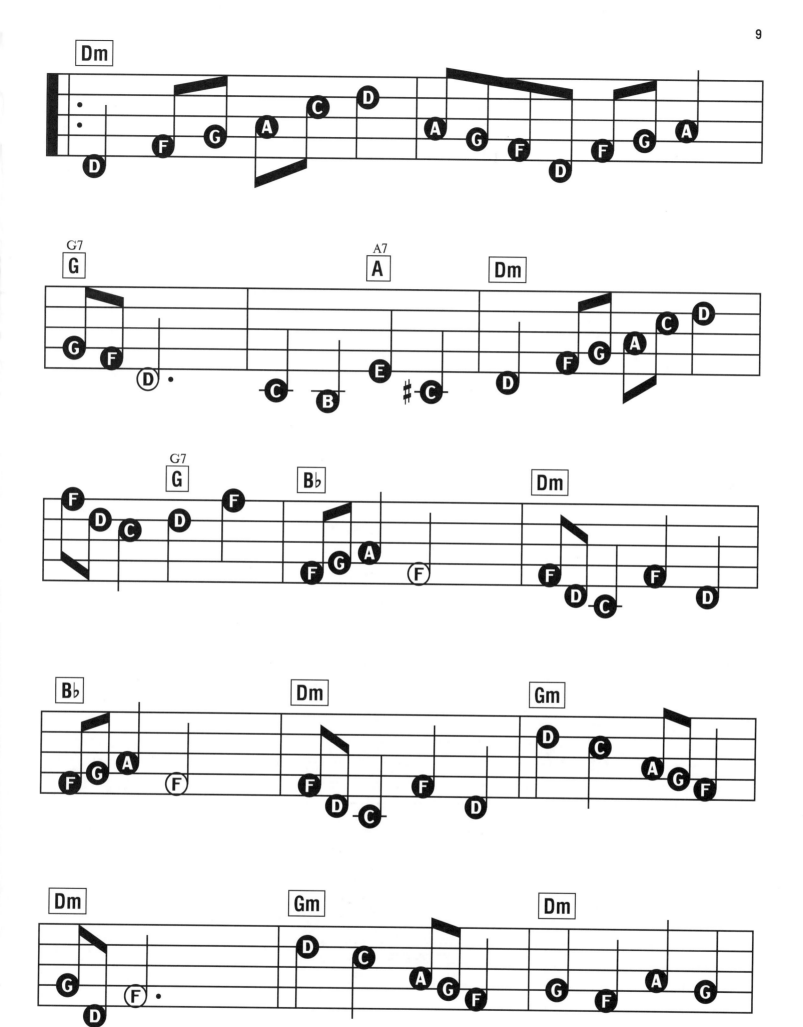

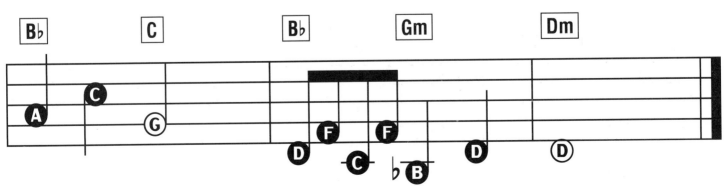

Any Dream Will Do

from JOSEPH AND THE AMAZING TECHNICOLOR® DREAMCOAT

Registration 6
Rhythm: Ballad or Shuffle

Music by Andrew Lloyd Webber
Lyrics by Tim Rice

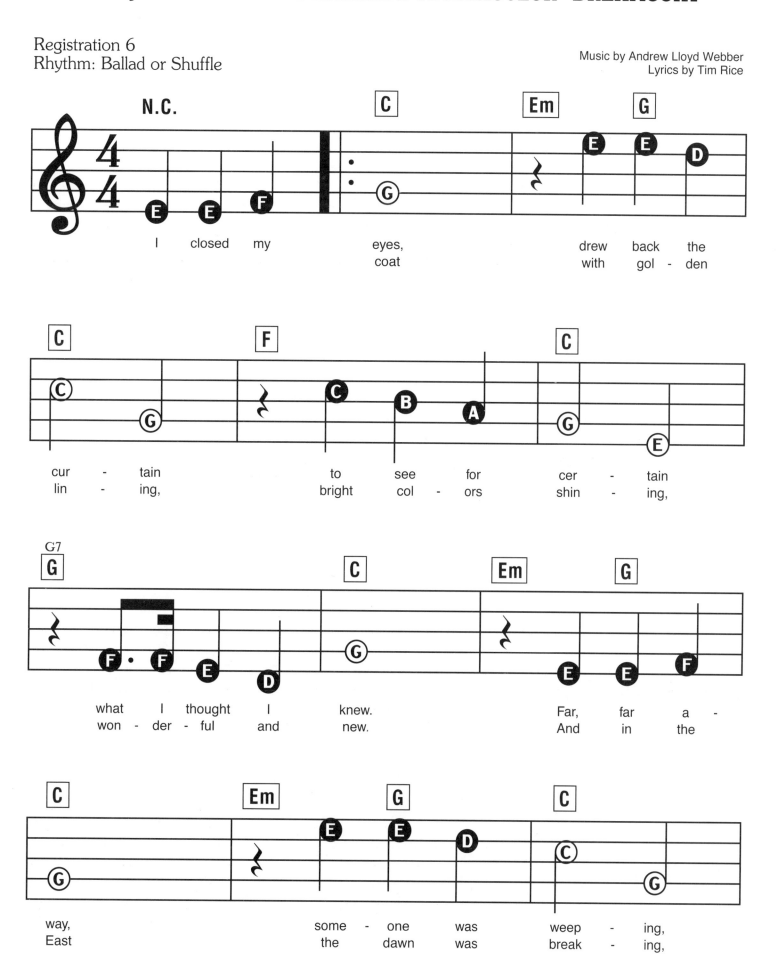

12

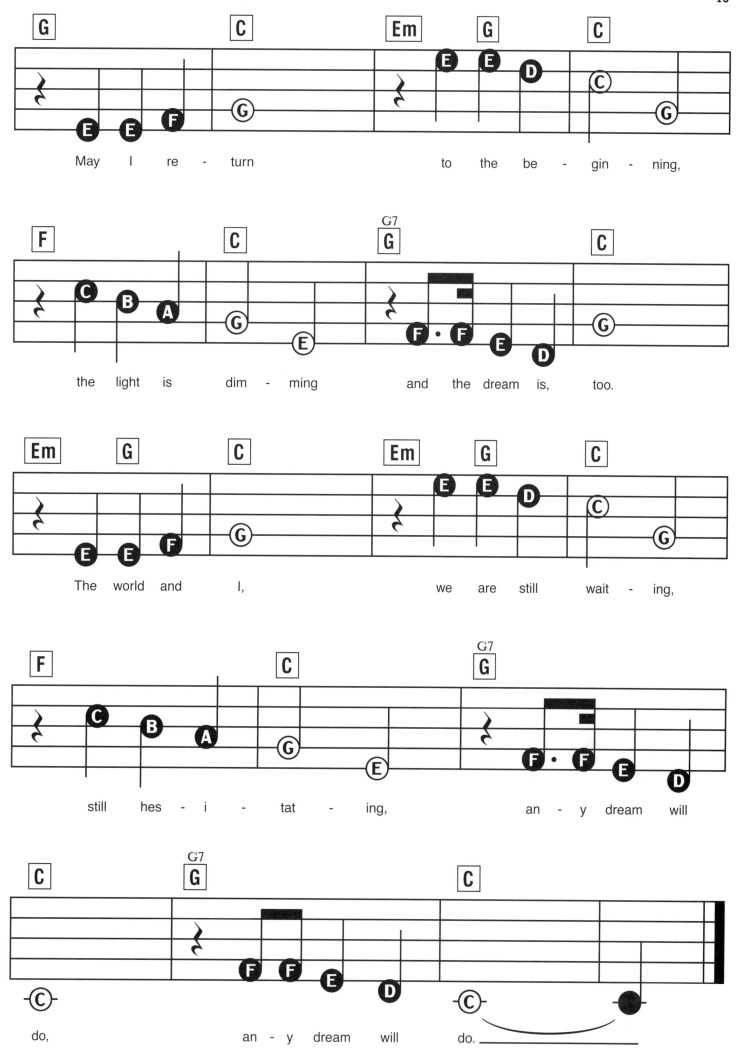

As Time Goes By
from CASABLANCA

Registration 8
Rhythm: Ballad

Words and Music by
Herman Hupfeld

You must re-mem-ber this, a kiss is still a kiss, A sigh is just a sigh; The fun-da-men-tal things ap-ply, As time goes by._____ And when two lov-ers woo, they still say, "I love you," On that you can re-ly; No mat-ter what the fu-ture brings, As time goes by._____

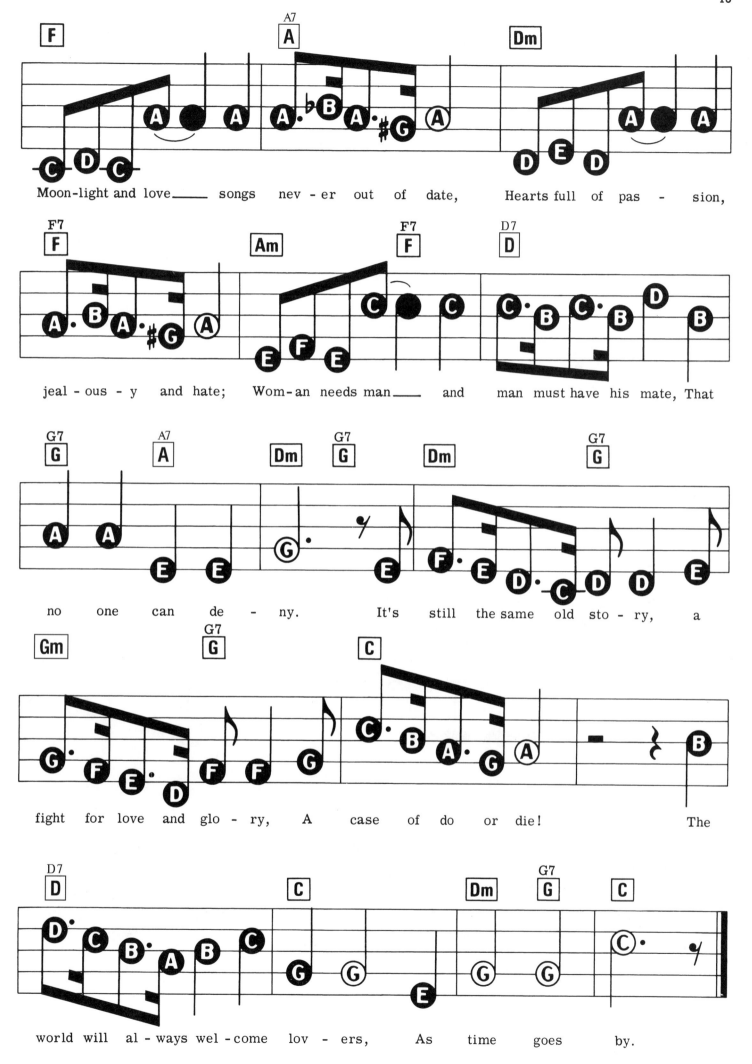

Axel F
Theme from the Paramount Motion Picture BEVERLY HILLS COP

Registration 5
Rhythm: Rock or 16-Beat

By Harold Faltermeyer

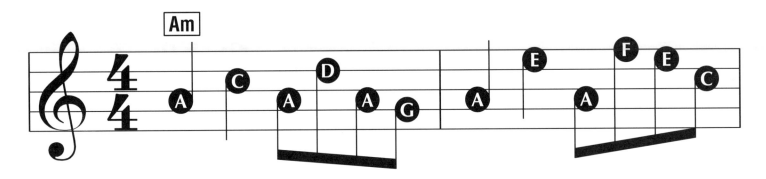

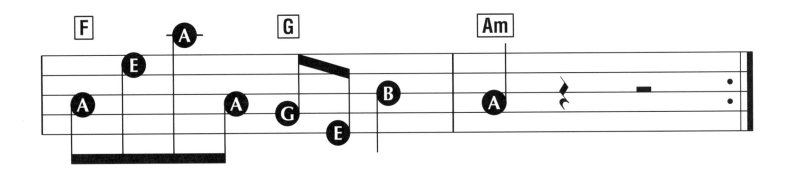

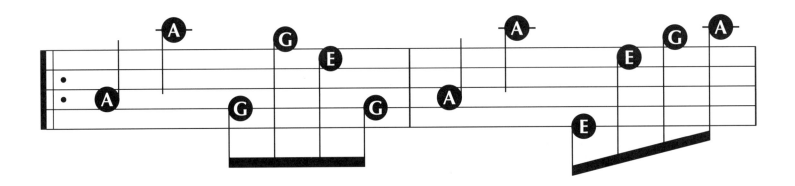

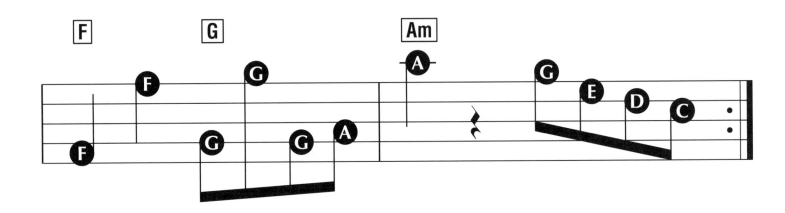

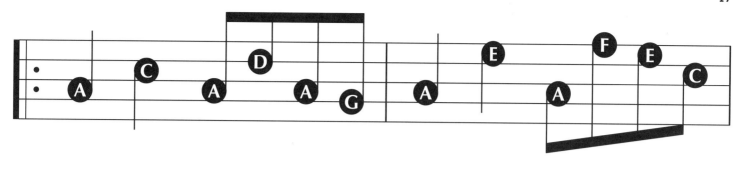

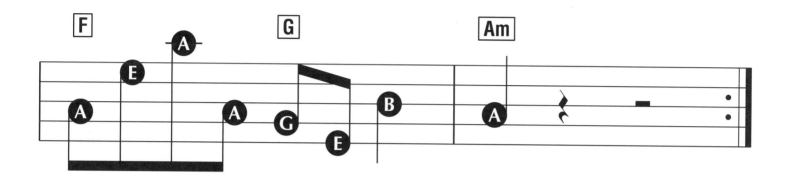

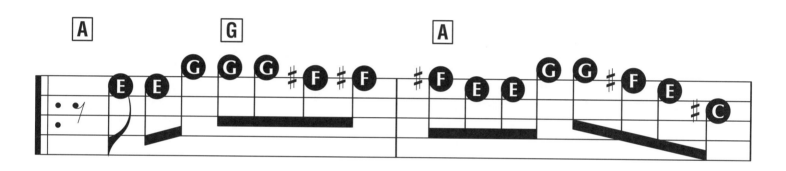

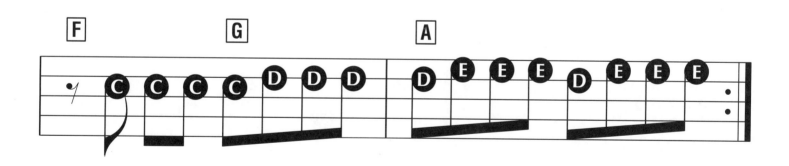

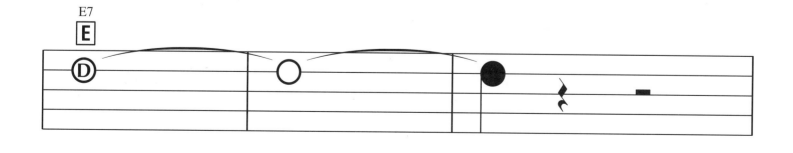

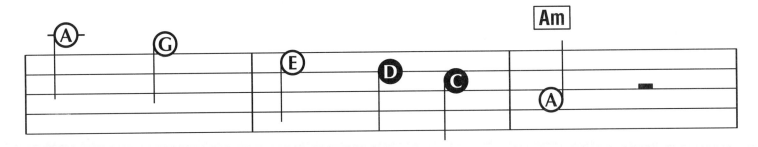

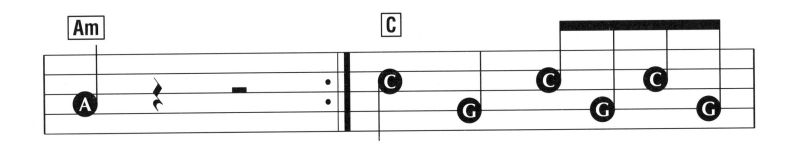

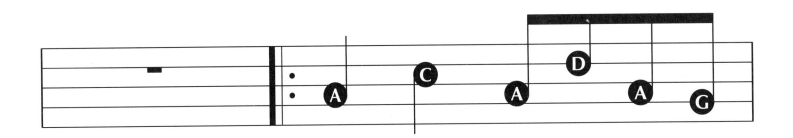

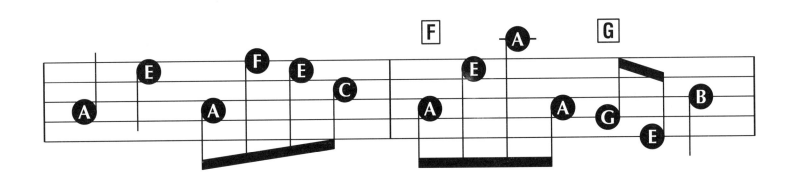

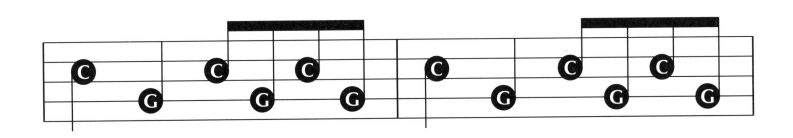

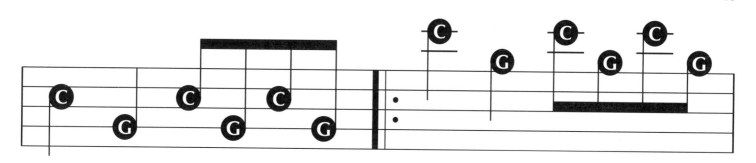

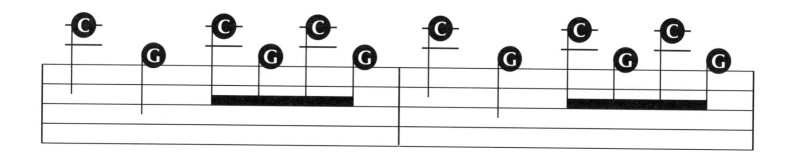

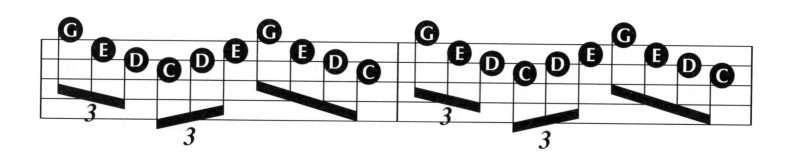

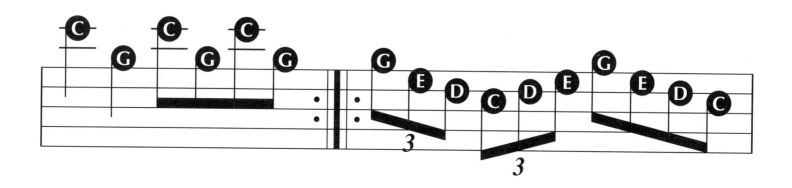

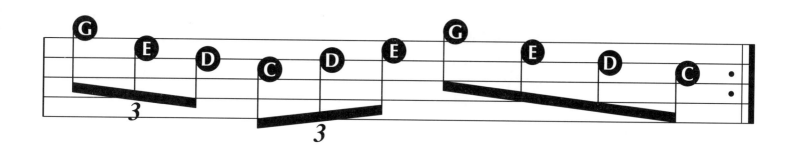

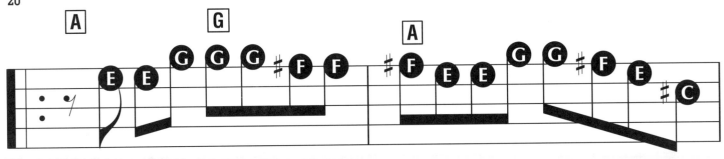
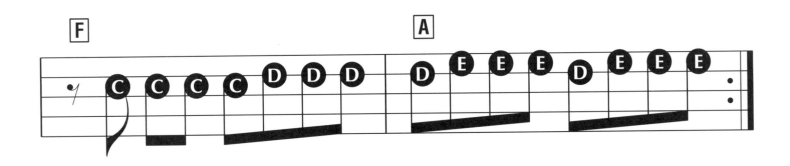
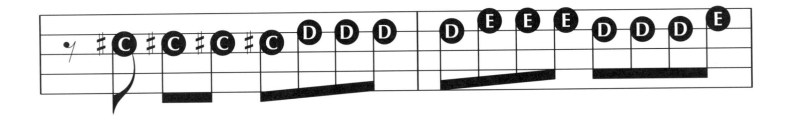
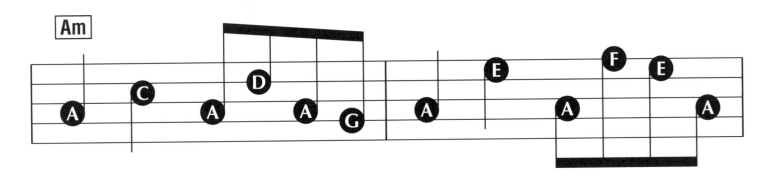
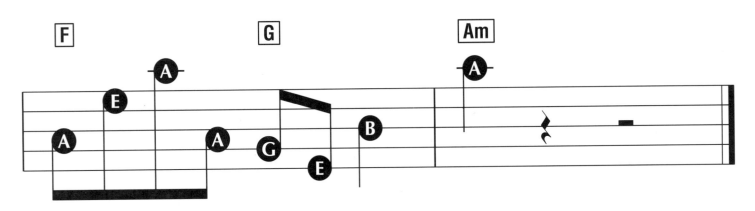

Breakdown

Registration 4
Rhythm: Shuffle or Rock

Words and Music by
Tom Petty

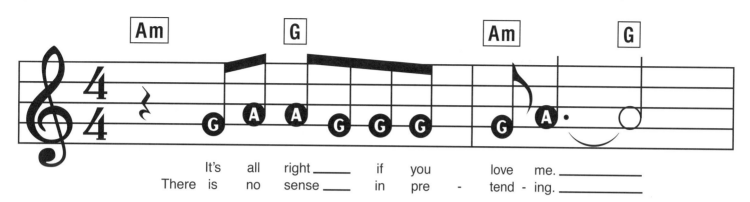

It's all right____ if you love me.____
There is no sense____ in pre - tend - ing.____

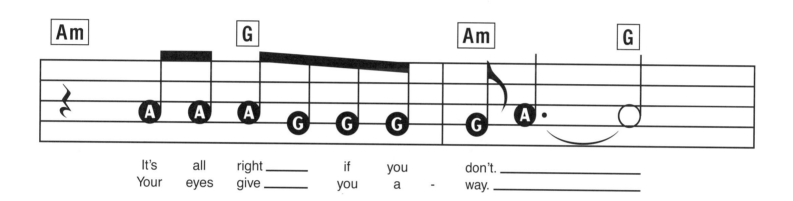

It's all right____ if you don't.____
Your eyes give____ you a - way.____

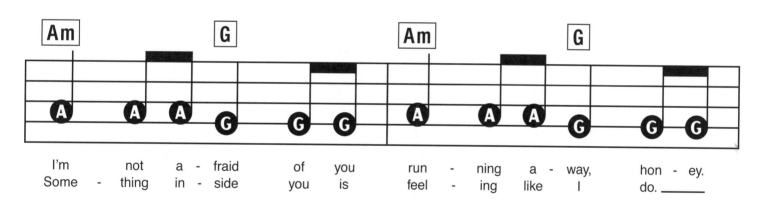

I'm not a - fraid of you run - ning a - way, hon - ey.
Some - thing in - side you is feel - ing like I do.____

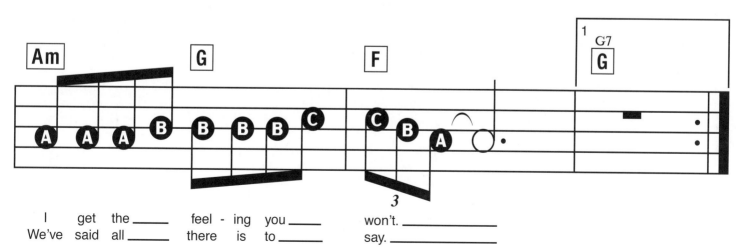

I get the____ feel - ing you____ won't.____
We've said all____ there is to____ say.____

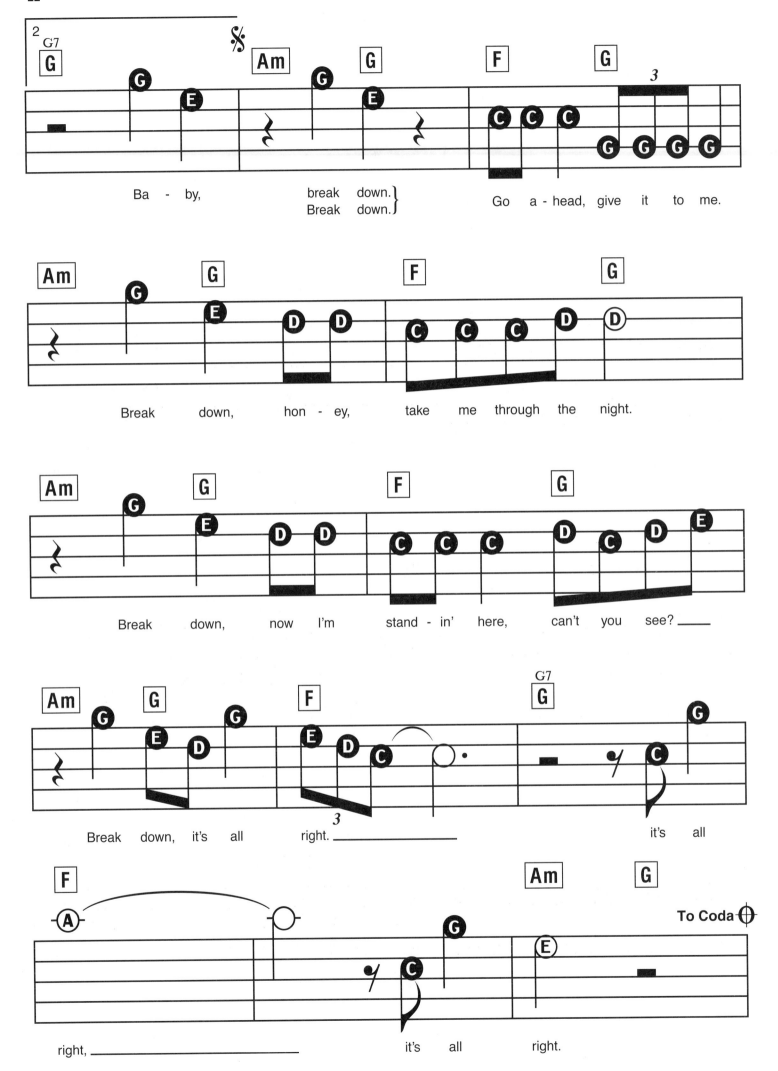

23

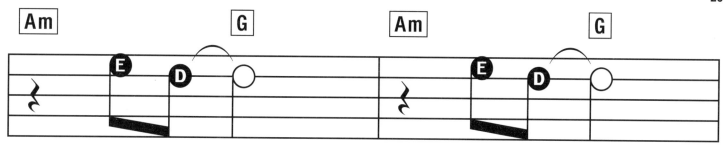

(Instrumental)

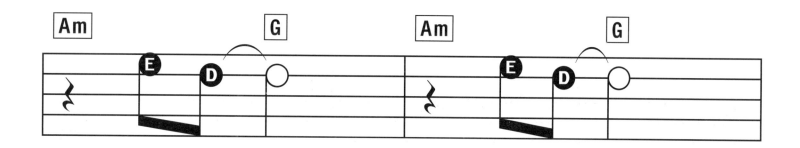

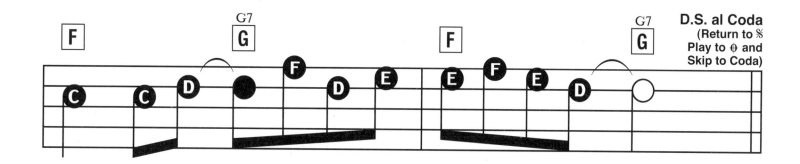

D.S. al Coda
(Return to ℅
Play to ⊕ and
Skip to Coda)

CODA

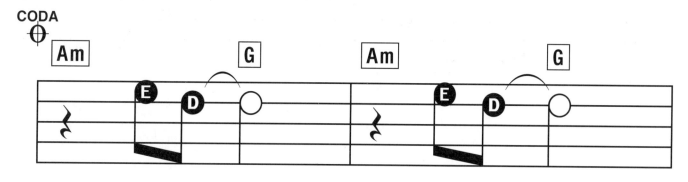

(Instrumental)

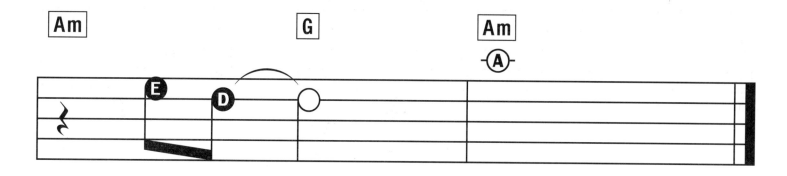

Babe

Words and Music by
Dennis DeYoung

Registration 1
Rhythm: Pops or Rock

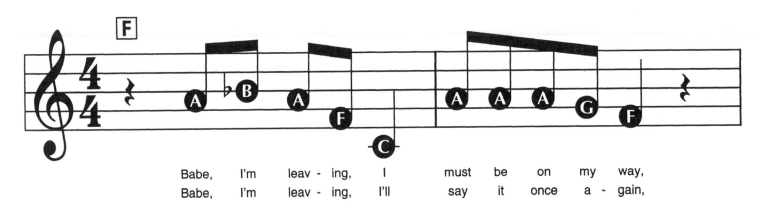

Babe, I'm leav - ing, I   must be on my way,
Babe, I'm leav - ing, I'll   say it once a - gain,

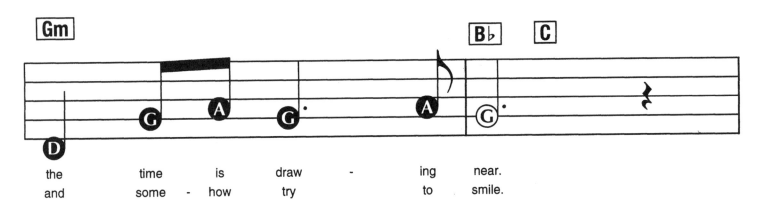

the   time is draw   -   ing   near.
and   some - how try   to   smile.

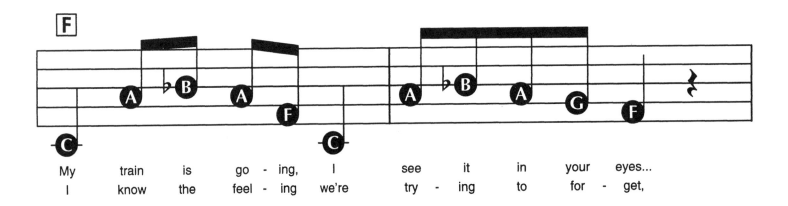

My   train is go - ing, I   see it in your eyes...
I   know the feel - ing we're   try - ing to for - get,

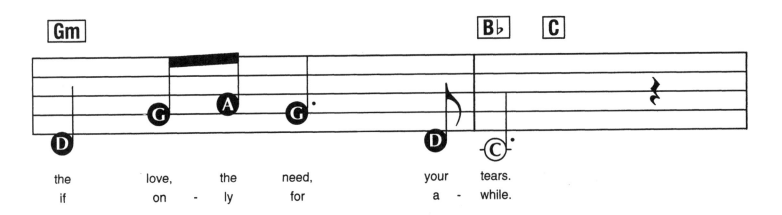

the   love, the need,   your   tears.
if   on - ly for   a   while.

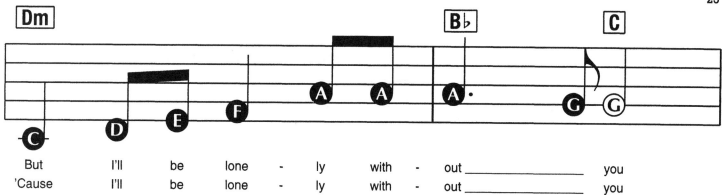

But / 'Cause I'll be lone - ly with - out _____ you

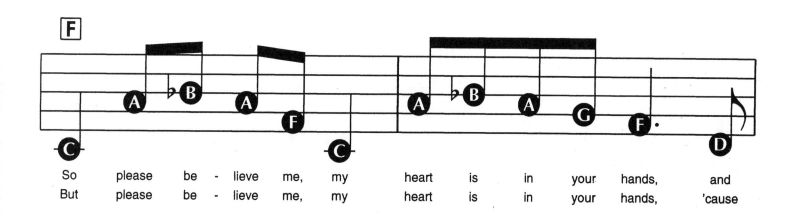

and I'll need your love to see me through.

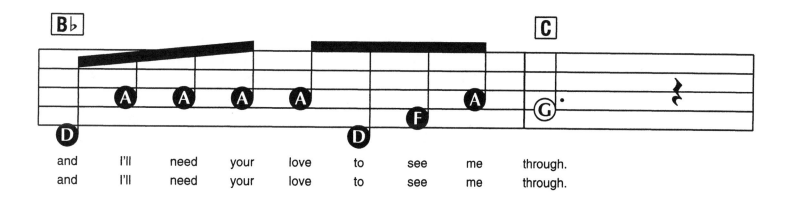

So / But please be - lieve me, my heart is in your hands, and / 'cause

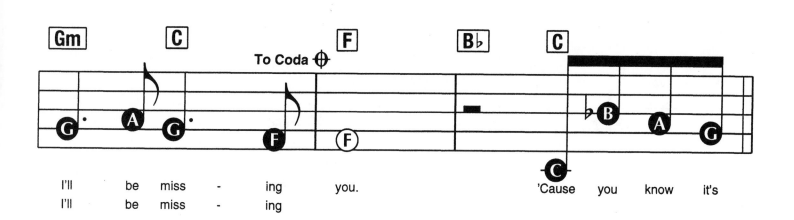

To Coda

I'll be miss - ing you. / 'Cause you know it's
I'll be miss - ing

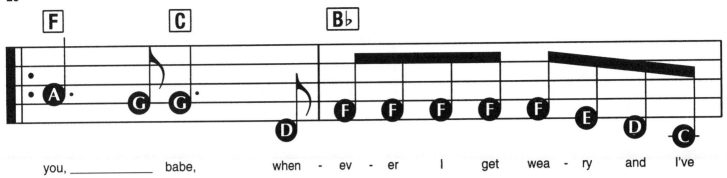

you, _____ babe, when - ev - er I get wea - ry and I've

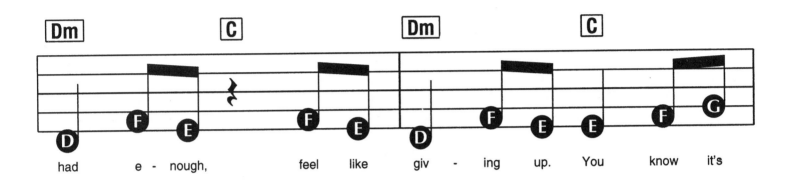

had e - nough, feel like giv - ing up. You know it's

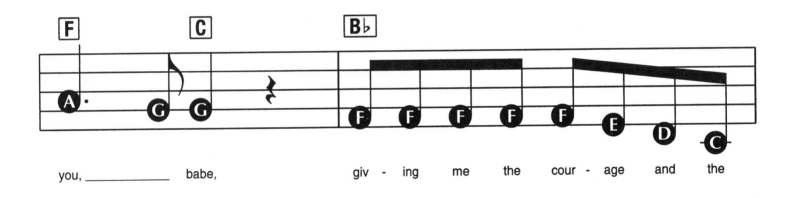

you, _____ babe, giv - ing me the cour - age and the

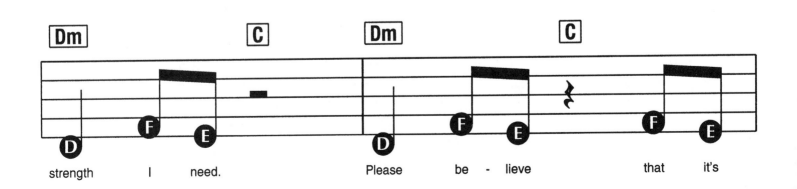

strength I need. Please be - lieve that it's

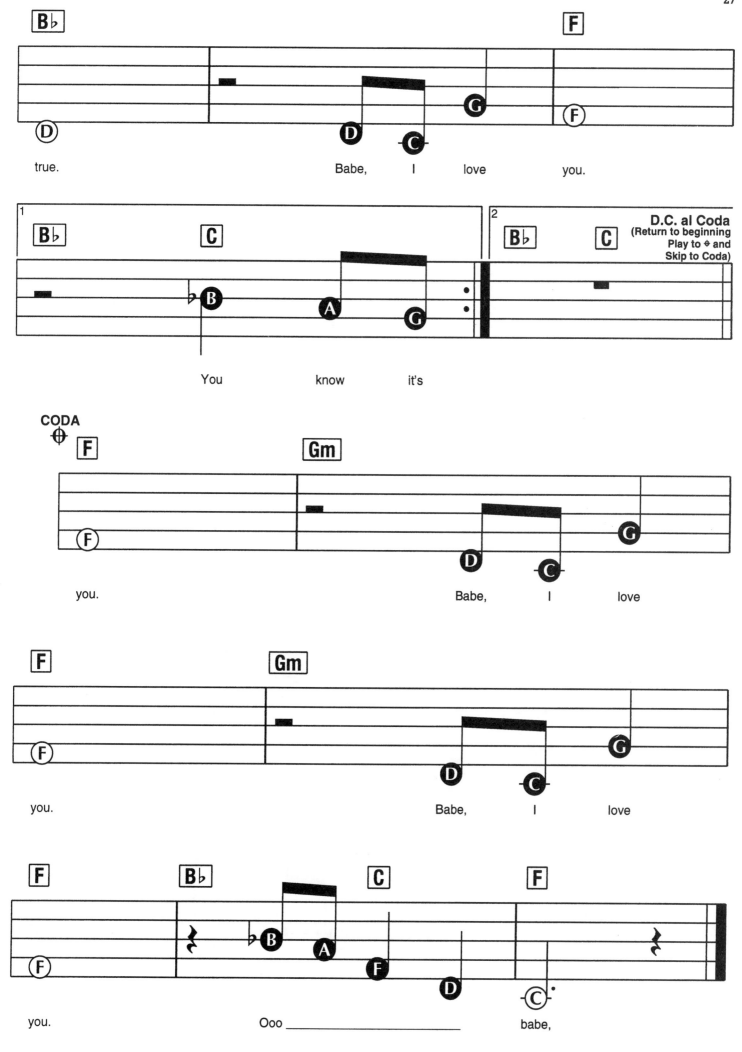

Billie Jean

Registration 4
Rhythm: Rock

Words and Music by
Michael Jackson

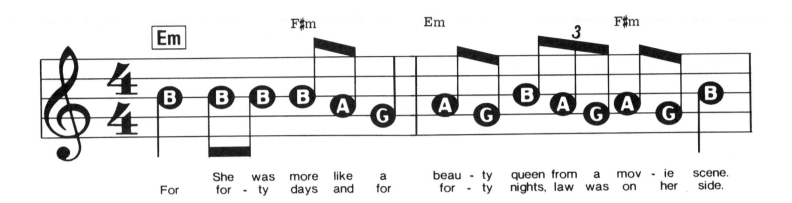

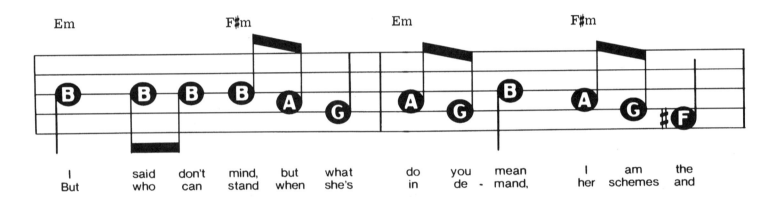

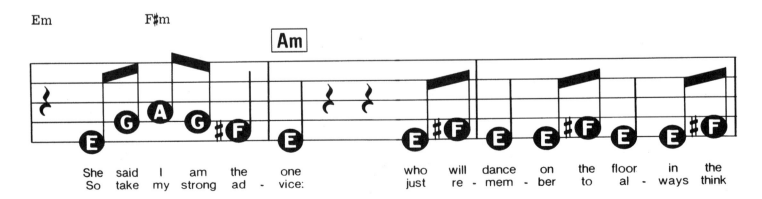

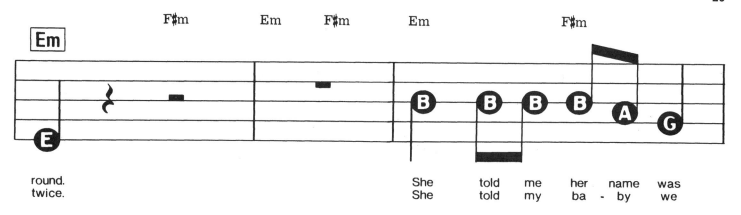

round.
twice.

She told me her name was
She told my ba - by we

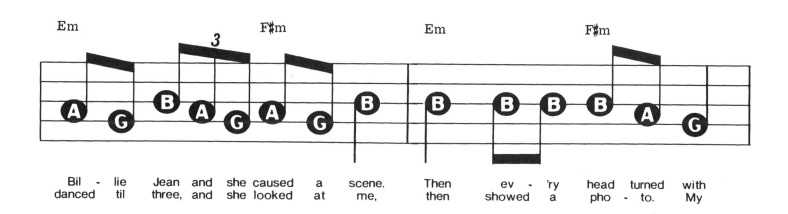

Bil - lie Jean and she caused a scene. Then ev - 'ry head turned with
danced til three, and she looked at me, then showed a pho - to. My

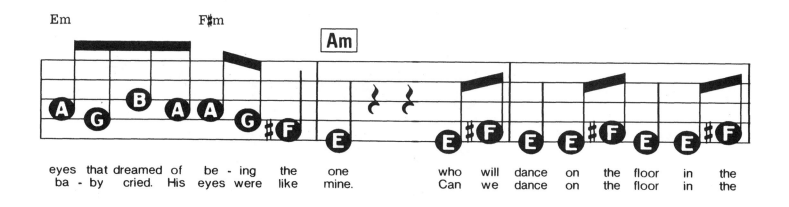

eyes that dreamed of be - ing the one who will dance on the floor in the
ba - by cried. His eyes were like one mine. Can we dance on the floor in the

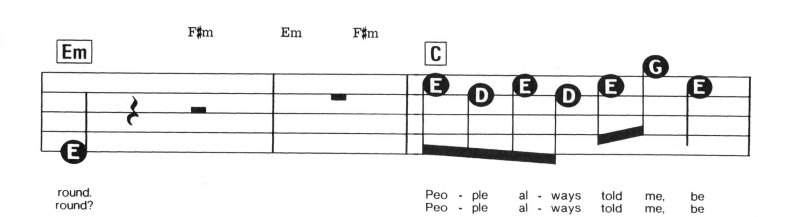

round.
round?

Peo - ple al - ways told me, be
Peo - ple al - ways told me, be

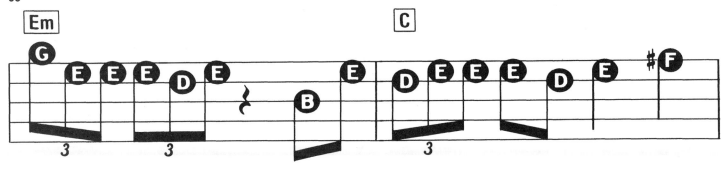

care - ful   of   what   you   do.   And   don't   go   a - round   break - in'   young   girls'
care - ful   of   what   you   do.   And   don't   go   a - round   break - in'   young   girls'

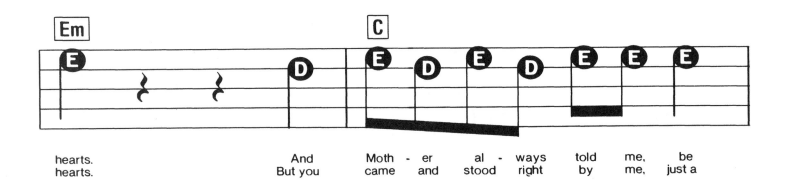

hearts.   And   Moth - er   al - ways   told   me,   be
hearts.   But you   came   and   stood   right   by   me,   just a

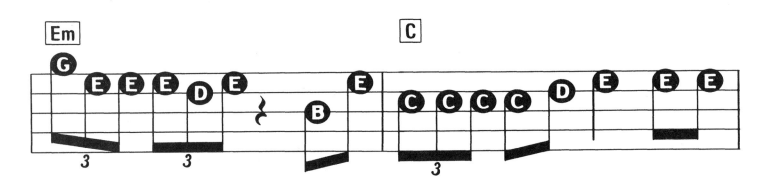

care - ful   of   who   you love.   And   be   care - ful   of   what   you   do.   'cause the
smell   of   sweet ___   per - fume.   This   hap - pened much ___   too   soon.   She ___

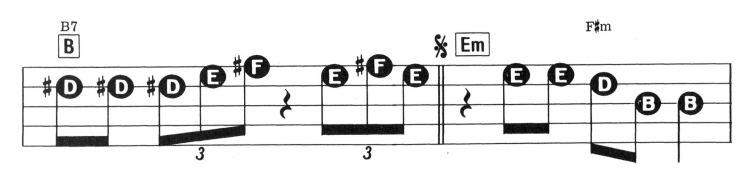

lie   be - comes   the   truth.   Hey. ___   Bil - lie   Jean ___   is
called   me   to   her   room.   Hey. ___

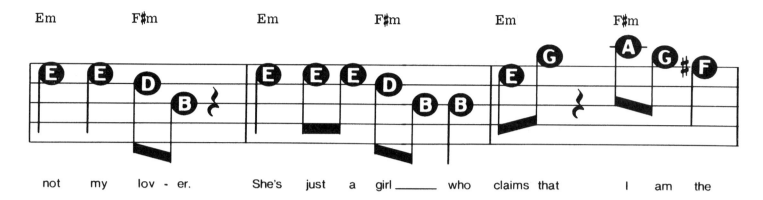

not my lov - er. She's just a girl ____ who claims that I am the

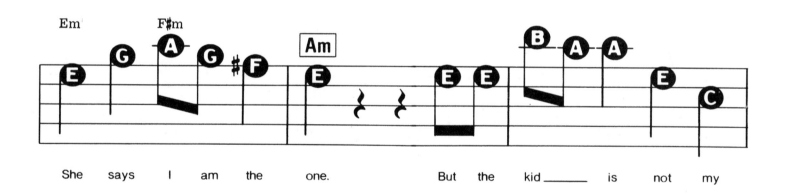

one. But the kid ____ is not my son.

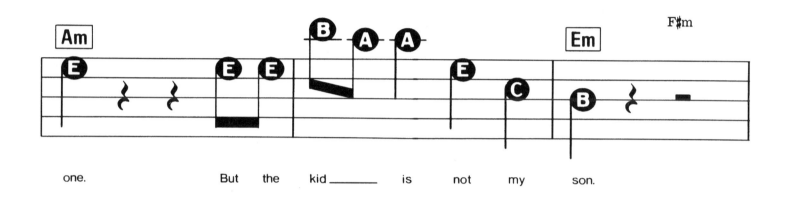

She says I am the one. But the kid ____ is not my

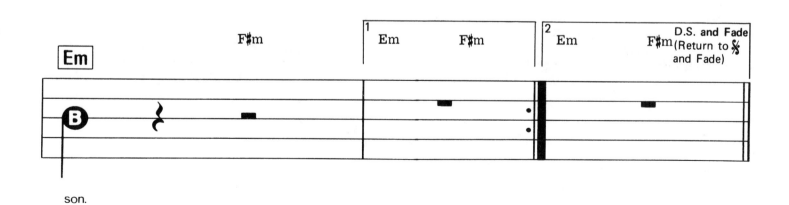

son.

Can't Help Falling in Love

from the Paramount Picture BLUE HAWAII

Registration 3
Rhythm: Ballad or Swing

Words and Music by George David Weiss,
Hugo Peretti and Luigi Creatore

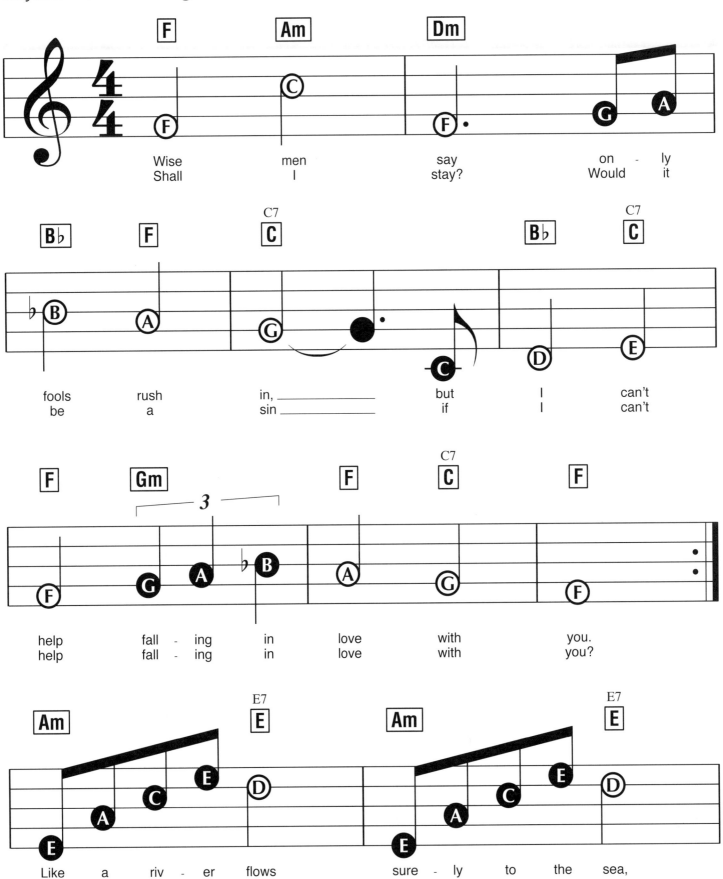

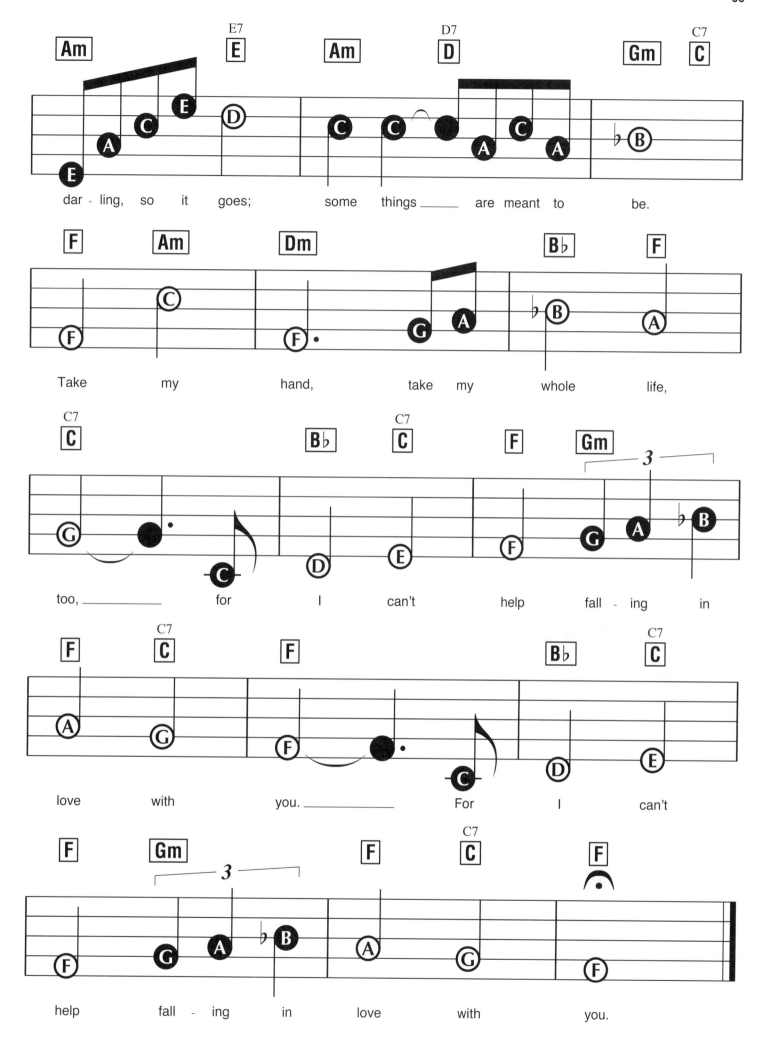

Daniel

Registration 2
Rhythm: Latin or Rock

Words and Music by Elton John
and Bernie Taupin

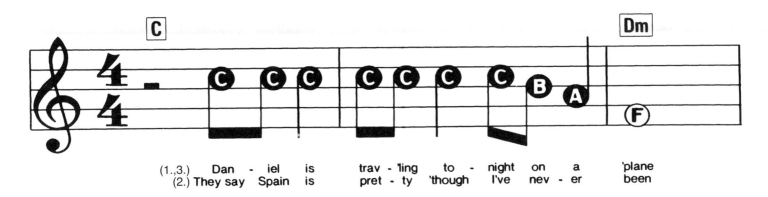

(1.,3.) Dan - iel is trav - 'ling to - night on a 'plane
(2.) They say Spain is pret - ty 'though I've nev - er been

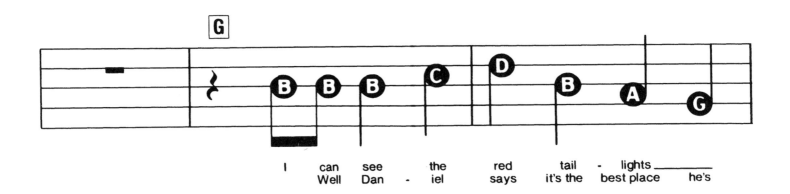

I can see the red tail - lights _____
Well Dan - iel says it's the best place he's

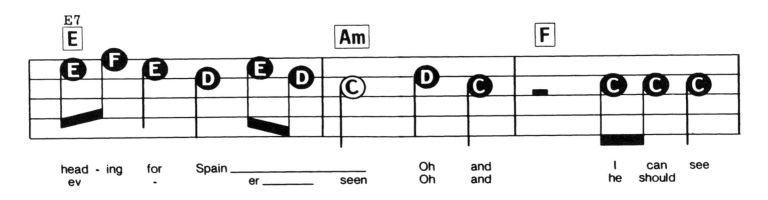

head - ing for Spain _____ Oh and I can see
ev - er _____ seen Oh and he should

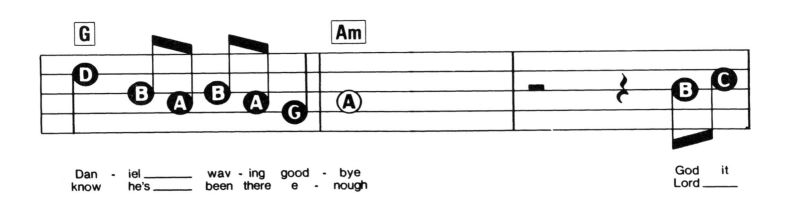

Dan - iel _____ wav - ing good - bye God it
know he's _____ been there e - nough Lord _____

35

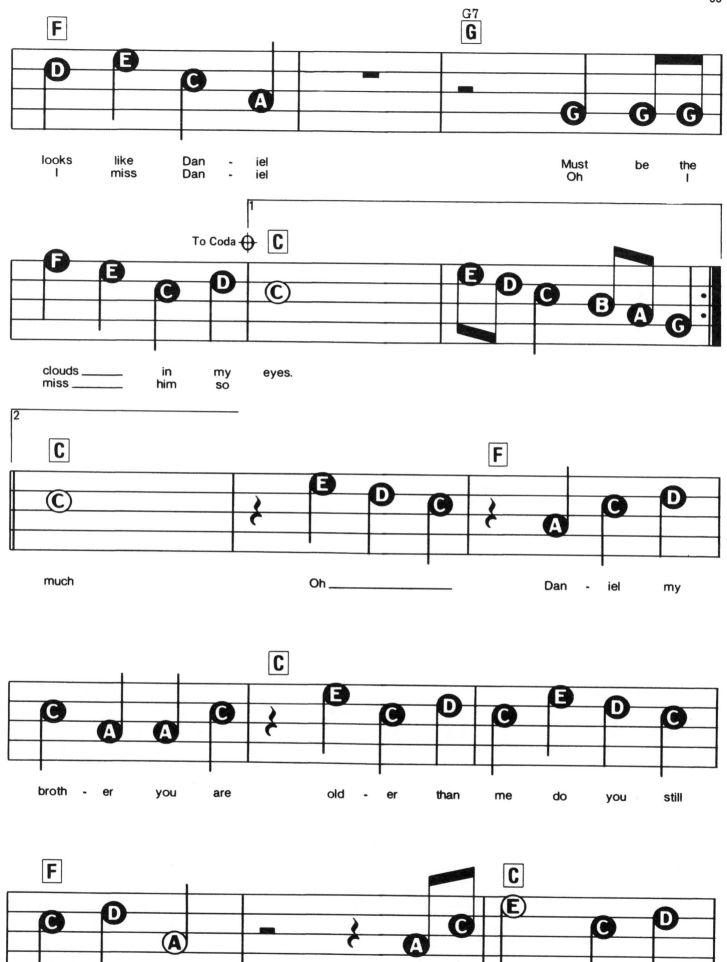

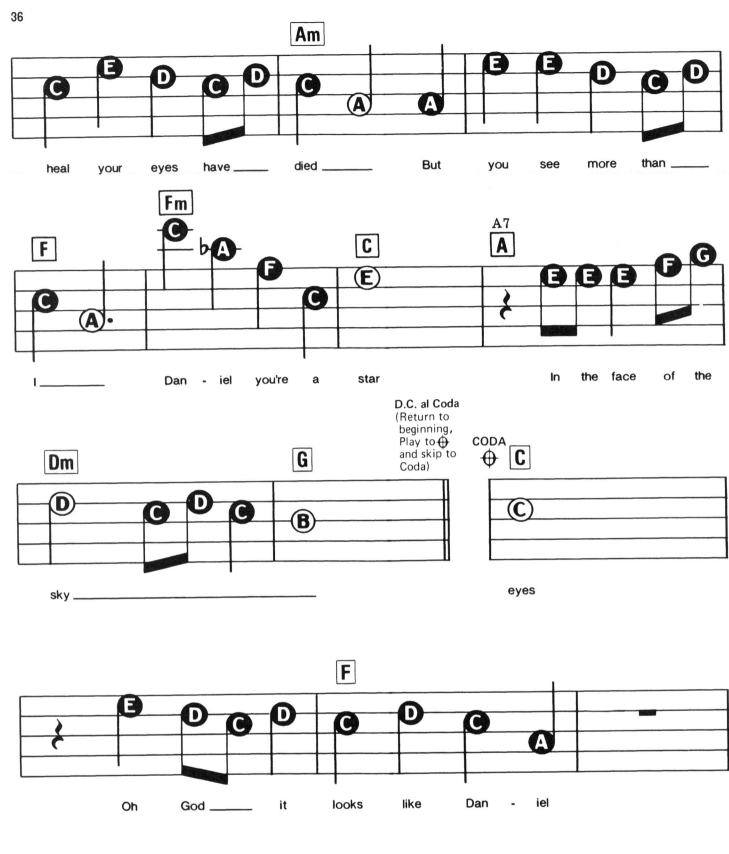

heal your eyes have _____ died _____ But you see more than _____

I _____ Dan - iel you're a star In the face of the

D.C. al Coda
(Return to beginning, Play to ⊕ and skip to Coda)

CODA

sky _____ eyes

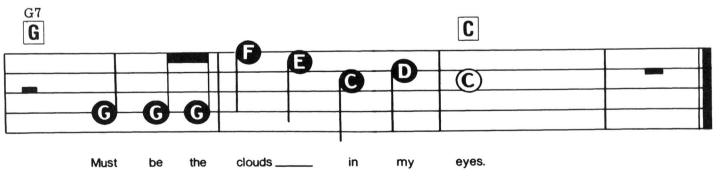

Oh God _____ it looks like Dan - iel

Must be the clouds _____ in my eyes.

(They Long to Be)
Close to You

Registration 2
Rhythm: Slow Rock

Lyrics by Hal David
Music by Burt Bacharach

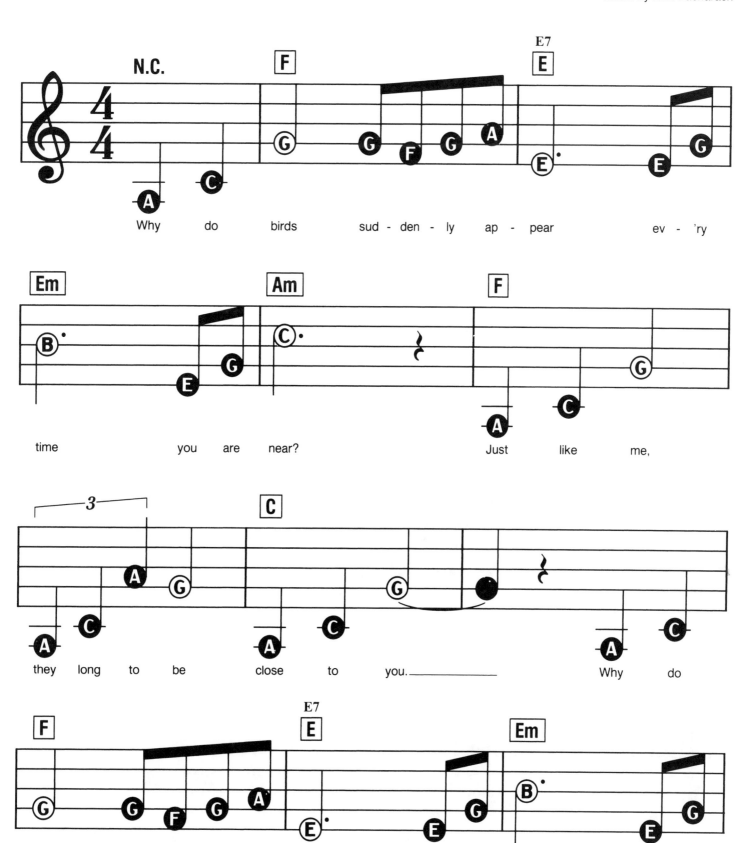

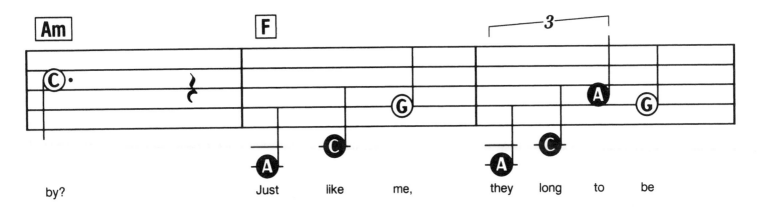

by? Just like me, they long to be

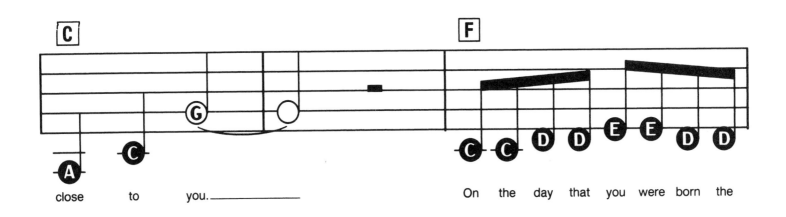

close to you. _____   On the day that you were born the

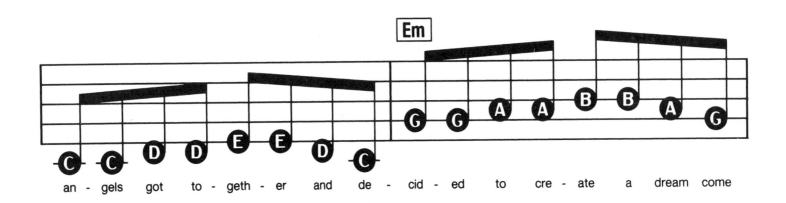

an - gels got to - geth - er and de - cid - ed to cre - ate a dream come

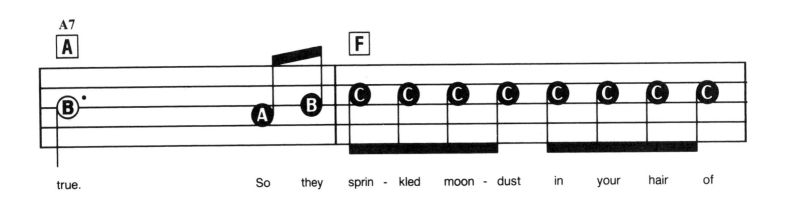

true. So they sprin - kled moon - dust in your hair of

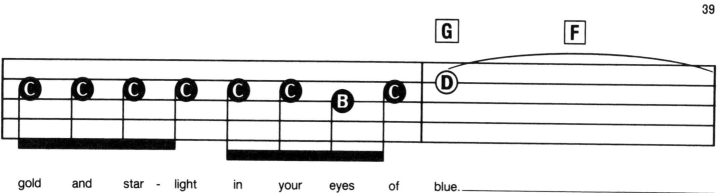

gold and star - light in your eyes of blue.

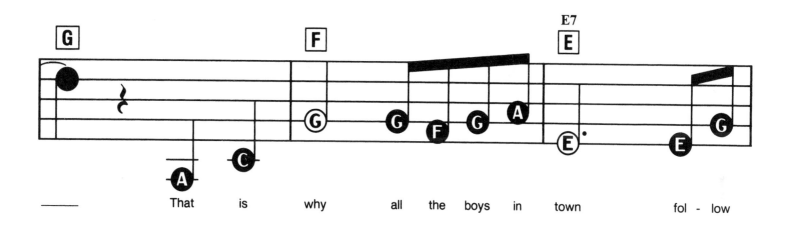

That is why all the boys in town fol - low

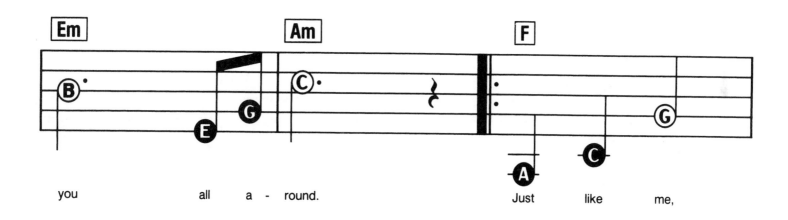

you all a - round. Just like me,

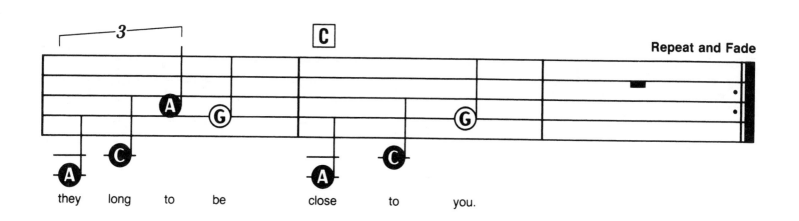

they long to be close to you.

Deacon Blues

Registration 7
Rhythm: Funk or Pop

Words and Music by Walter Becker
and Donald Fagen

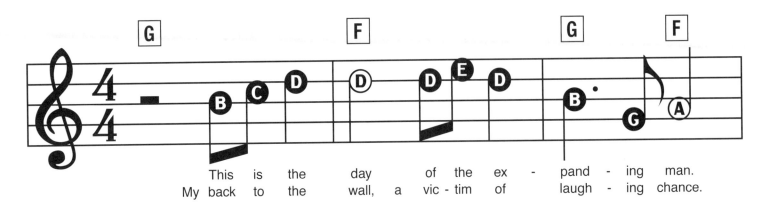

This is the day of the ex - pand - ing man.
My back to the wall, a vic - tim of laugh - ing chance.

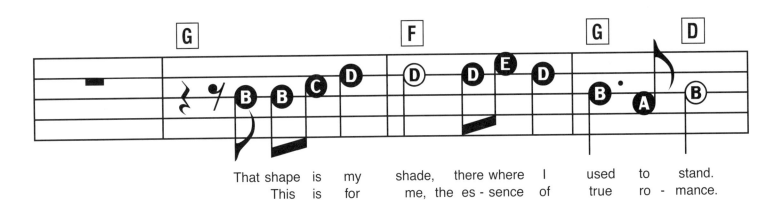

That shape is my shade, there where I used to stand.
This is for me, the es - sence of true ro - mance.

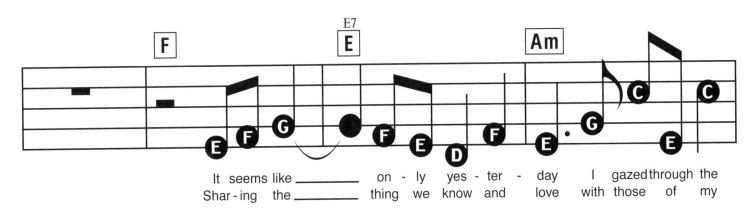

It seems like _____ on - ly yes - ter - day I gazed through the
Shar - ing the _____ thing we know and love with those of my

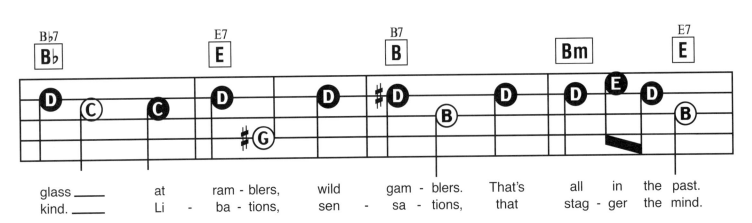

glass _____ at ram - blers, wild gam - blers. That's all in the past.
kind. _____ Li - ba - tions, sen - sa - tions, that stag - ger the mind.

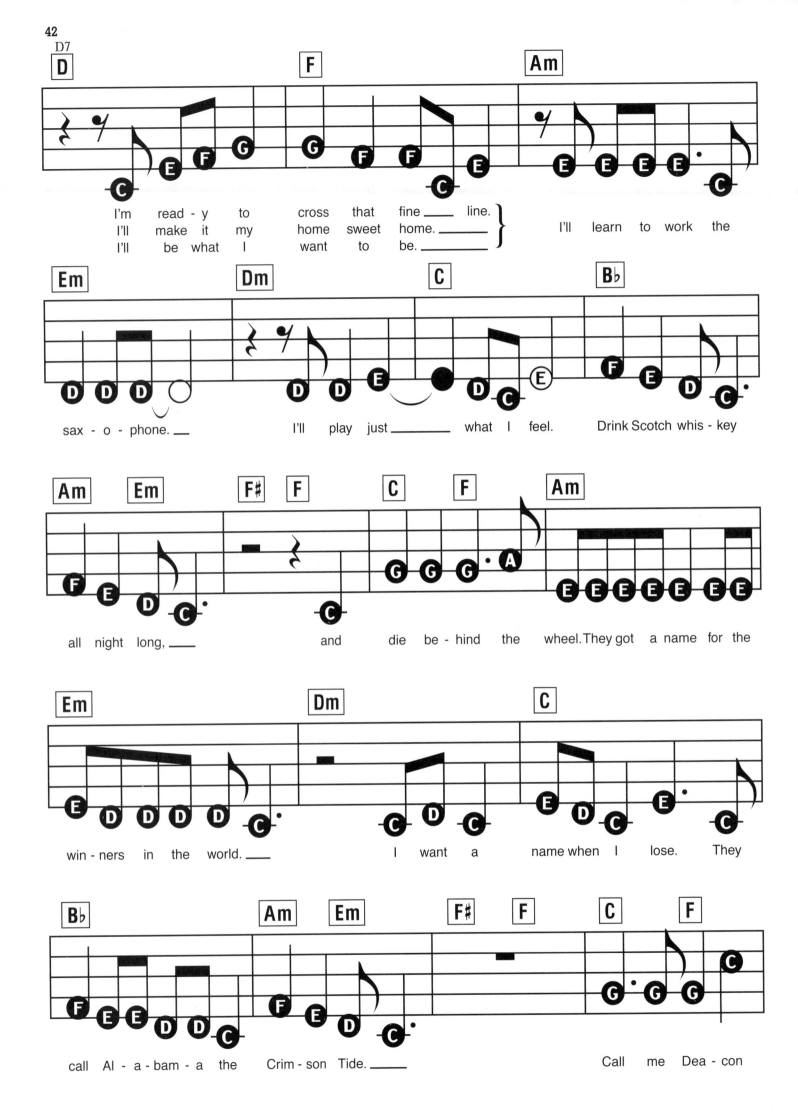

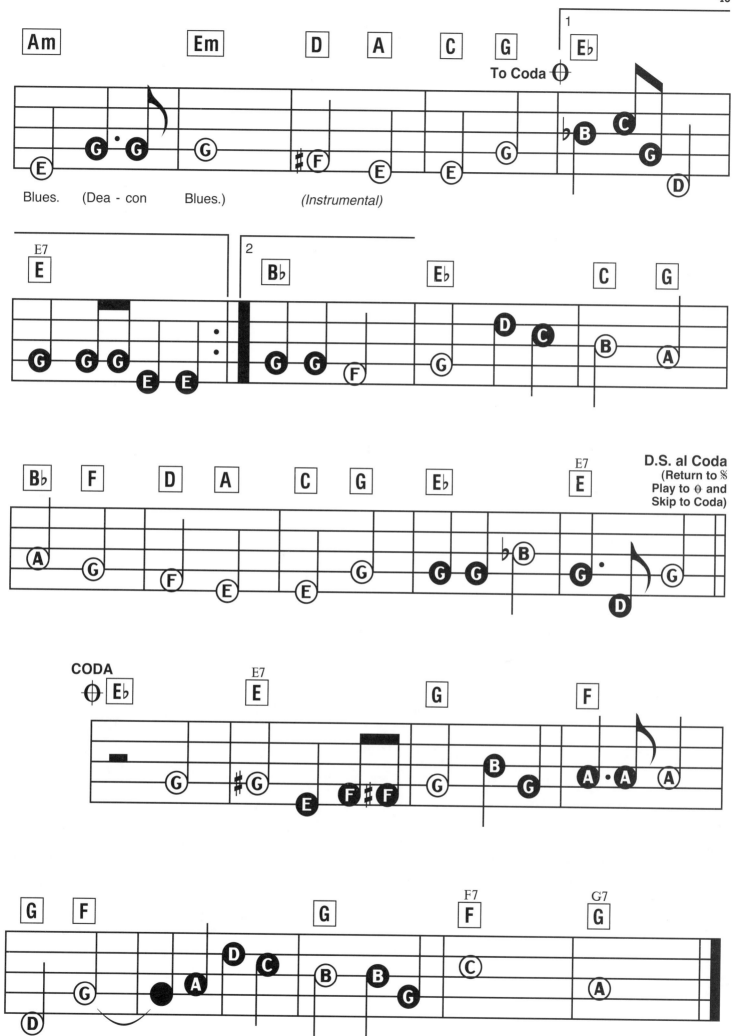

Defying Gravity
from the Broadway Musical WICKED

Registration 7
Rhythm: Pop or Rock

Music and Lyrics by
Stephen Schwartz

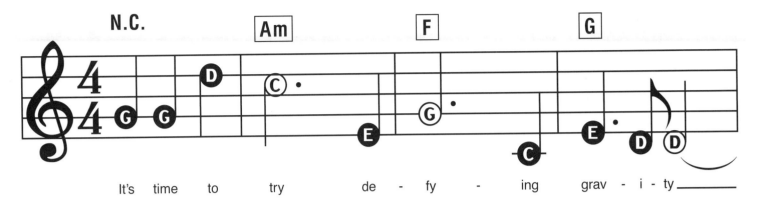

It's time to try de - fy - ing grav - i - ty ____

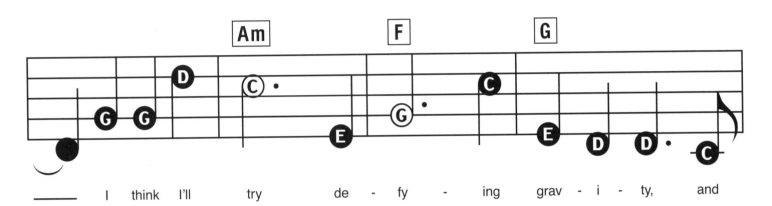

____ I think I'll try de - fy - ing grav - i - ty, and

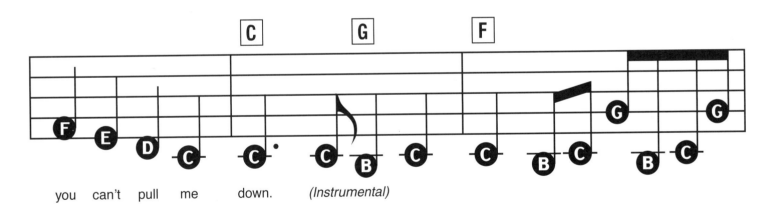

you can't pull me down. *(Instrumental)*

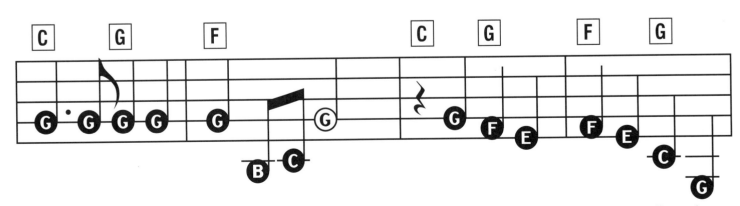

I'm through ac - cept - ing lim - its

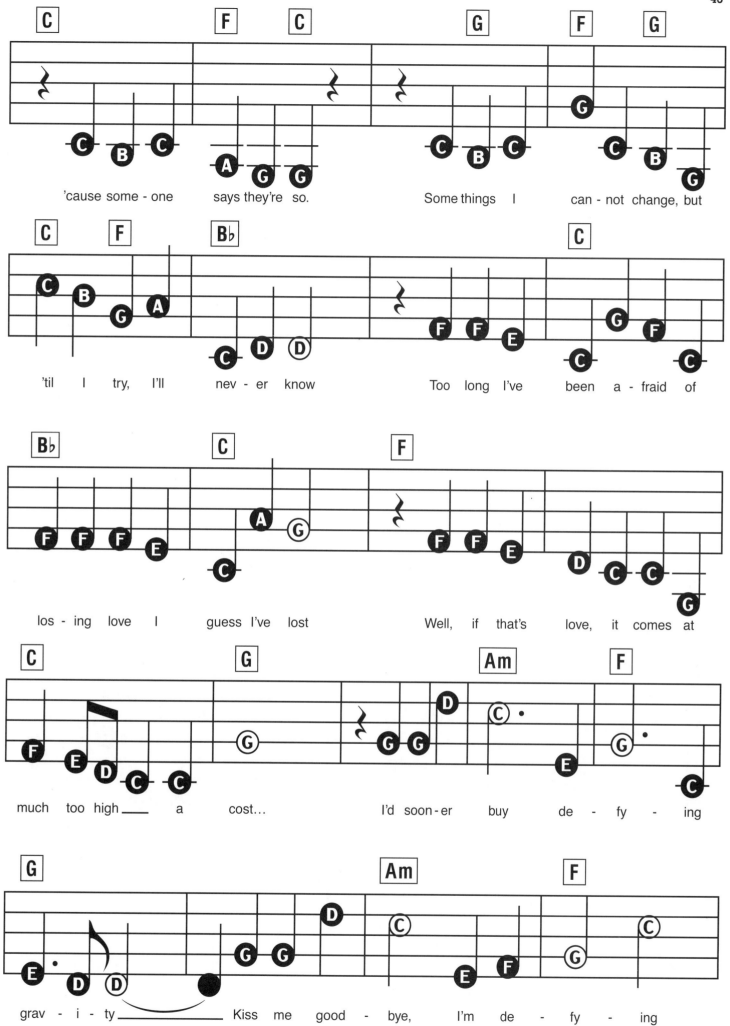

45

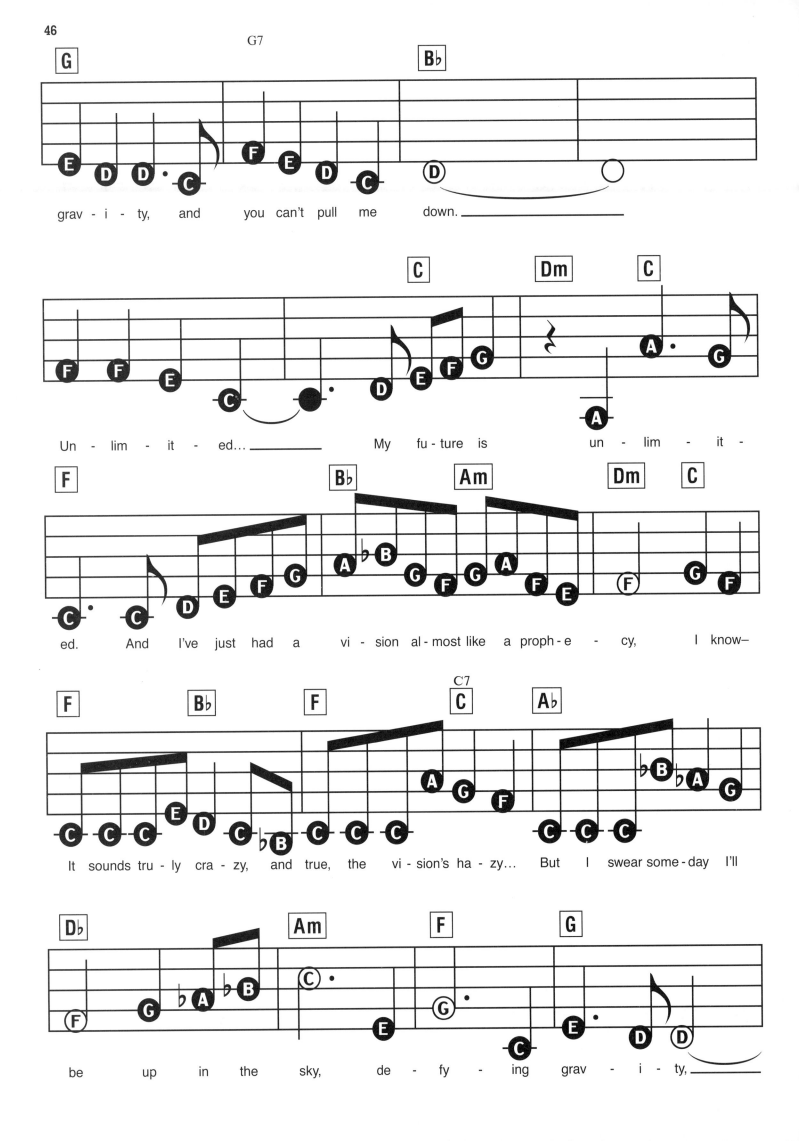

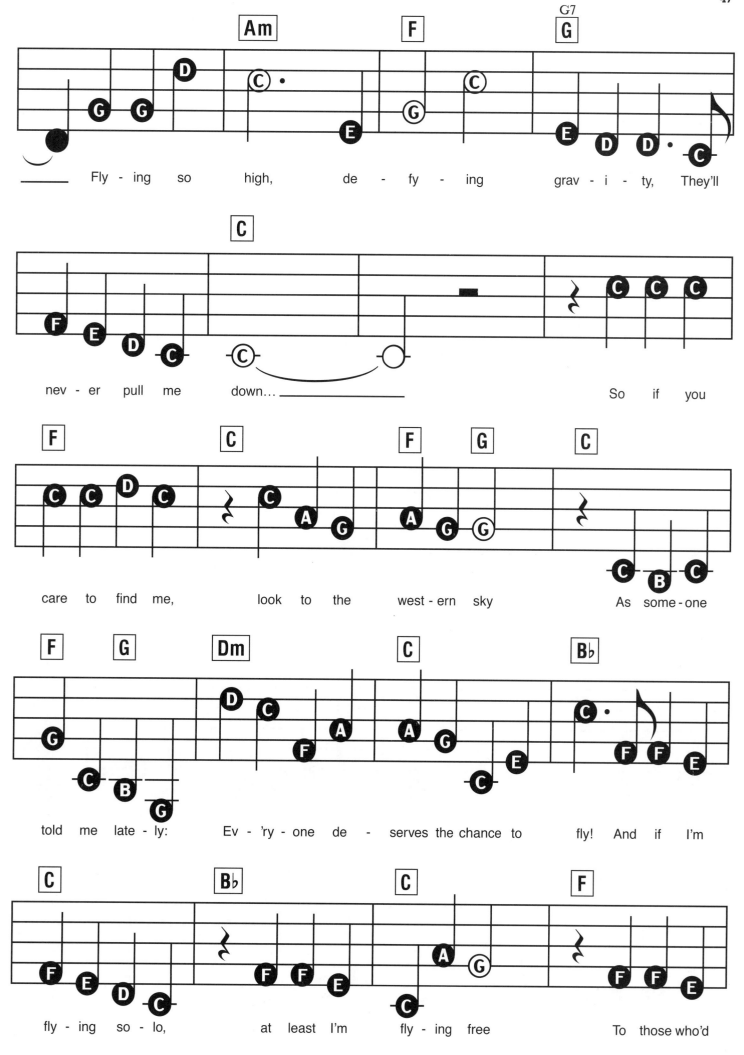

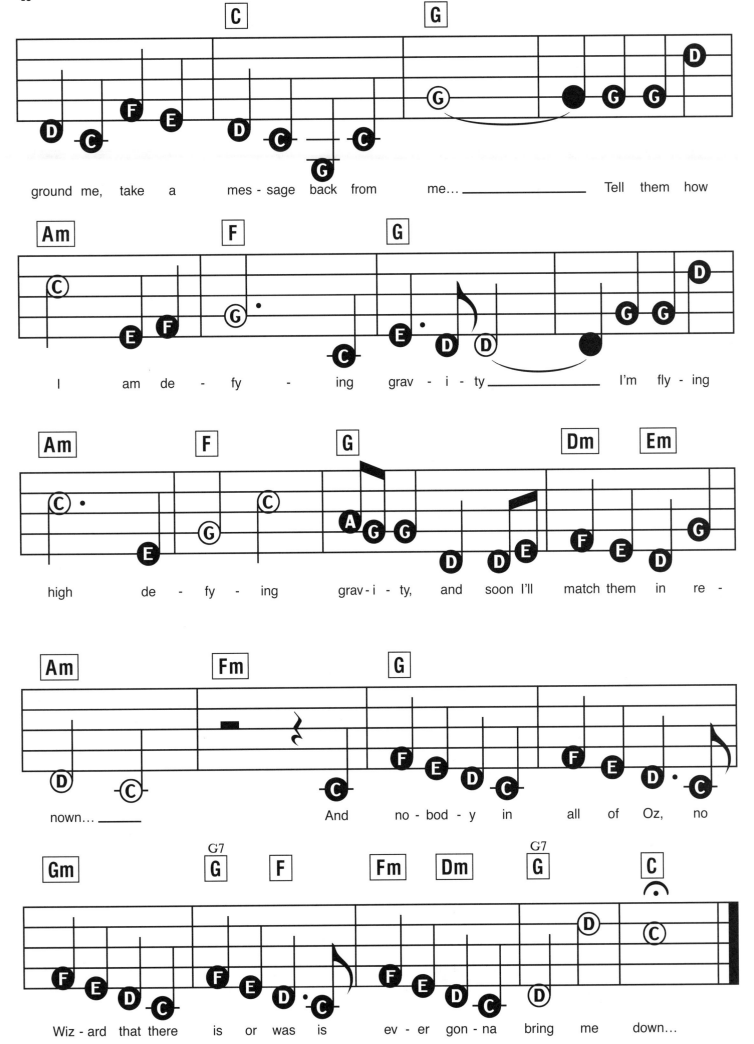

Dream Weaver

Registration 10
Rhythm: Rock or Pops

Words and Music by
Gary Wright

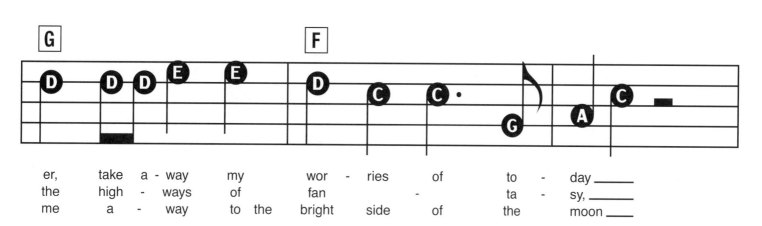

I've	just	closed	my _____	eyes		a	- gain, ___
Fly	me	high	through the	star	-	ry	skies, ___
Though	the	dawn	may be	com	-	ing	soon, ___

climbed a - board the	Dream _____		Weav - er	train. ___
or may - be	to _____		an	as - tral plane. ___
there still may	_____		be some	time. ___

	Driv -
	Cross
	Fly

er,	take a -	way	my	wor -	ries	of	to - day _____
the	high - ways	of	fan	-		ta	- sy, _____
me a -	way	to the	bright	side	of	the	moon ___

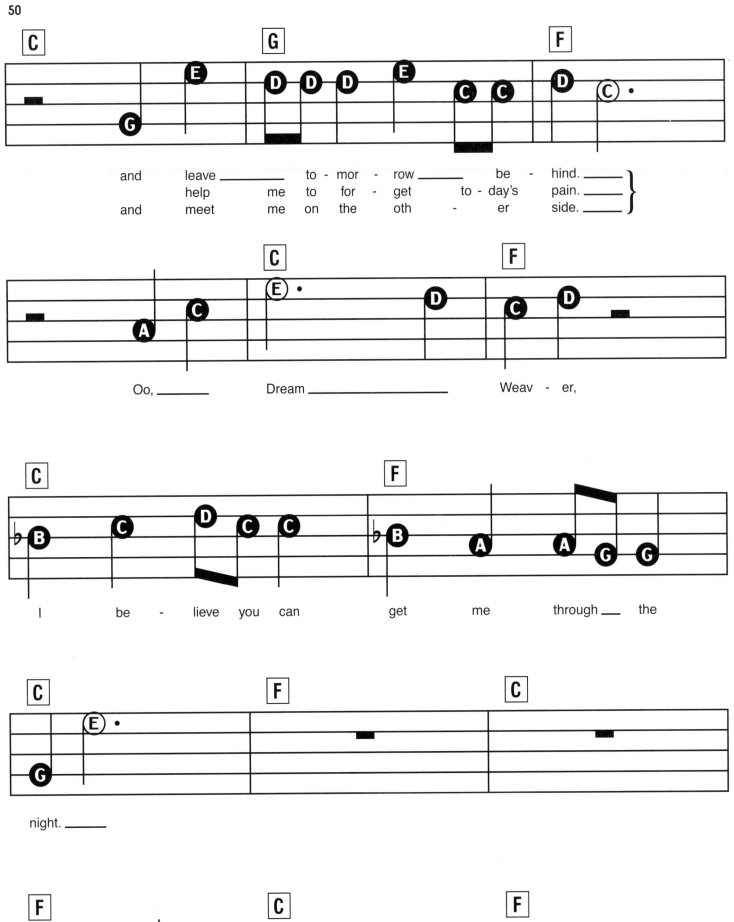

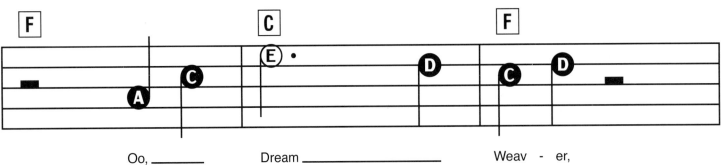

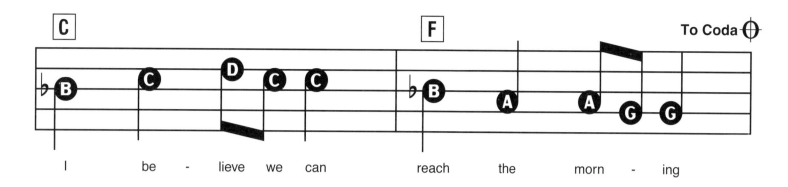

I be - lieve we can reach the morn - ing

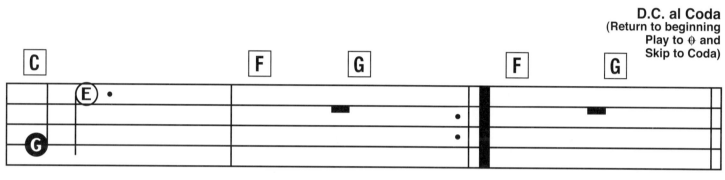

D.C. al Coda
(Return to beginning
Play to ⊕ and
Skip to Coda)

light. _____

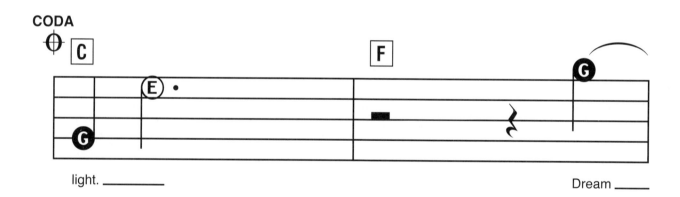

CODA

light. _____ Dream _____

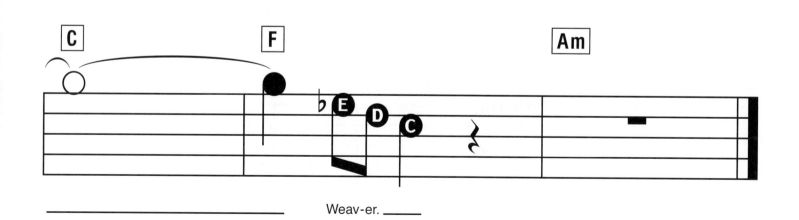

_____ Weav-er. _____

Don't Stop Believin'

Registration 1
Rhythm: 8-Beat or Rock

Words and Music by Steve Perry,
Neal Schon and Jonathan Cain

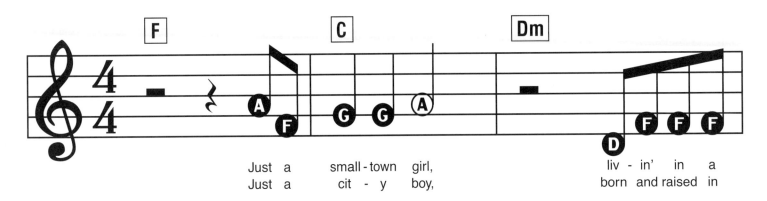

Just a   small-town girl,   liv - in' in a
Just a   cit - y   boy,   born and raised in

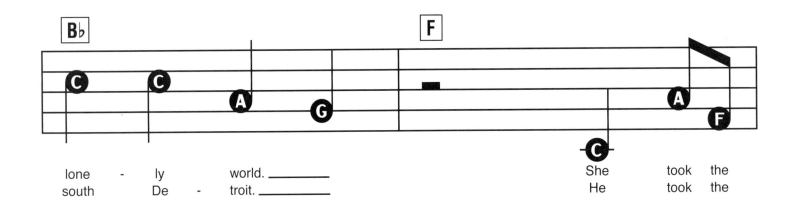

lone - ly   world. _____   She   took the
south   De - troit. _____   He   took the

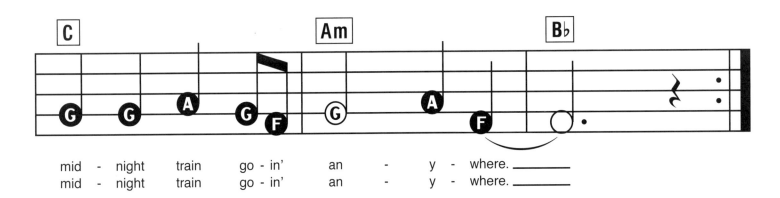

mid - night train go - in' an   -   y - where. _____
mid - night train go - in' an   -   y - where. _____

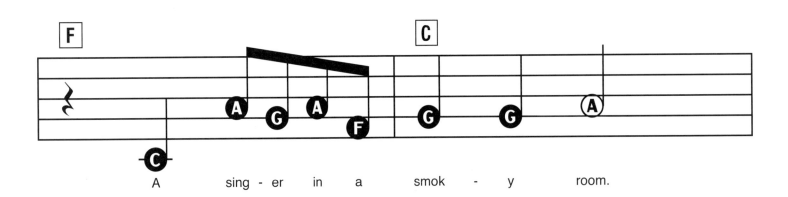

A   sing - er in a smok - y   room.

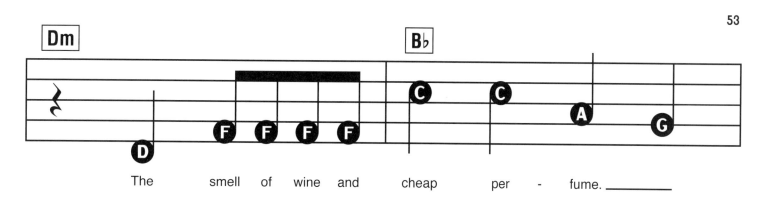

The smell of wine and cheap per - fume. _____

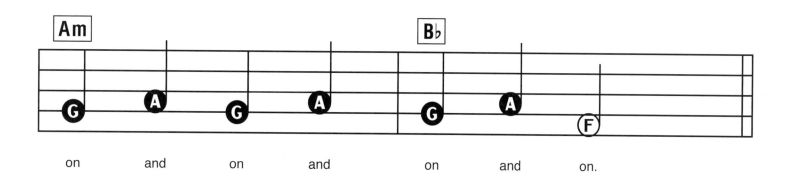

For a smile ___ they can share the night. It goes

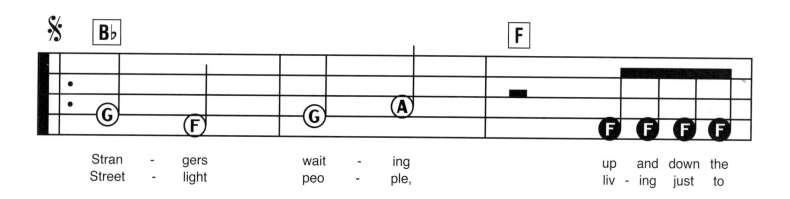

on and on and on and on.

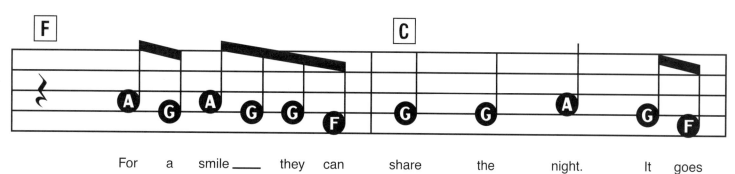

Stran - gers wait - ing up and down the
Street - light peo - ple, liv - ing just to

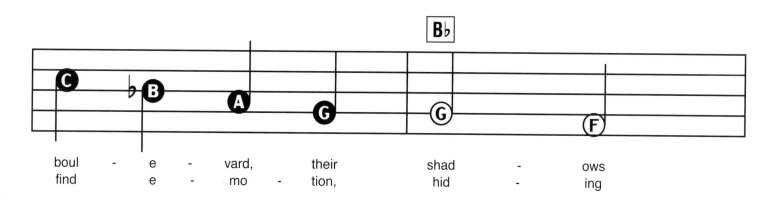

boul - e - vard, their shad - ows
find e - mo - tion, hid - ing

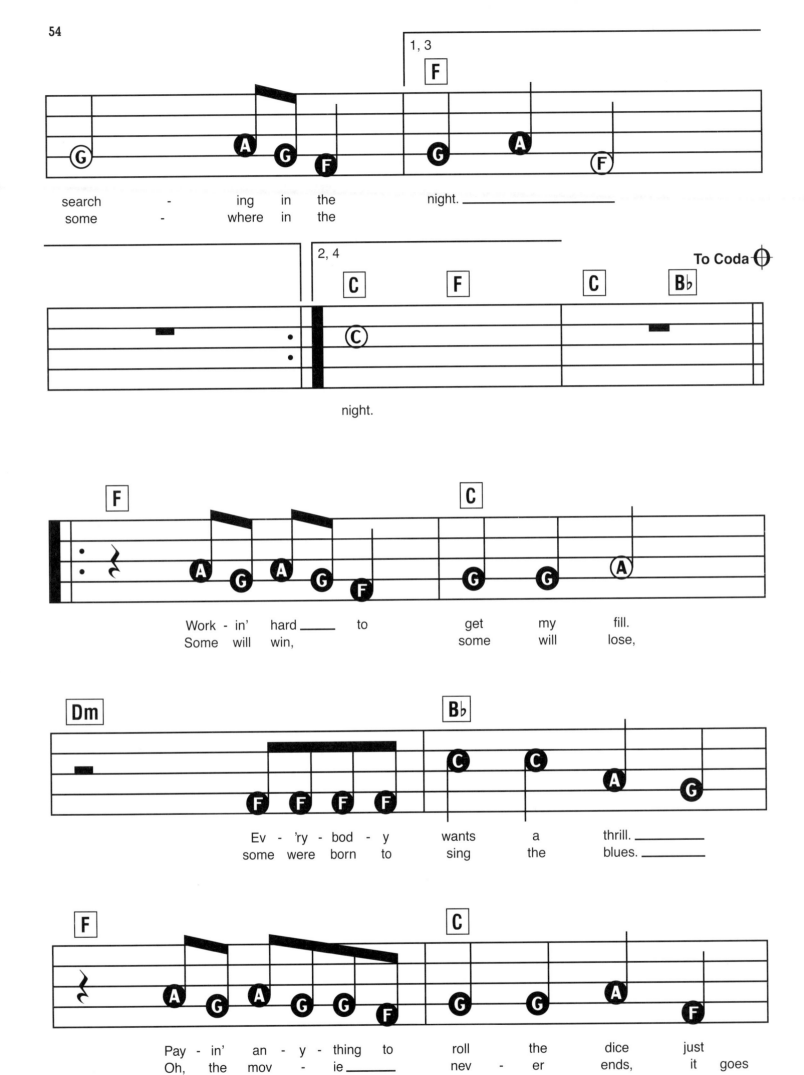

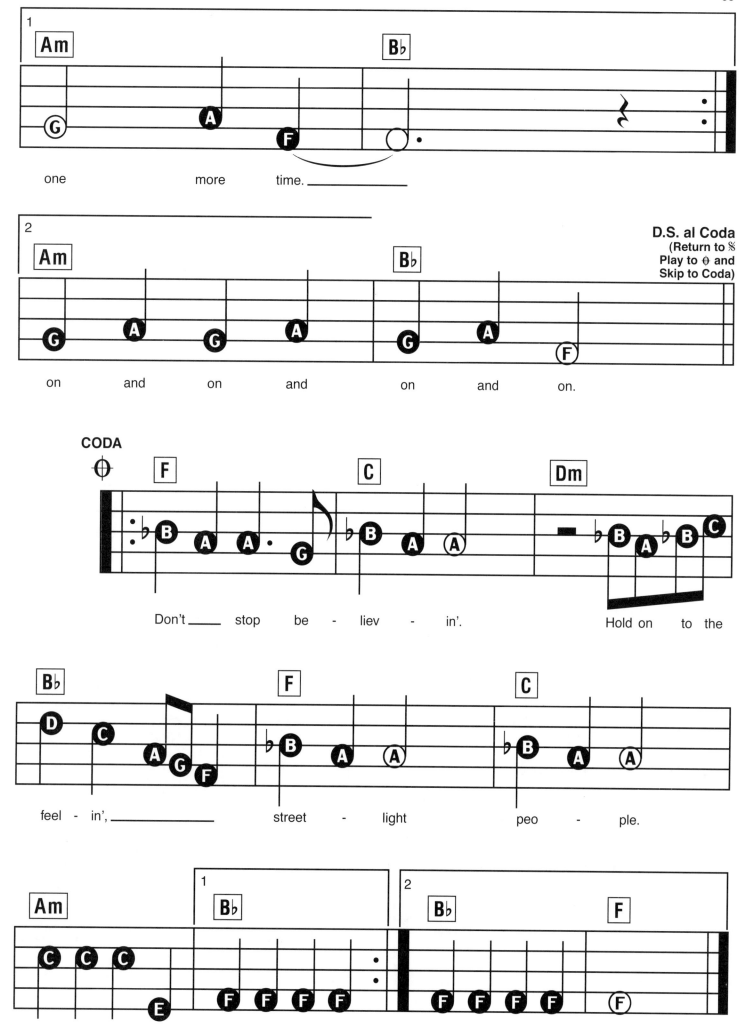

Dream a Little Dream of Me

Registration 4
Rhythm: Ballad or Fox Trot

Words by Gus Kahn
Music by Wilbur Schwandt and Fabian Andree

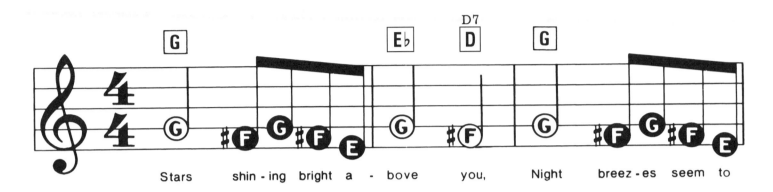

Stars shin - ing bright a - bove you, Night breez - es seem to

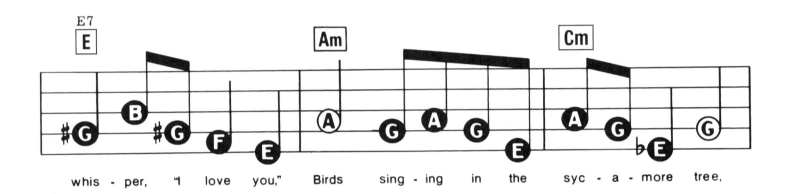

whis - per, "I love you," Birds sing - ing in the syc - a - more tree,

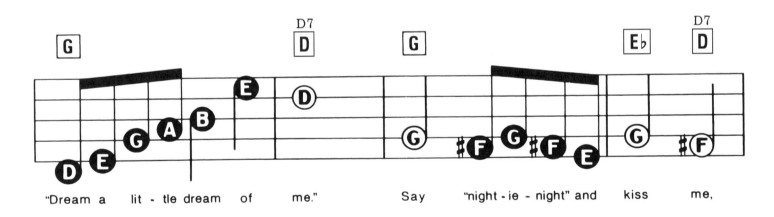

"Dream a lit - tle dream of me." Say "night - ie - night" and kiss me,

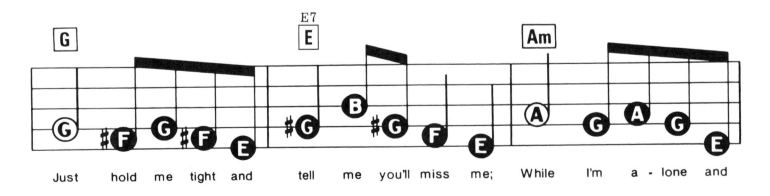

Just hold me tight and tell me you'll miss me; While I'm a - lone and

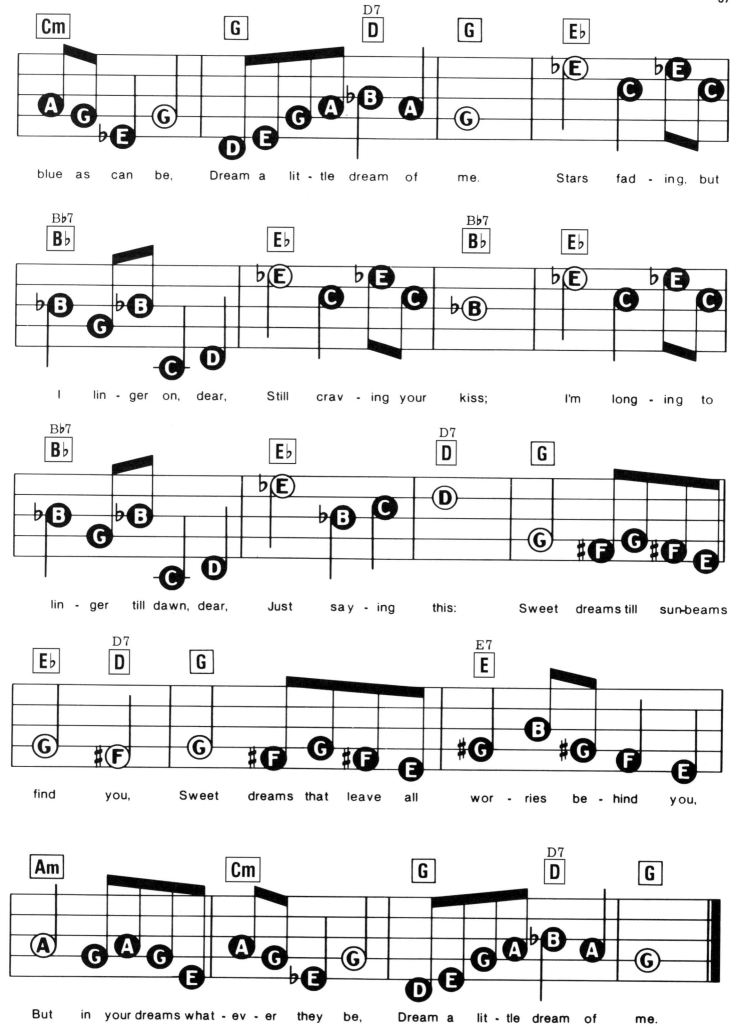

Dreamer

Registration 1
Rhythm: Rock or 8-Beat

Words and Music by Rick Davies
and Roger Hodgson

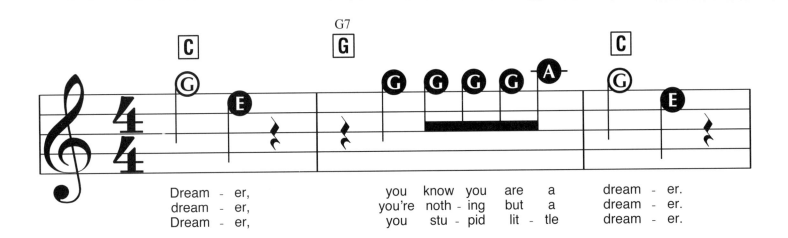

Dream - er,   you know you are a   dream - er.
dream - er,   you're noth - ing but a   dream - er.
Dream - er,   you stu - pid lit - tle   dream - er.

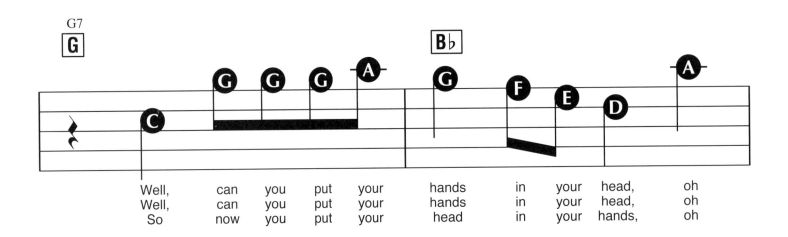

Well, can you put your hands in your head, oh
Well, can you put your hands in your head, oh
So now you put your head in your hands, oh

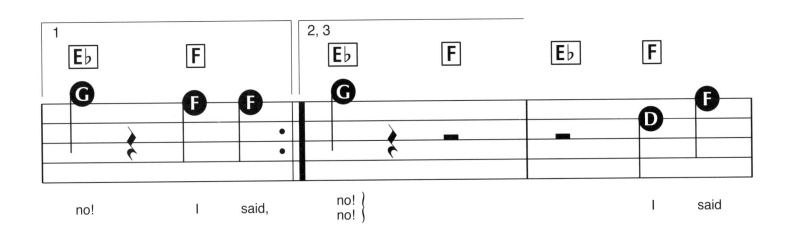

no!   I said,   no! no!   I said

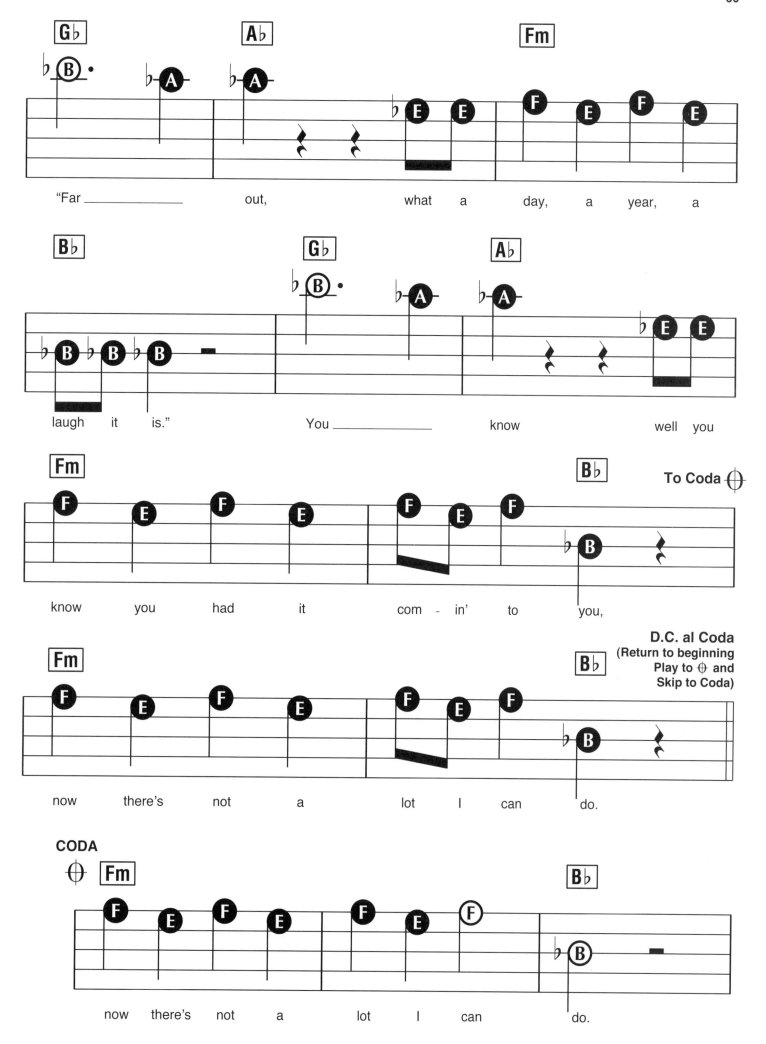

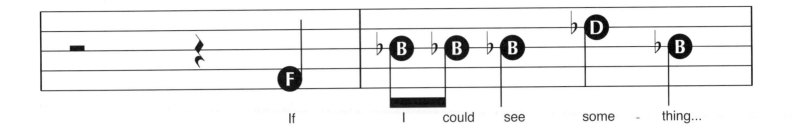

If I could see some - thing...

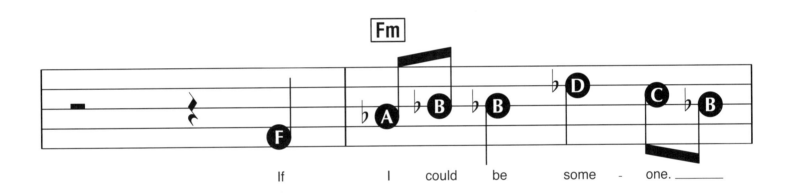

(You can see an - y - thing you want, boy.)

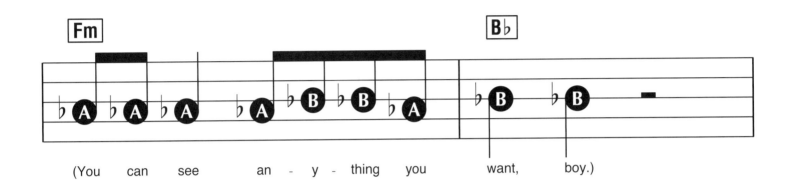

If I could be some - one. _____

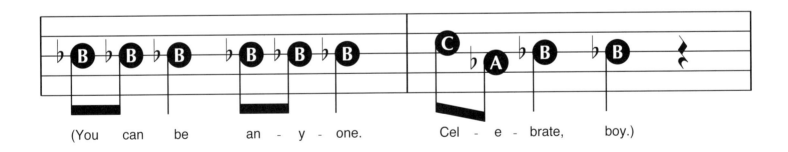

(You can be an - y - one. Cel - e - brate, boy.)

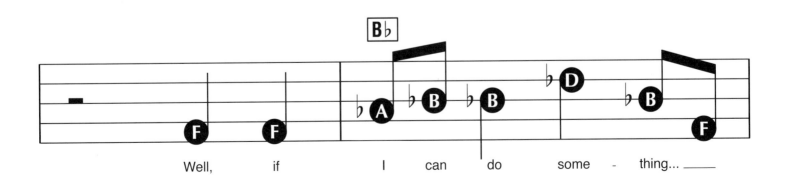

Well, if I can do some - thing... _____

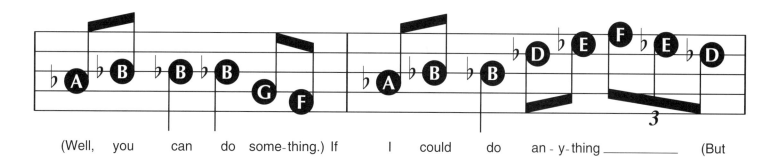

(Well, you can do some-thing.) If I could do an - y-thing _____ (But

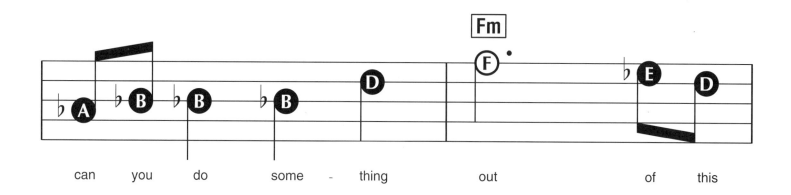

can you do some - thing out of this

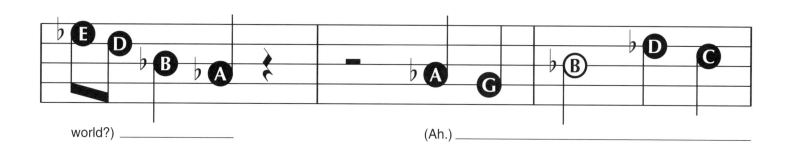

world?) _____ (Ah.) _____

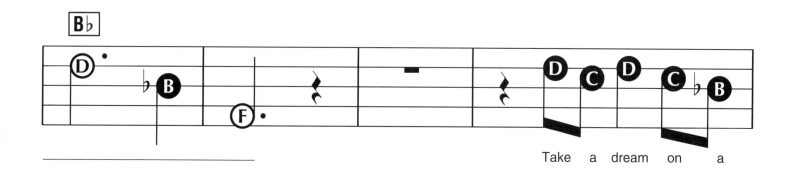

Take a dream on a

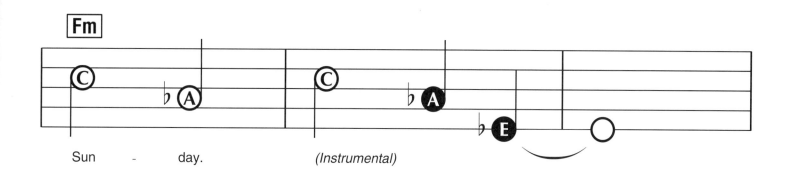

Sun - day. (Instrumental)

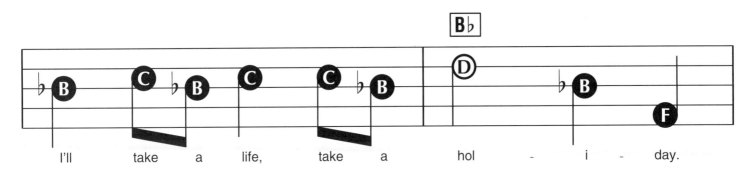

I'll take a life, take a hol - i - day.

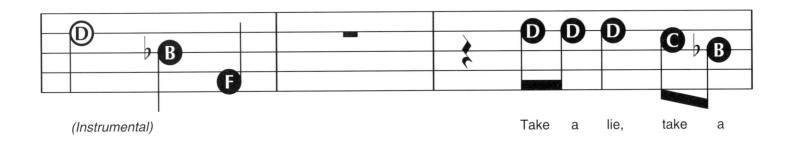

(Instrumental)　　　　　　　　Take a lie, take a

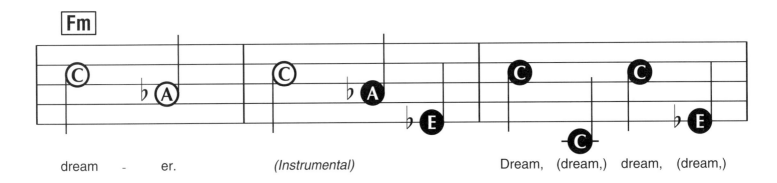

dream - er.　(Instrumental)　Dream, (dream,) dream, (dream,)

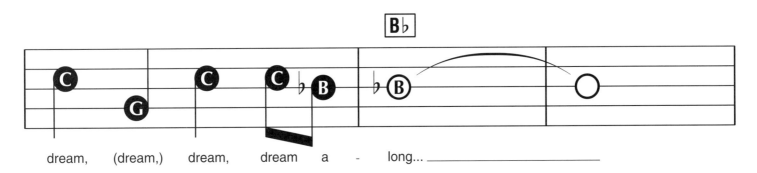

dream, (dream,) dream, dream a - long...

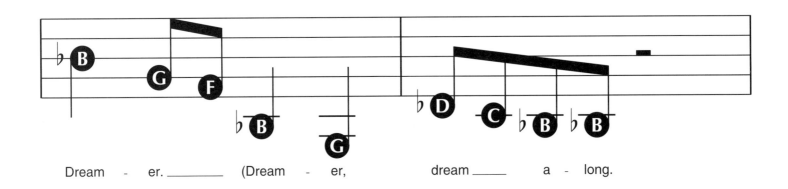

Dream - er.　(Dream - er, dream a - long.

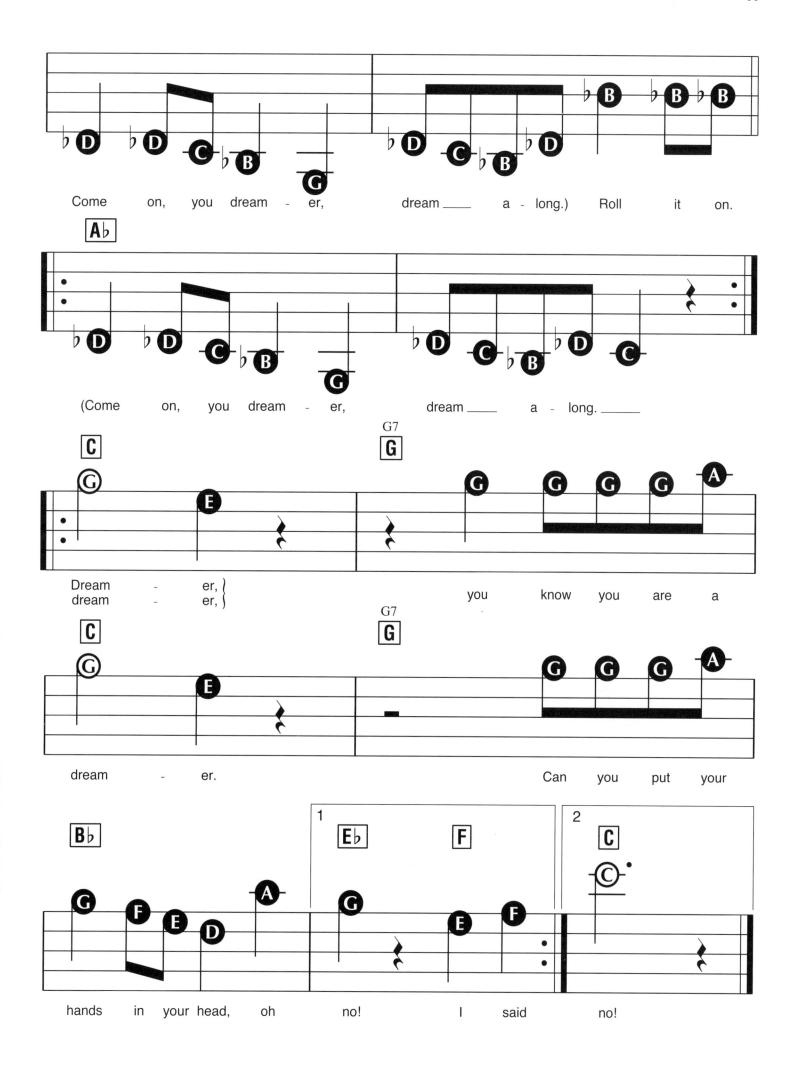

Ebony and Ivory

Registration 1
Rhythm: Rock or 8-Beat

Words and Music by
Paul McCartney

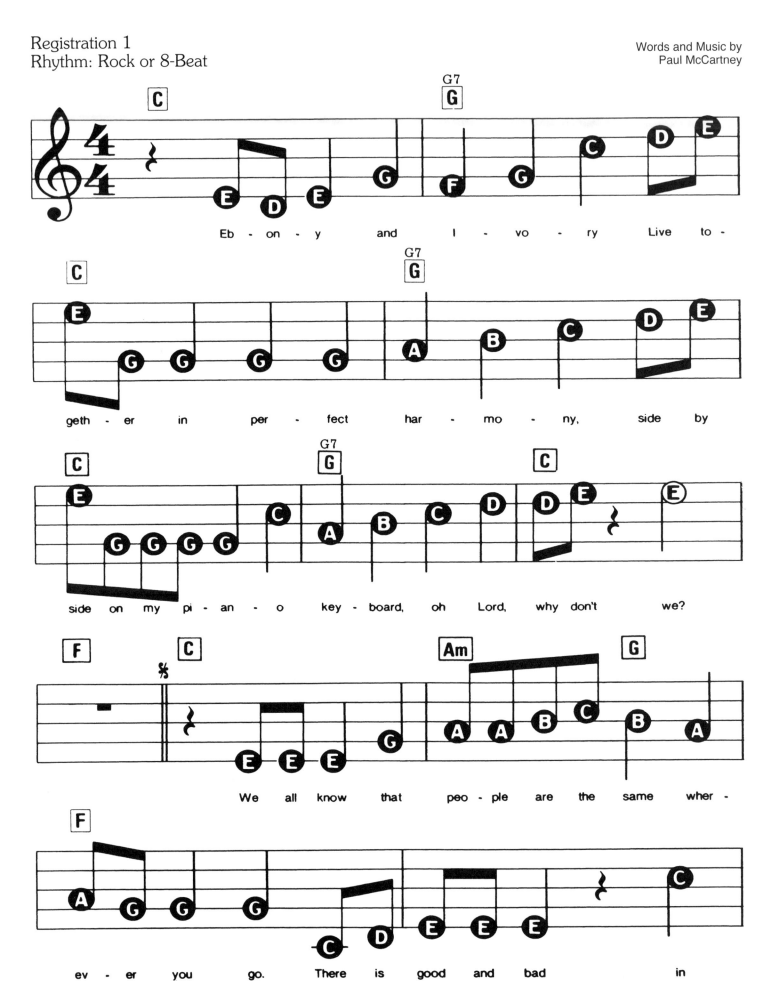

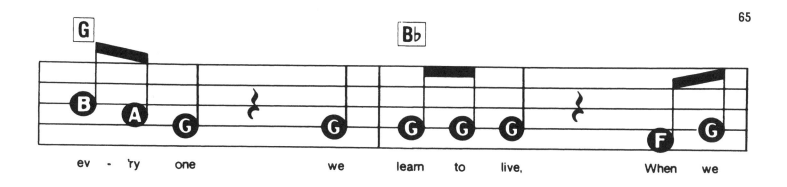

ev - 'ry one   we   learn to live,   When we

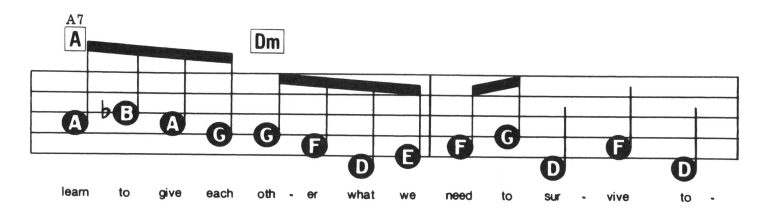

learn   to   give each oth - er   what we   need   to sur - vive to -

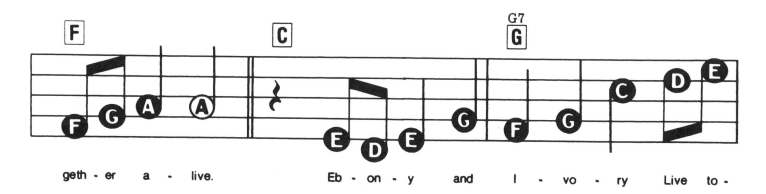

geth - er a - live.   Eb - on - y   and   I - vo - ry   Live to -

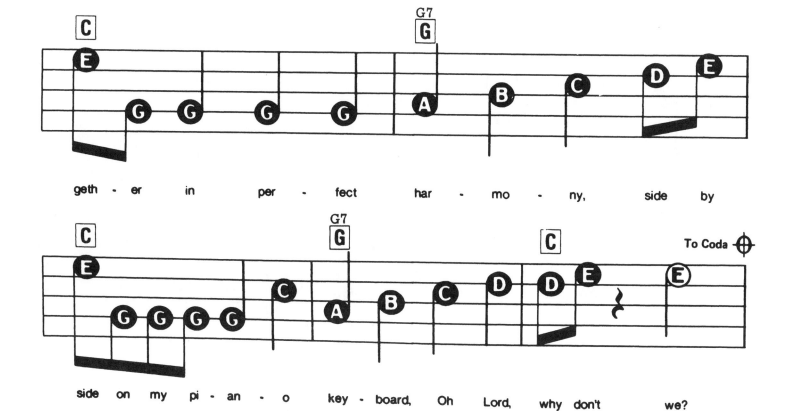

geth - er   in   per - fect   har - mo - ny,   side by

side on my pi - an - o   key - board, Oh Lord, why don't   we?

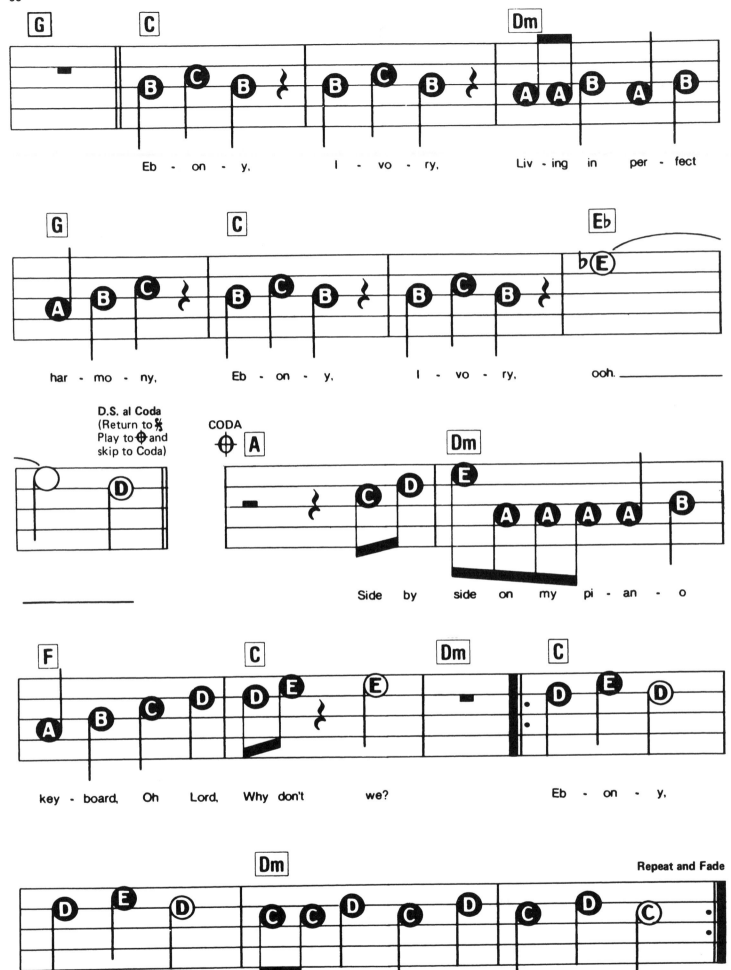

Escape
(The Piña Colada Song)

Registration 4
Rhythm: Rock

Words and Music by
Rupert Holmes

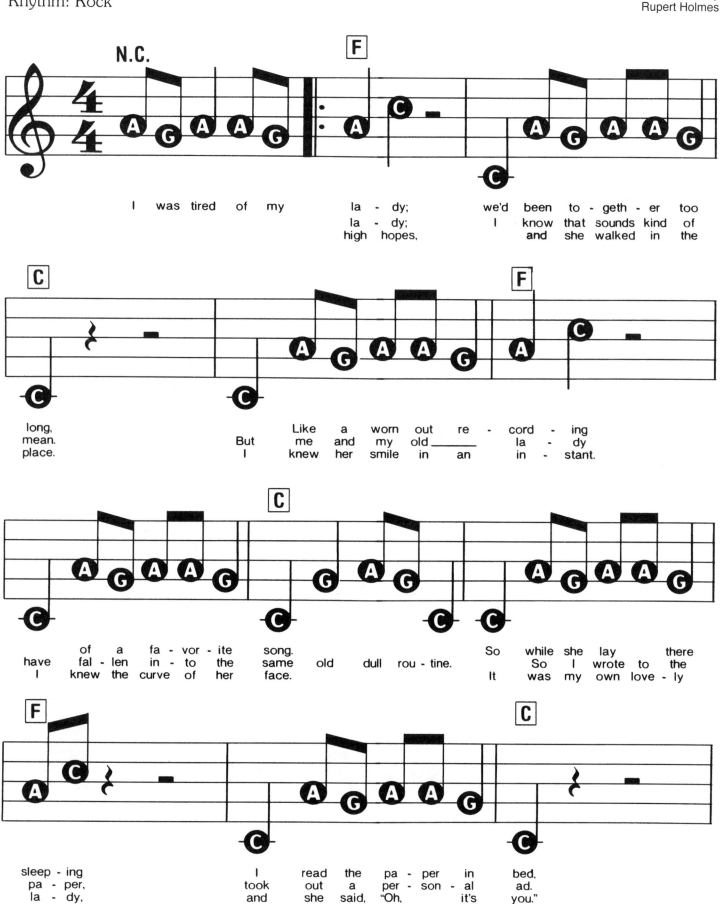

68

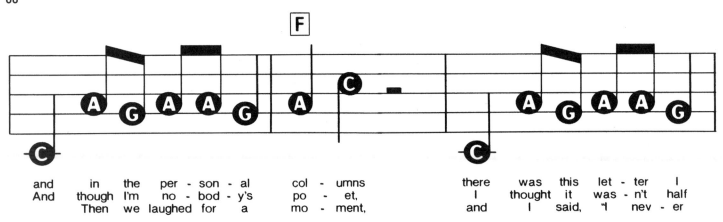

and   in   the   per - son - al   col - umns   there   was this   let - ter   I
And   though I'm   no - bod - y's   po - et,   I   thought it   was - n't   half
Then   we   laughed for   a   mo - ment,   and   I   said, "I   nev - er

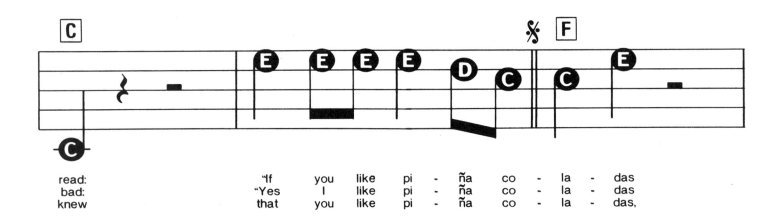

read: "If   you   like   pi - ña   co - la - das
bad: "Yes   I   like   pi - ña   co - la - das
knew   that   you   like   pi - ña   co - la - das,

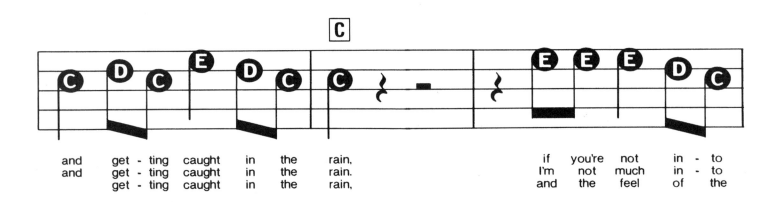

and   get - ting caught   in   the   rain,   if   you're   not   in - to
and   get - ting caught   in   the   rain.   I'm   not   much   in - to
        get - ting caught   in   the   rain,   and   the   feel   of   the

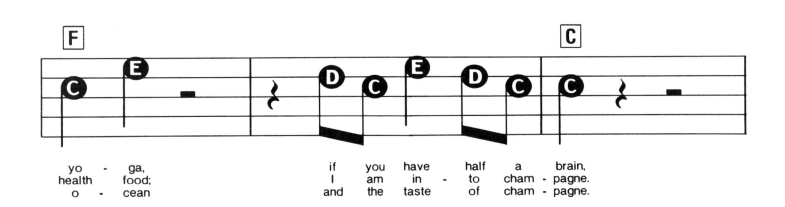

yo - ga,   if   you   have   half   a   brain,
health   food;   I   am   in - to   cham - pagne.
o - cean   and   the   taste   of   cham - pagne.

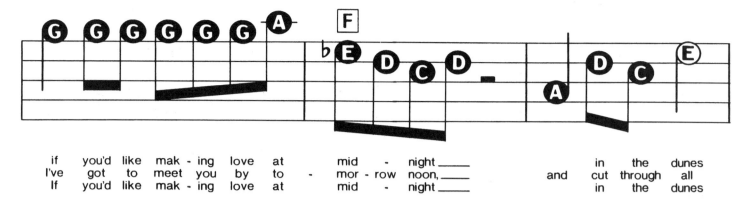

if you'd like mak - ing love at mid - night _____ in the dunes
I've got to meet you by to - mor - row noon, _____ and cut through all
If you'd like mak - ing love at mid - night _____ in the dunes

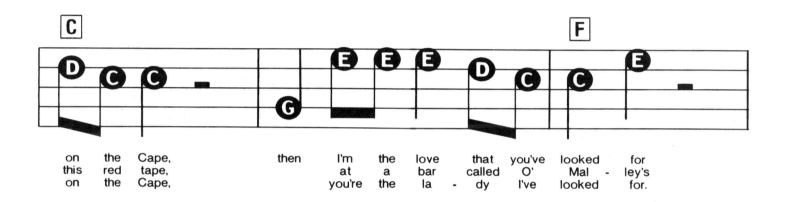

on the Cape, then I'm the love that you've looked for
this red tape, at a bar called O' Mal - ley's
on the Cape, you're the la - dy I've looked for.

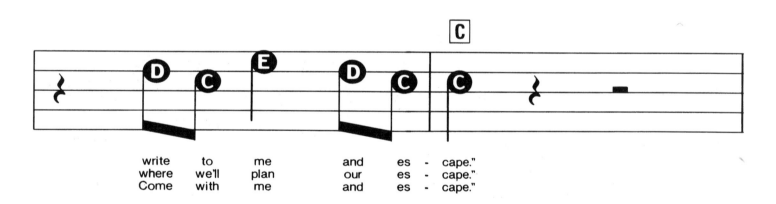

write to me and es - cape."
where we'll plan our es - cape."
Come with me and es - cape."

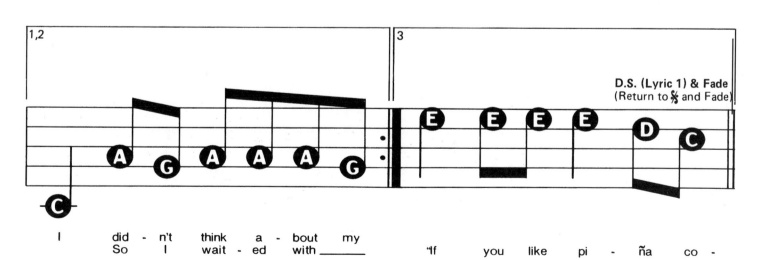

D.S. (Lyric 1) & Fade
(Return to 𝄋 and Fade)

I did - n't think a - bout my
So I wait - ed with _____ "If you like pi - ña co -

Fallin'

Registration 8
Rhythm: Slow Rock or 6/8 Waltz

Words and Music by
Alicia Keys

N.C.

I keep on fall - in' in and out of love ___

with - a you.

Some - times ___ I

love you, some - times you make me blue.

Some - times I feel good.

At times I feel

used.

Lov - ing you, dar - ling, ___

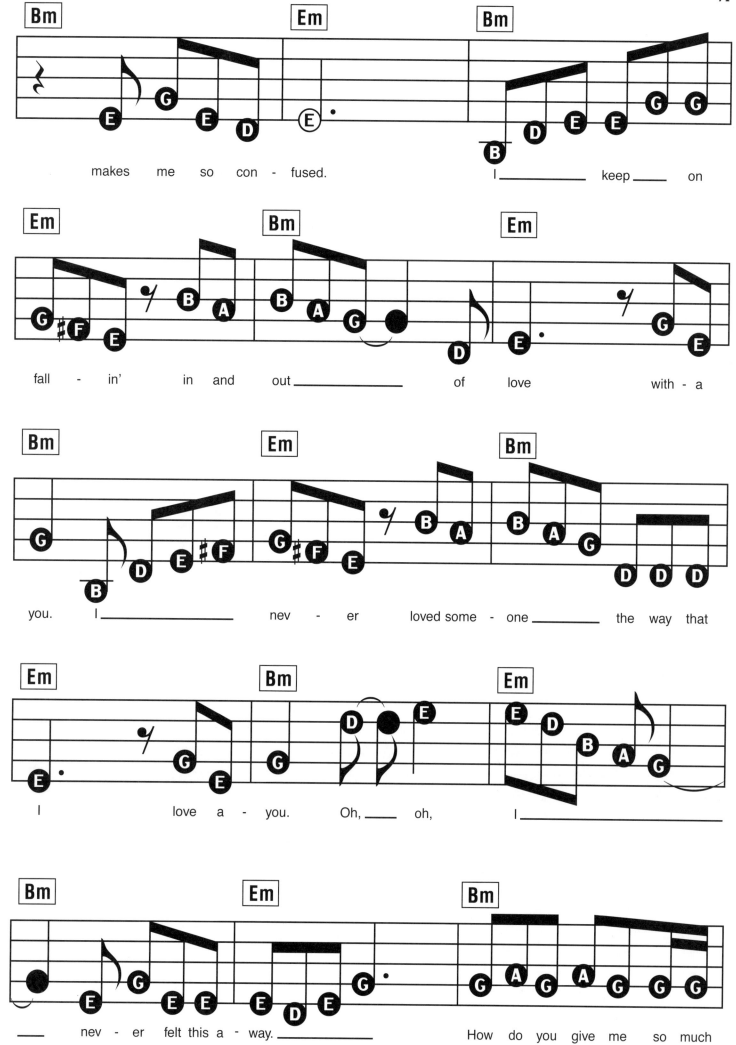

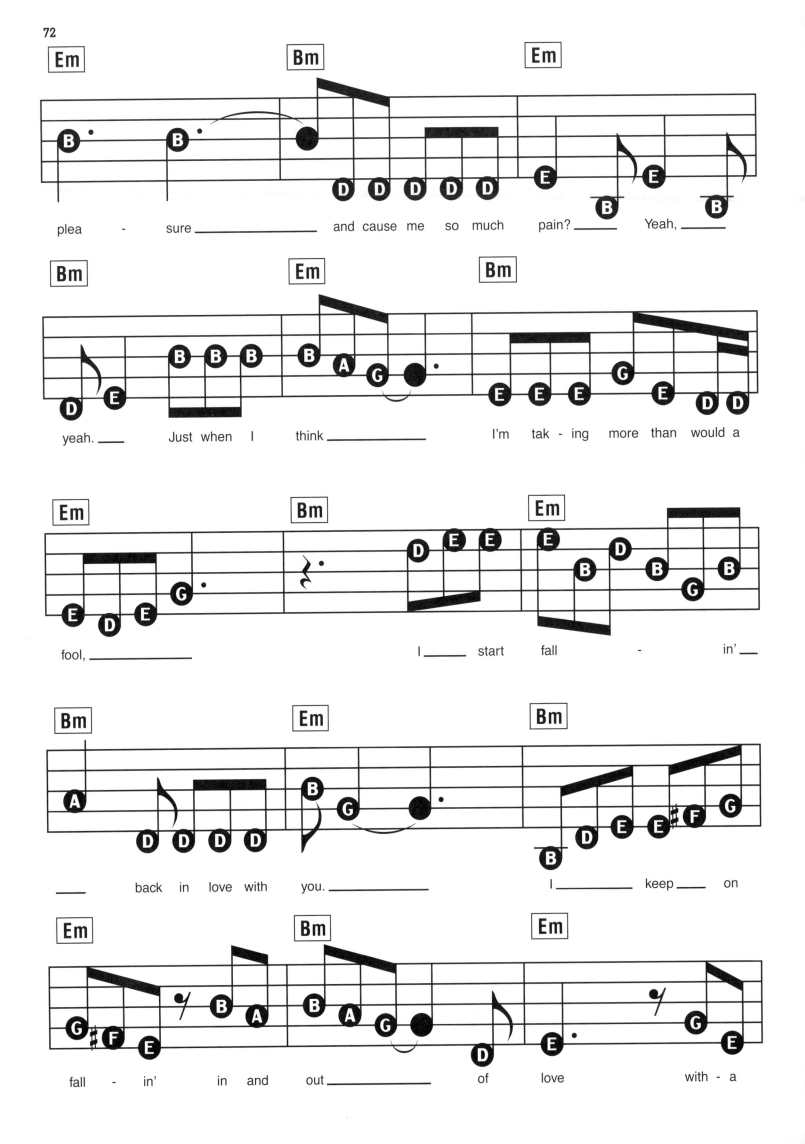

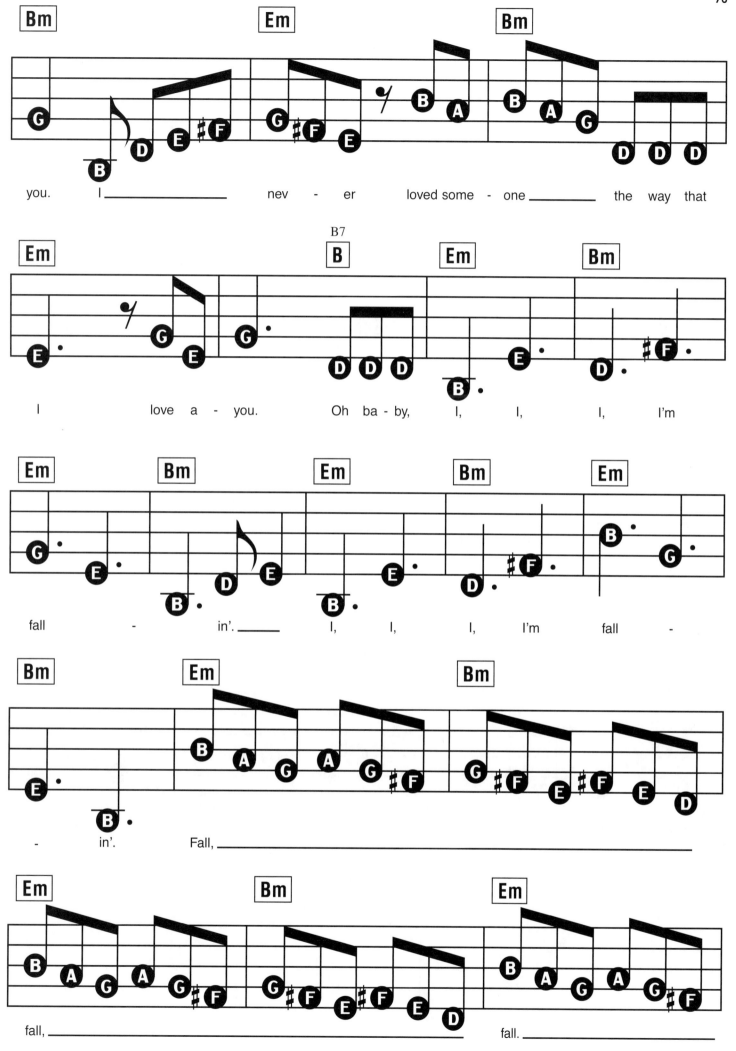

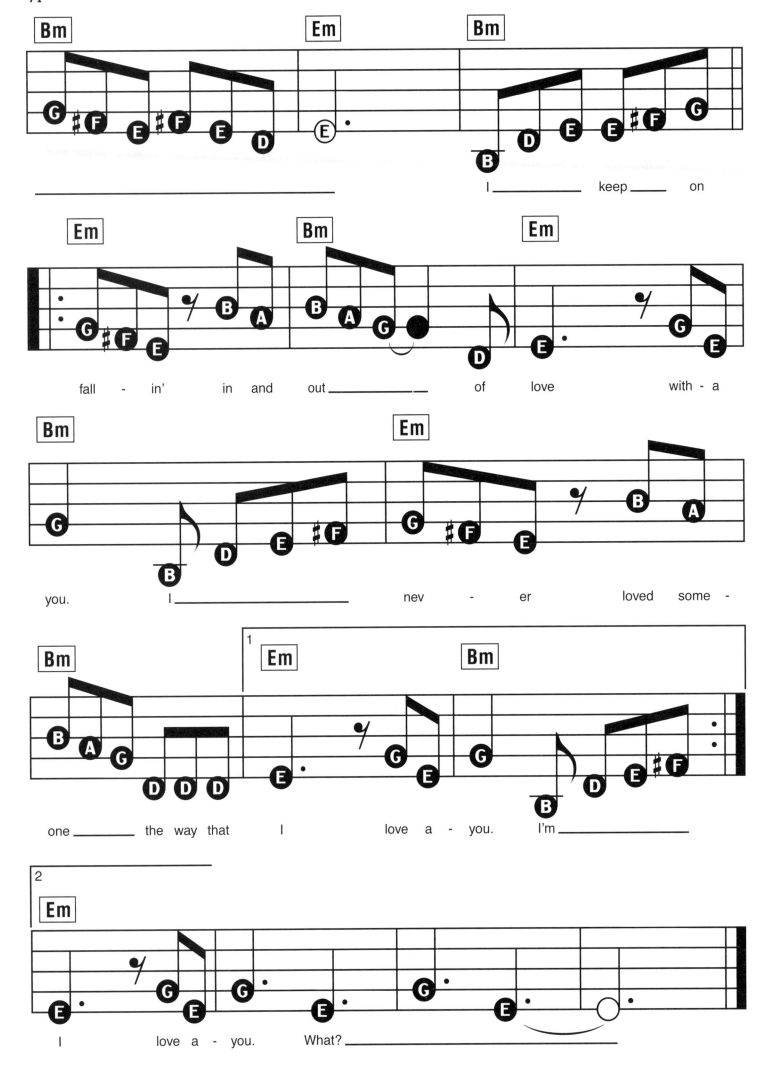

How Deep Is Your Love
from the Motion Picture SATURDAY NIGHT FEVER

Registration 4
Rhythm: Rock or Disco

Words and Music by Barry Gibb,
Robin Gibb and Maurice Gibb

E♭7

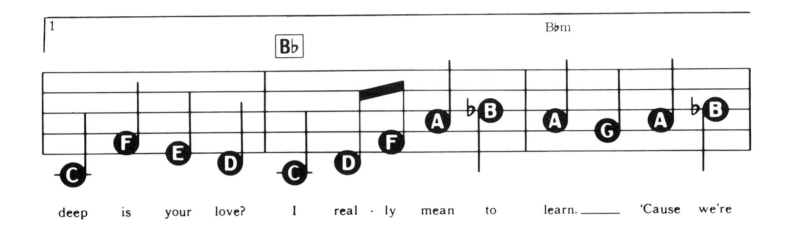

soft · ly leave.⎱ And it's me you need to show: How deep is your love? How
real · ly do. ⎰

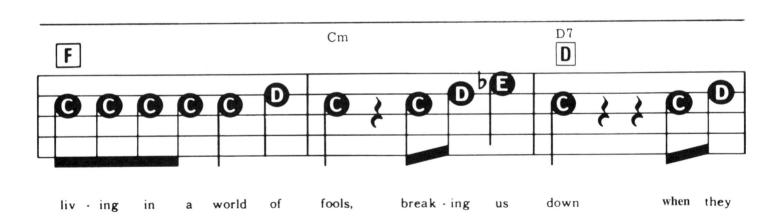

deep is your love? I real · ly mean to learn.____ 'Cause we're

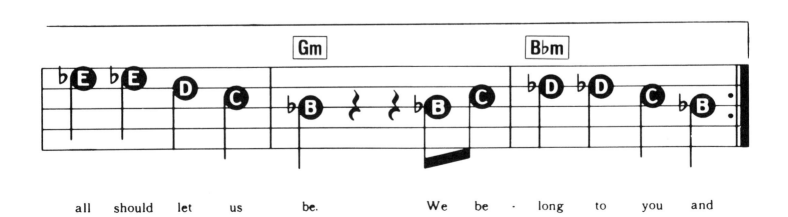

liv · ing in a world of fools, break · ing us down when they

all should let us be. We be · long to you and

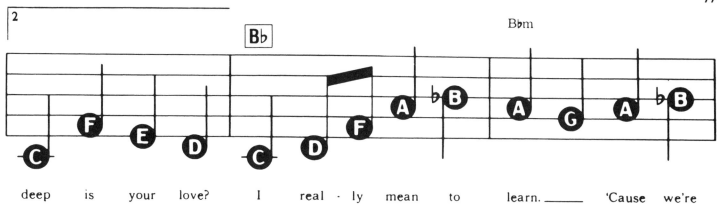

deep   is   your   love?   I   real · ly   mean   to   learn. _____ 'Cause   we're

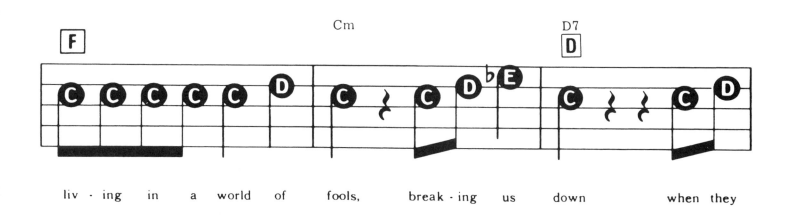

liv · ing   in   a   world   of   fools,   break · ing   us   down   when   they

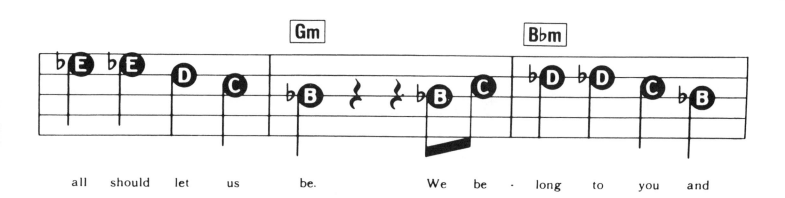

all   should   let   us   be.   We   be · long   to   you   and

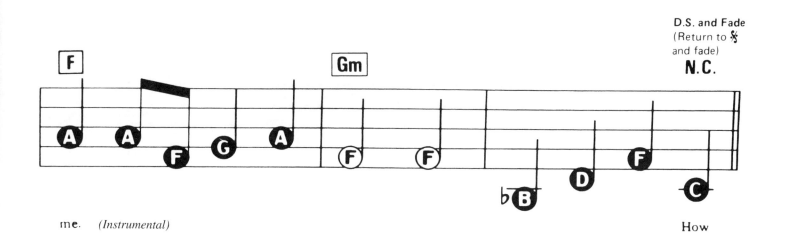

me.   *(Instrumental)*   How

Fields of Gold

Registration 4
Rhythm: Rock or 8-Beat

Music and Lyrics by
Sting

You'll re - mem - ber me,   when the   west wind moves up a -
stay with me,   will you   be my love a -

on   the   fields   of   bar - ley.   You'll for - get   the   sun   in   his
mong   the   fields   of   bar - ley?   We'll for - get   the   sun   in   his

jeal - ous   sky   as   we   walk   in   fields   of   gold.
jeal - ous   sky   as   we   lie   in   fields   of   gold.

So   she
See   the

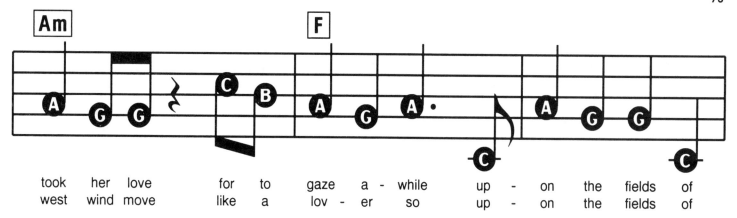

took her love for to gaze a - while up - on the fields of
west wind move like a lov - er so up - on the fields of

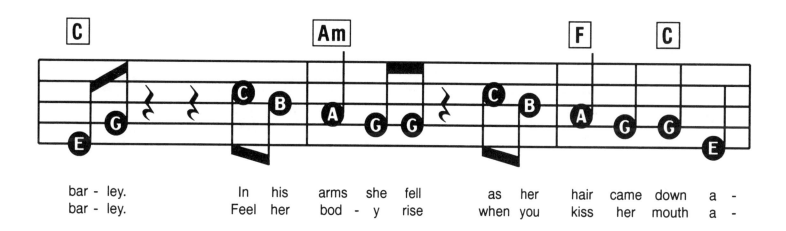

bar - ley. In his arms she fell as her hair came down a -
bar - ley. Feel her bod - y rise when you kiss her mouth a -

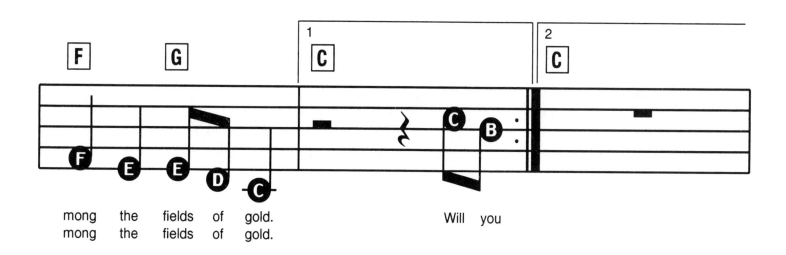

mong the fields of gold.
mong the fields of gold. Will you

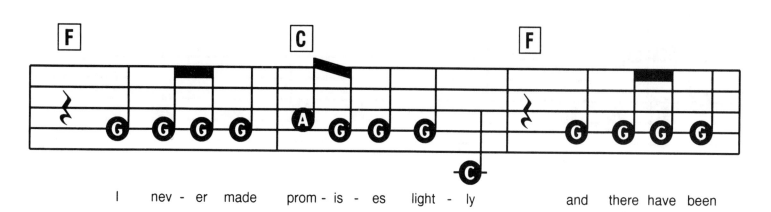

I nev - er made prom - is - es light - ly and there have been

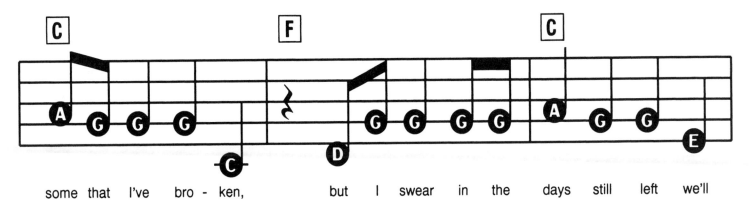

some that I've bro - ken,   but I swear in the days still left we'll

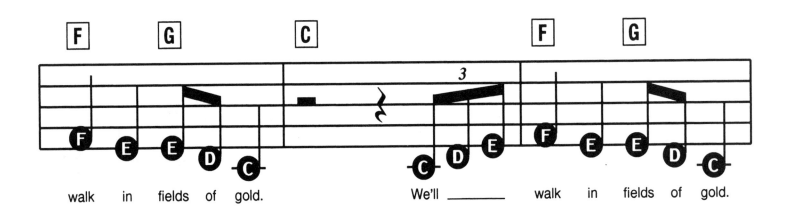

walk in fields of gold.   We'll _____ walk in fields of gold.

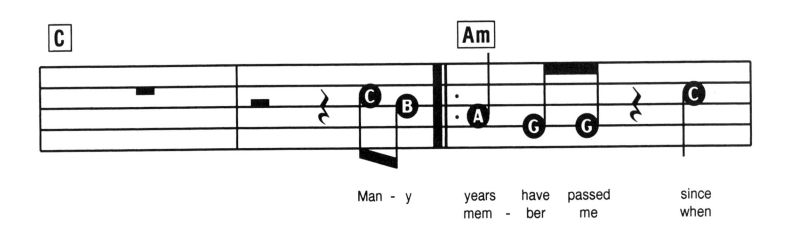

Man - y   years have passed   since
mem - ber   me   when

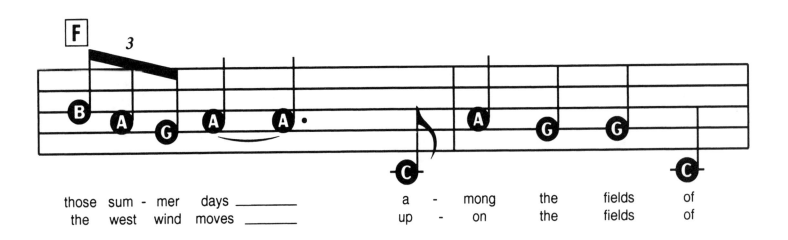

those sum - mer days _____   a - mong the fields of
the west wind moves _____   up - on the fields of

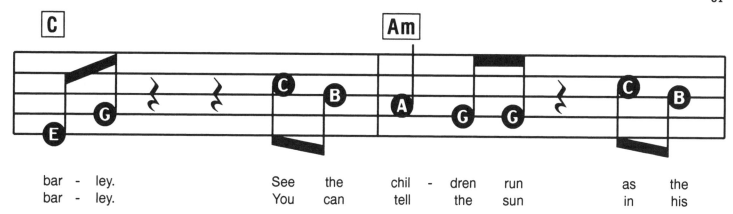

bar - ley.   See the chil - dren run   as the
bar - ley.   You can tell the sun   in his

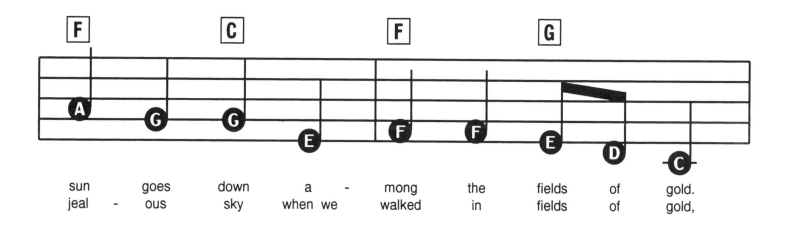

sun goes down a - mong the fields of gold.
jeal - ous sky when we walked in fields of gold,

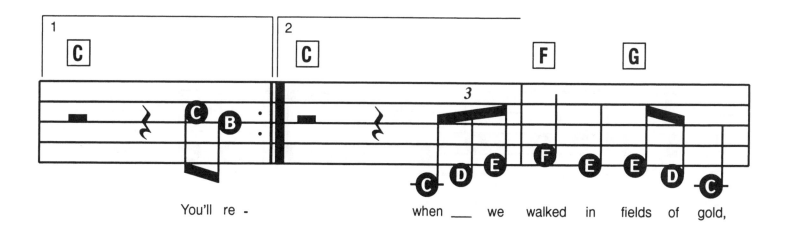

You'll re -   when ___ we walked in fields of gold,

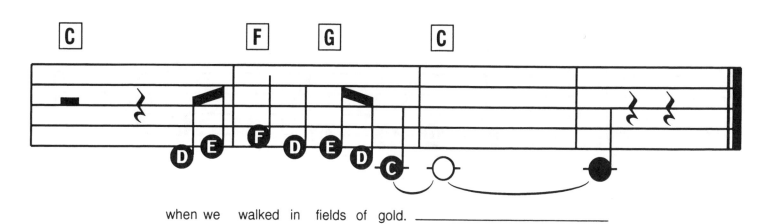

when we walked in fields of gold. _____

Hallelujah

Registration 4
Rhythm: 6/8 March

Words and Music by
Leonard Cohen

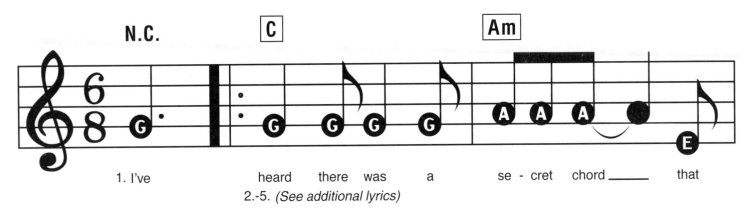

1. I've   heard   there   was   a   se - cret chord _____   that
2.-5. *(See additional lyrics)*

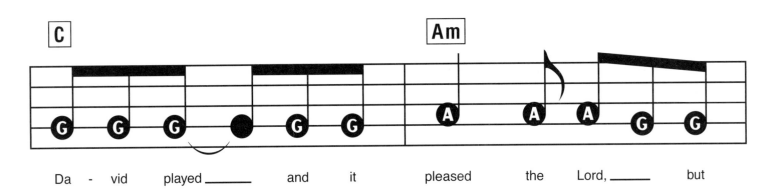

Da - vid   played _____   and   it   pleased the   Lord, _____   but

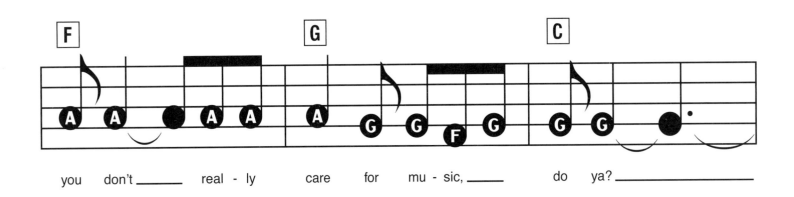

you   don't _____   real - ly care   for   mu - sic, _____   do   ya? _____

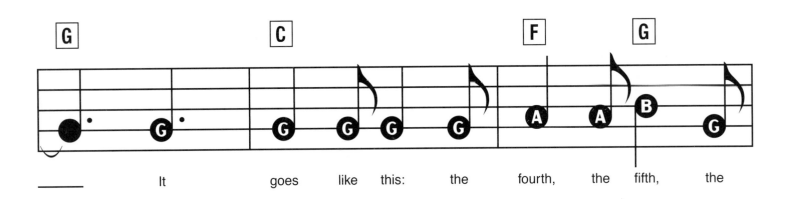

_____   It   goes   like   this: the   fourth, the   fifth,   the

83

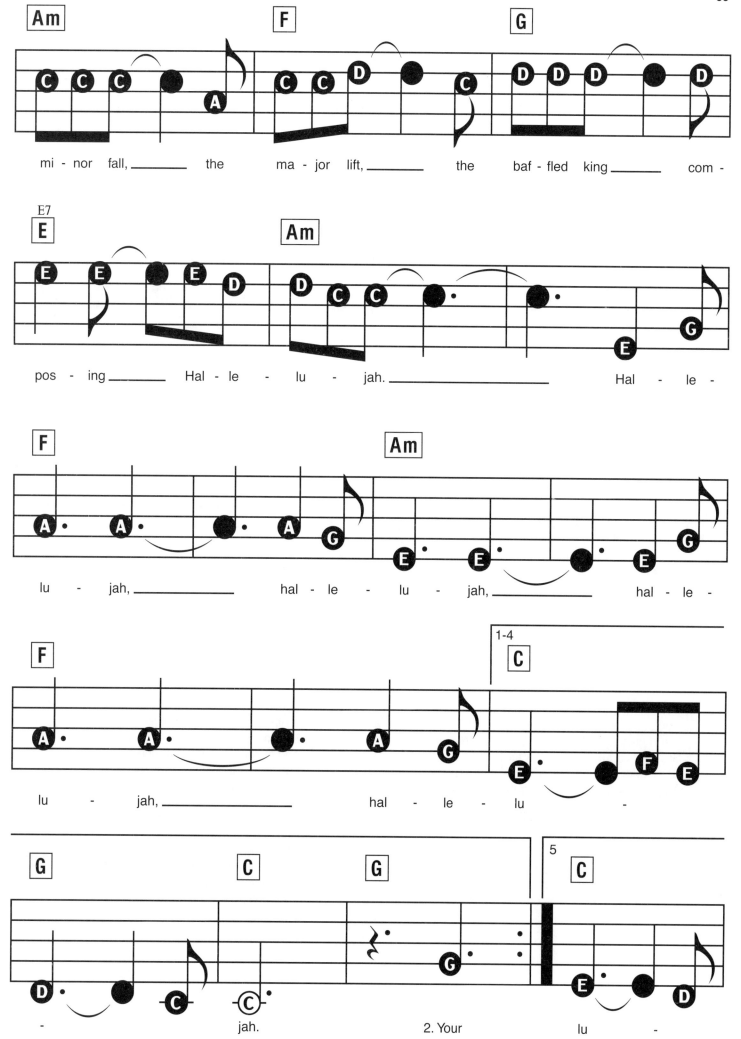

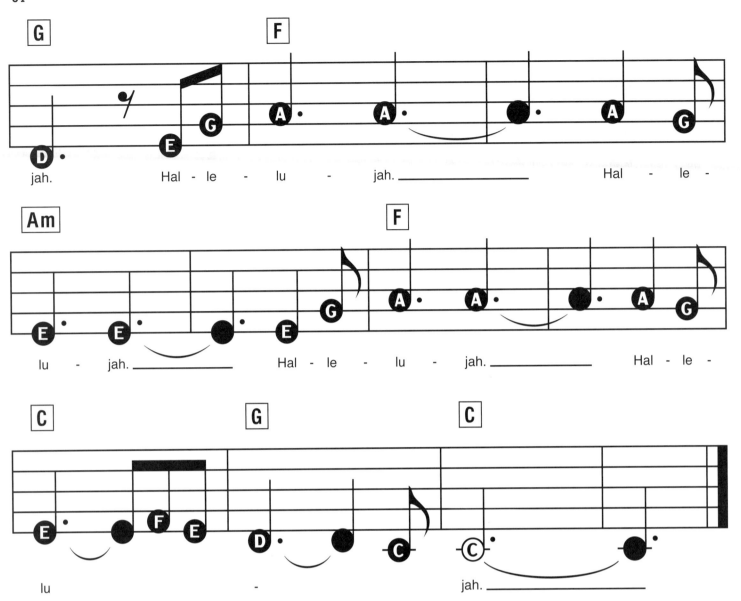

Additional Lyrics

2. Your faith was strong but you needed proof.
   You saw her bathing on the roof.
   Her beauty and the moonlight overthrew ya.
   She tied you to a kitchen chair.
   She broke your throne, she cut your hair.
   And from your lips she drew the Hallelujah.

3. Maybe I have been here before.
   I know this room, I've walked this floor.
   I used to live alone before I knew ya.
   I've seen your flag on the marble arch.
   Love is not a vict'ry march.
   It's a cold and it's a broken Hallelujah.

4. There was a time you let me know
   What's real and going on below.
   But now you never show it to me, do ya?
   And remember when I moved in you.
   The holy dark was movin', too,
   And every breath we drew was Hallelujah.

5. Maybe there's a God above,
   And all I ever learned from love
   Was how to shoot at someone who outdrew ya.
   And it's not a cry you can hear at night.
   It's not somebody who's seen the light.
   It's a cold and it's a broken Hallelujah.

I Feel the Earth Move

Registration 4
Rhythm: Rock

Words and Music by
Carole King

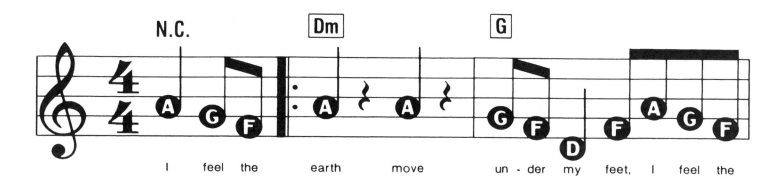

I feel the earth move un-der my feet, I feel the

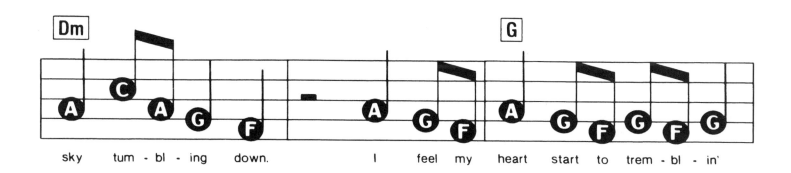

sky tum-bl-ing down. I feel my heart start to trem-bl-in'

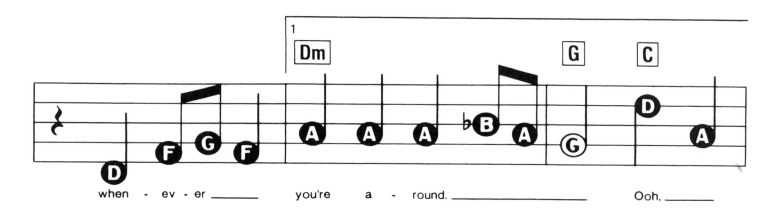

when-ev-er _____ you're a-round. _____ Ooh, _____

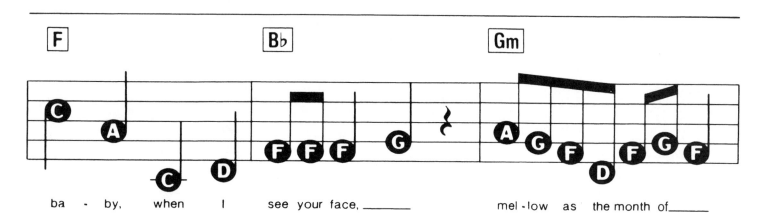

ba-by, when I see your face, _____ mel-low as the month of _____

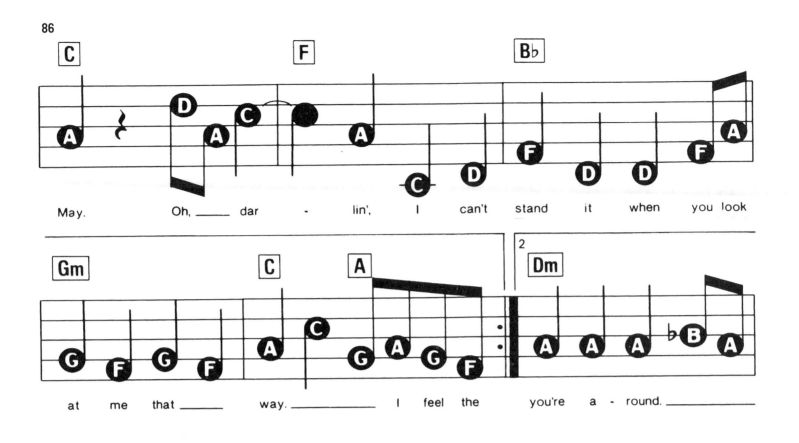

May.   Oh, _____ dar - lin',   I   can't   stand   it   when   you   look

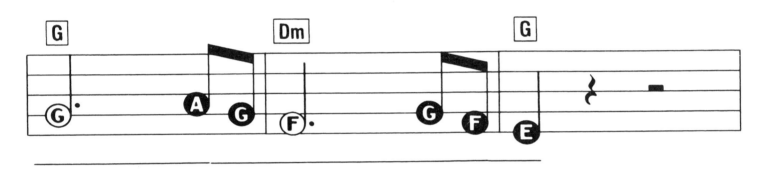

at   me   that _____   way. _____ I   feel   the   you're   a - round. _____

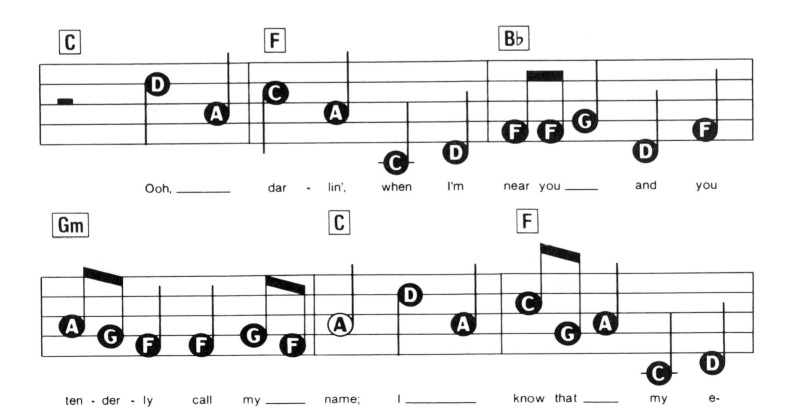

Ooh, _____ dar - lin',   when   I'm   near   you _____   and   you

ten - der - ly   call   my _____ name;   I _____ know   that _____   my   e-

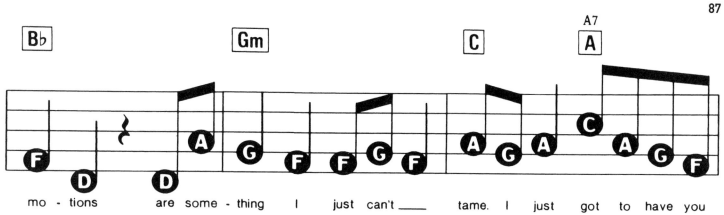

mo - tions   are some - thing   I   just can't ____   tame.   I   just   got   to   have   you

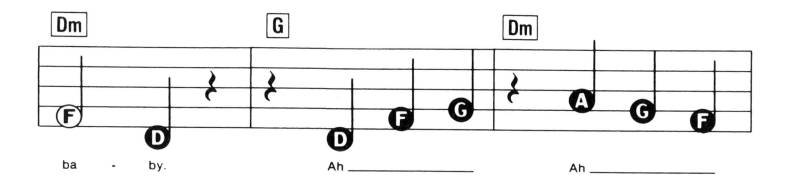

ba - by.   Ah _____   Ah _____

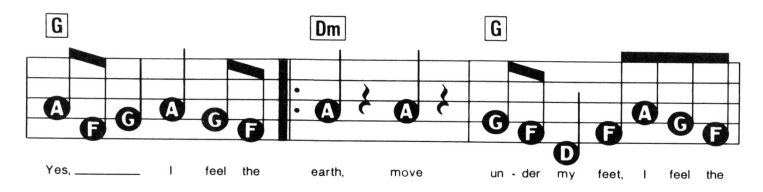

Yes, _____   I   feel   the   earth,   move   un - der   my   feet,   I   feel   the

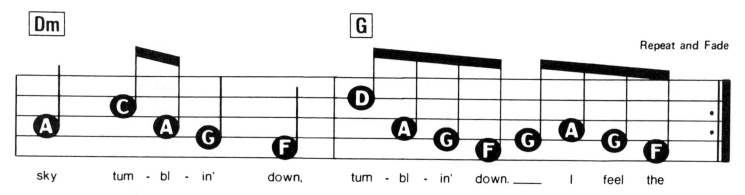

Repeat and Fade

sky   tum - bl - in'   down,   tum - bl - in'   down. ____   I   feel   the

Additional Lyrics

I just lose control down to my very soul,
I get hot and cold all over, all over, all over.

I'm a Believer

Registration 5
Rhythm: Rock

Words and Music by
Neil Diamond

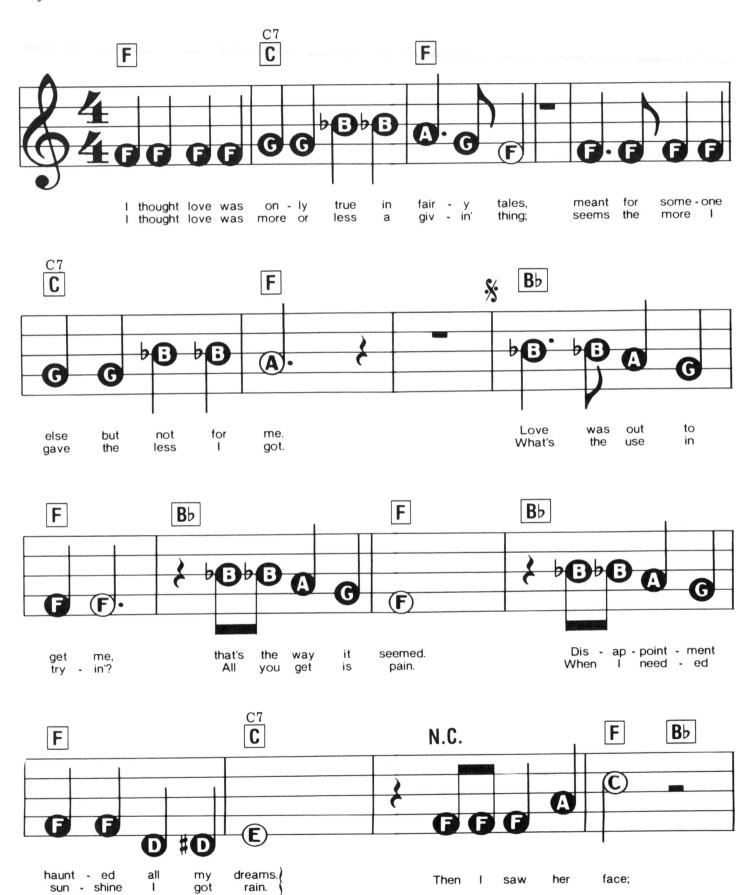

I thought love was on-ly true in fair-y tales,
I thought love was more or less a giv-in' thing;

meant for some-one
seems the more I

else but not for me.
gave the not less I got.

Love was out to
What's the use in

get me,
try-in'?

that's the way it seemed.
All you get is pain.

Dis-ap-point-ment
When I need-ed

haunt-ed all my dreams.
sun-shine I got rain.

Then I saw her face;

89

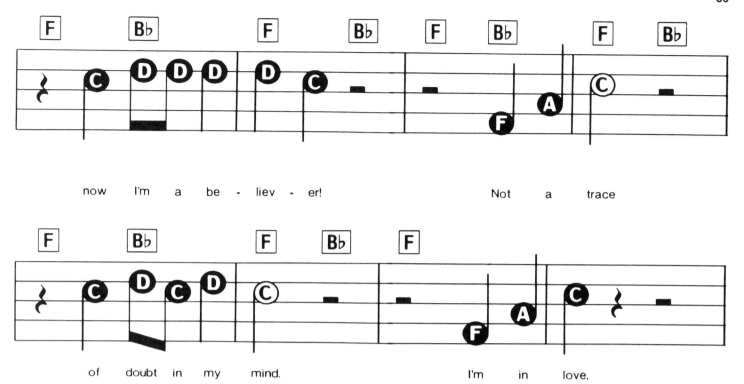

now I'm a be - liev - er! Not a trace

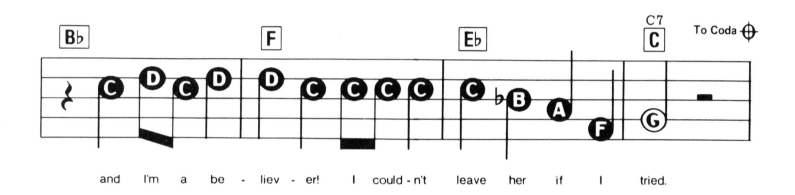

of doubt in my mind. I'm in love,

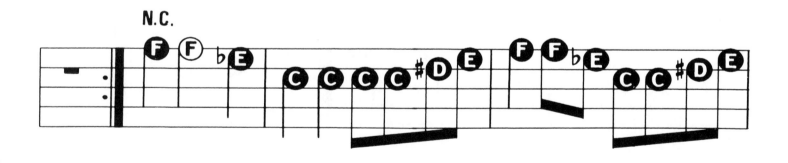

and I'm a be - liev - er! I could-n't leave her if I tried.

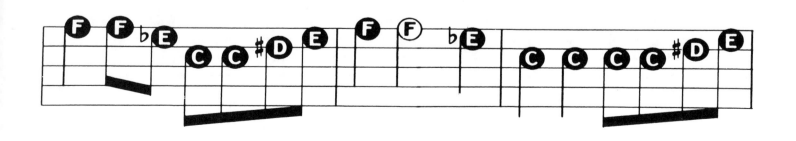

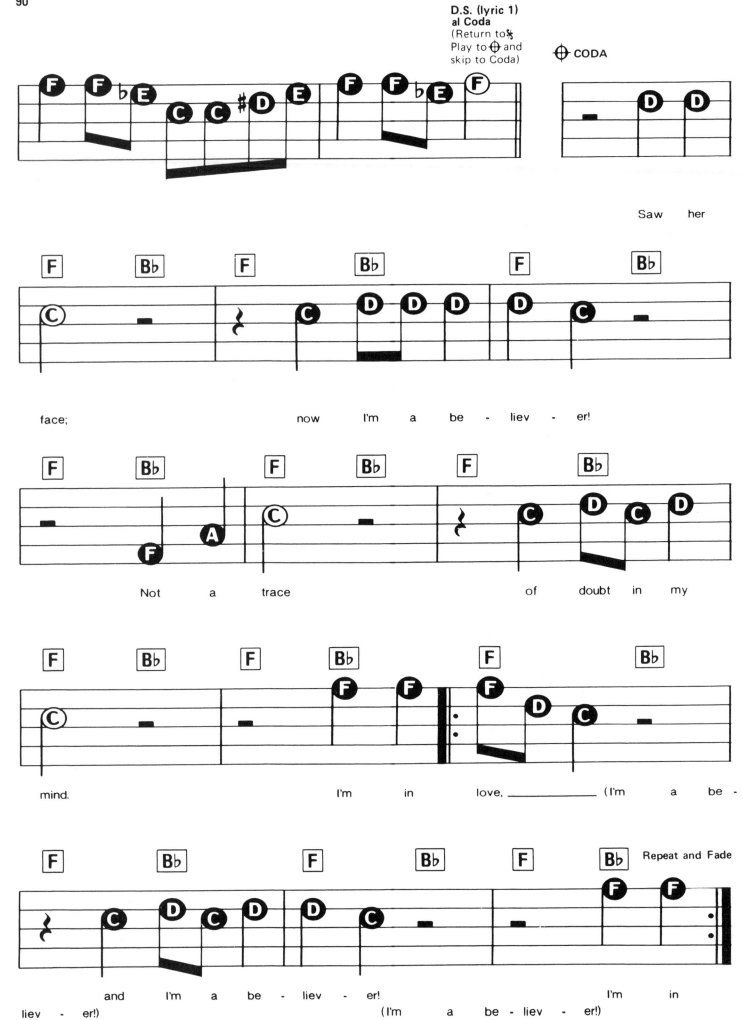

Living for the City

Registration 9
Rhythm: Rock

Words and Music by
Stevie Wonder

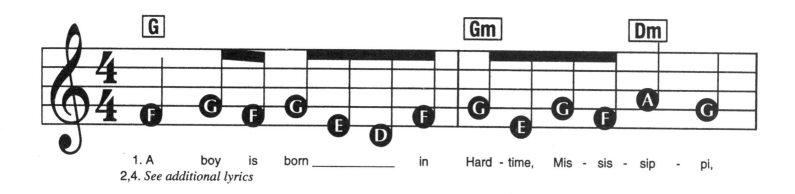

1. A boy is born _____ in Hard - time, Mis - sis - sip - pi,
2,4. *See additional lyrics*

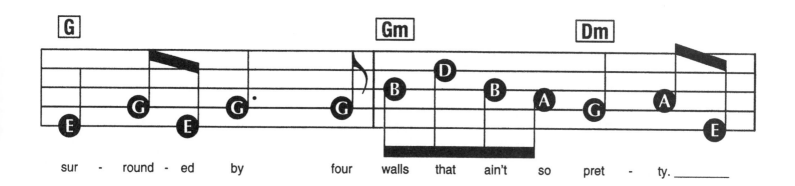

sur - round - ed by four walls that ain't so pret - ty. _____

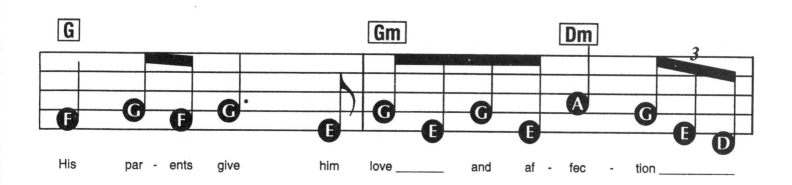

His par - ents give him love _____ and af - fec - tion _____

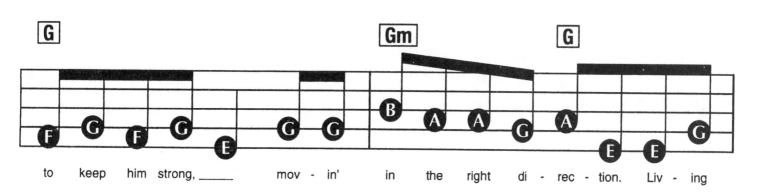

to keep him strong, _____ mov - in' in the right di - rec - tion. Liv - ing

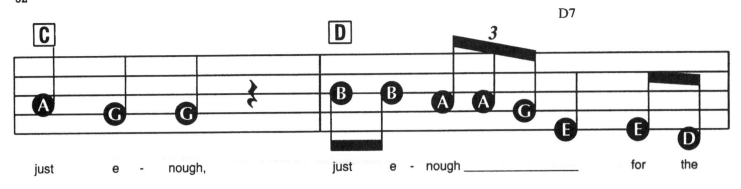

just e - nough, just e - nough _____ for the

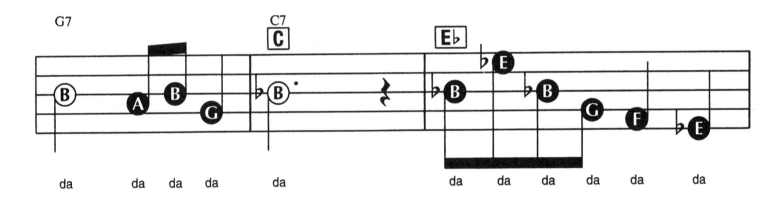

ci - ty. Yeah, Da da da

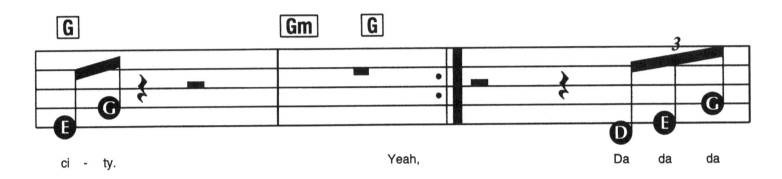

da da da da da da da da da da da

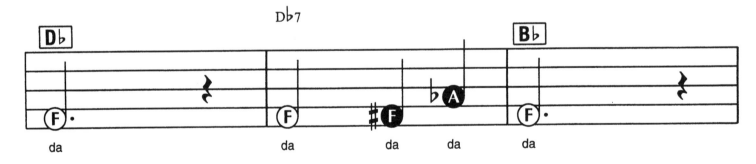

da da da da da

D.C. al Coda
(Return to beginning,
Play to ✛ and
Skip to Coda)

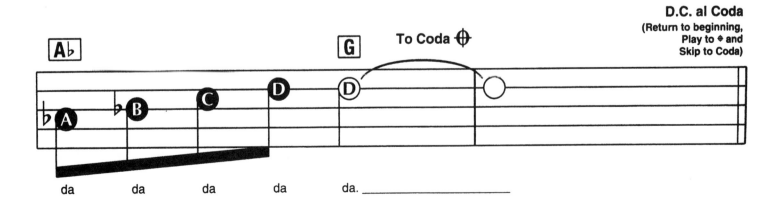

To Coda ✛

da da da da da. _____

CODA

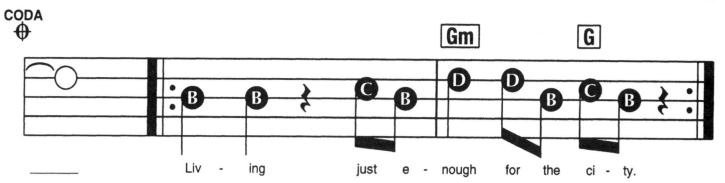

Liv - ing   just   e - nough   for   the   ci - ty.

Additional Lyrics

2. His father works some days for fourteen hours,
   And you can bet he barely makes a dollar.
   His mother goes to scrub the follrs for many,
   And you'd best believe she hardly gets a penny.
   Living just enough, just enough for the city.

3. His sister's black, but she is sho'nuff pretty.
   Her skirt is short, but Lord her legs are sturdy.
   To walk to school, she's got to get up early.
   Her clothes are old, but never are they dirty.
   Living just enough, just enough for the city.

4. Her brother's smart, he's got more sense than many.
   His patience's long, but soon he won't have any.
   To find a job is like a haaystack needle, 'cause
   Where he lives, they don't use colored people.
   Living just enough, just enough for the city.

In My Life

Registration 2
Rhythm: Rock or Jazz Rock

Words and Music by John Lennon
and Paul McCartney

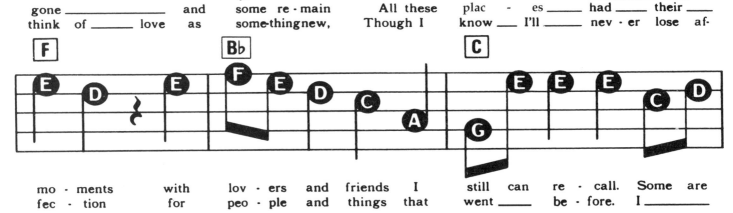

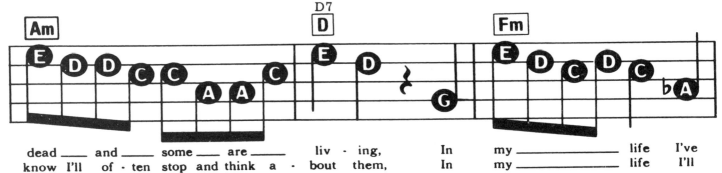

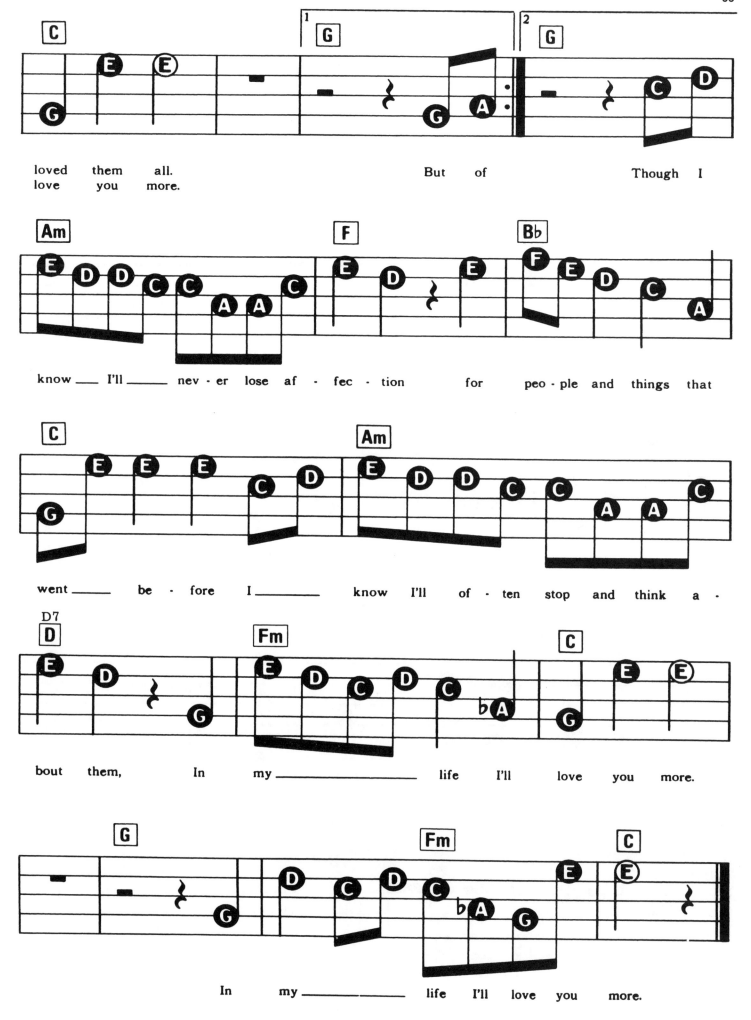

loved them all.
love you more.
But of
Though I

know ___ I'll ___ nev - er lose af - fec - tion for peo - ple and things that

went ___ be - fore I ___ know I'll of - ten stop and think a -

bout them, In my ___ life I'll love you more.

In my ___ life I'll love you more.

Just the Two of Us

Registration 4
Rhythm: Latin

Words and Music by Ralph MacDonald,
William Salter and Bill Withers

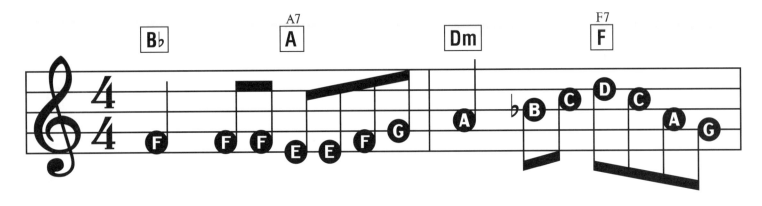

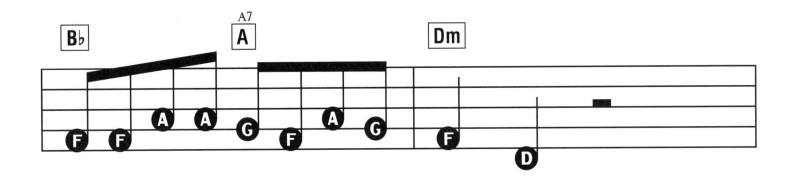

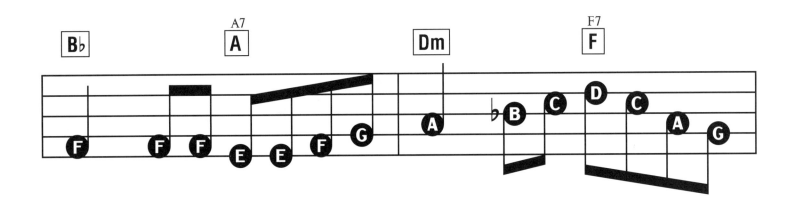

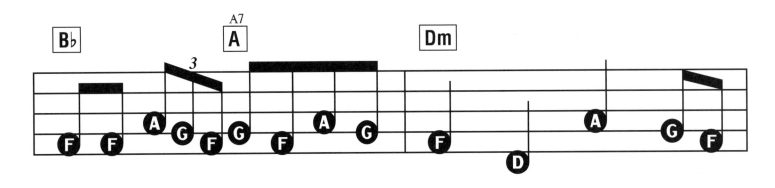

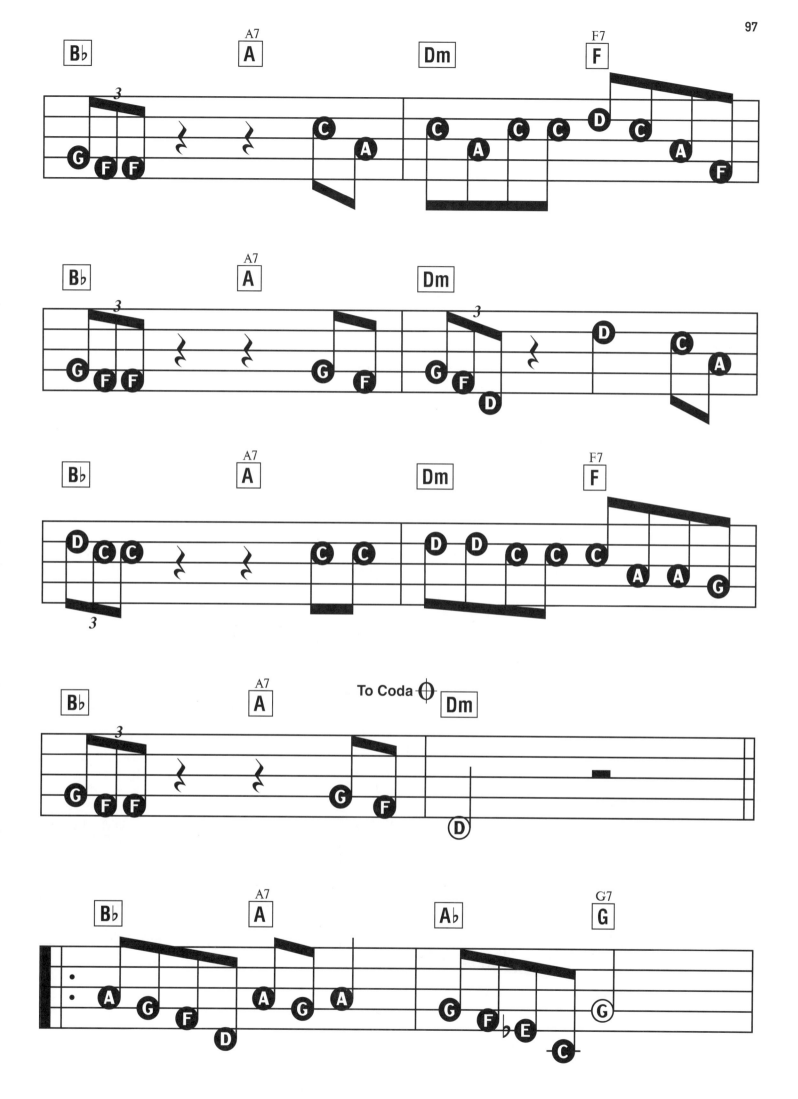

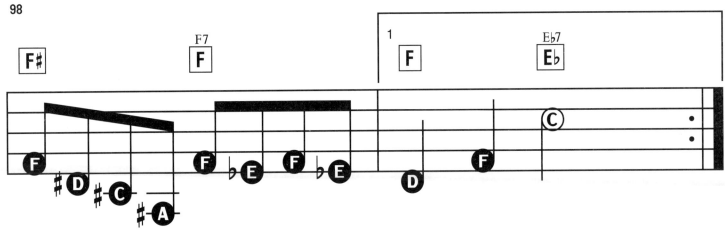

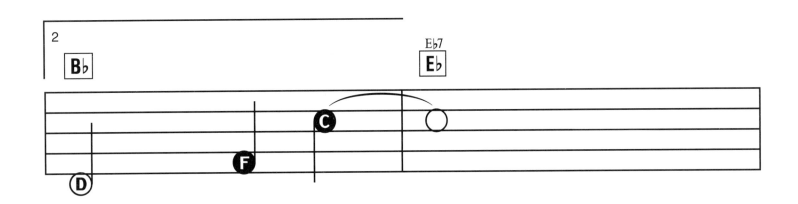

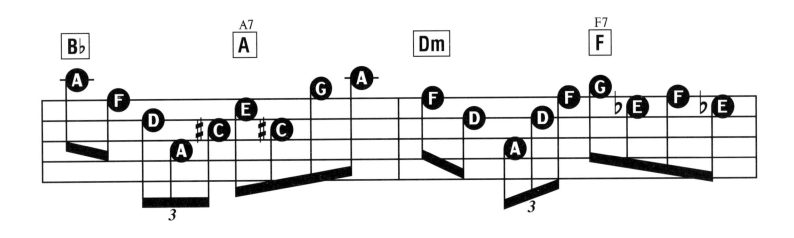

D.C. al Coda
(Return to beginning
Play to ⊕ and
Skip to Coda)

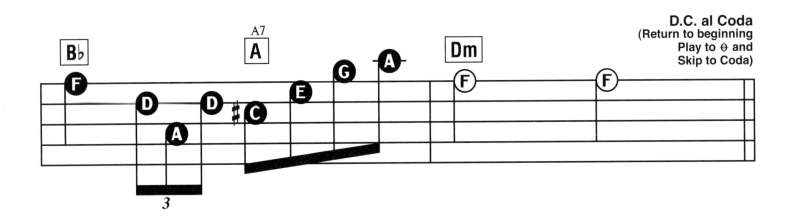

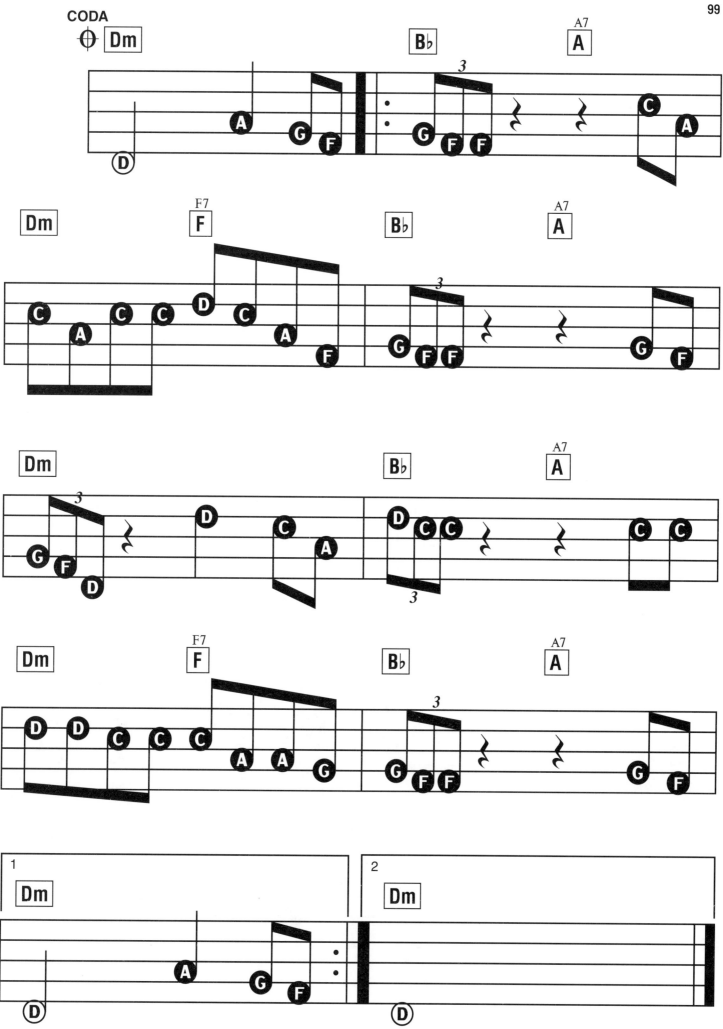

Just the Way You Are

Registration 4
Rhythm: Rock or Jazz Rock

Words and Music by
Billy Joel

C   **Am**   **F**

C E C A· A C
E

Don't   go   chang - ing   to   try   and
Don't   go   try - ing   some ____   new
said   I   love you,   and   that's for -

C (C7)   **F**   **Fm**

A   E·   E F G   E C C ♭A

please   me.   You   nev - er   let   me   down   be -
fash - ion.   Don't change the   col - or   of   your
ev - er,   and   this   I   prom - ise from   the

C   **F** (C7)   **F**

E   F G E D   E E E

fore.   Mm, ____ mm. ____   Don't   i -
hair.   Mm, ____ mm. ____   You   always
heart.   Mm, ____ mm. ____   I   could not

Fm   **C**   **Am**   **To Coda** ⊕

D C·   C E G   B C

mag - ine   you're too fa - mil - iar
have   my   un - spok - en pas - sion,
love   you   an - y   bet - ter.

101

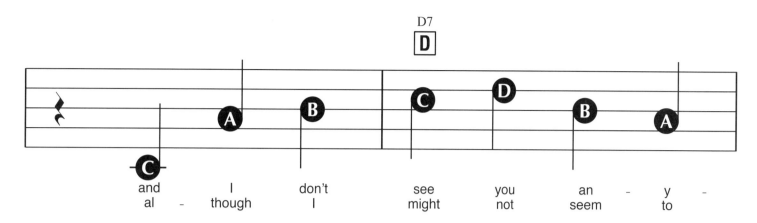

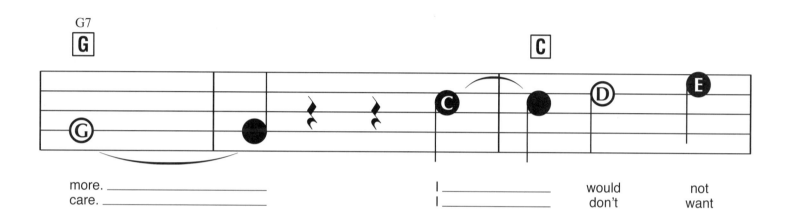

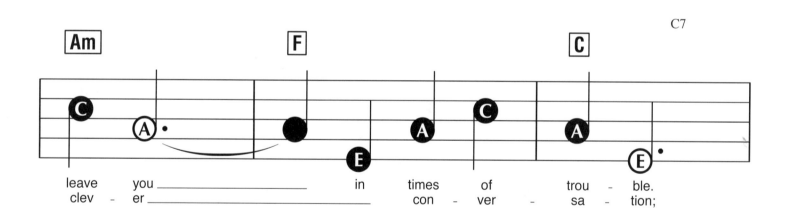

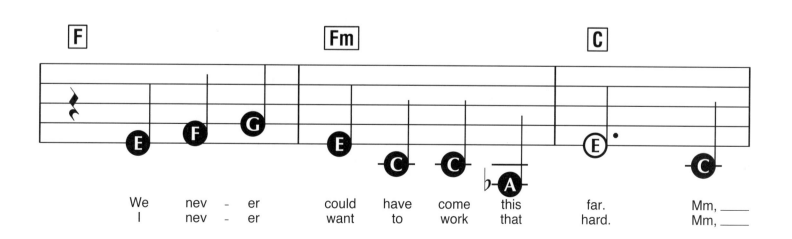

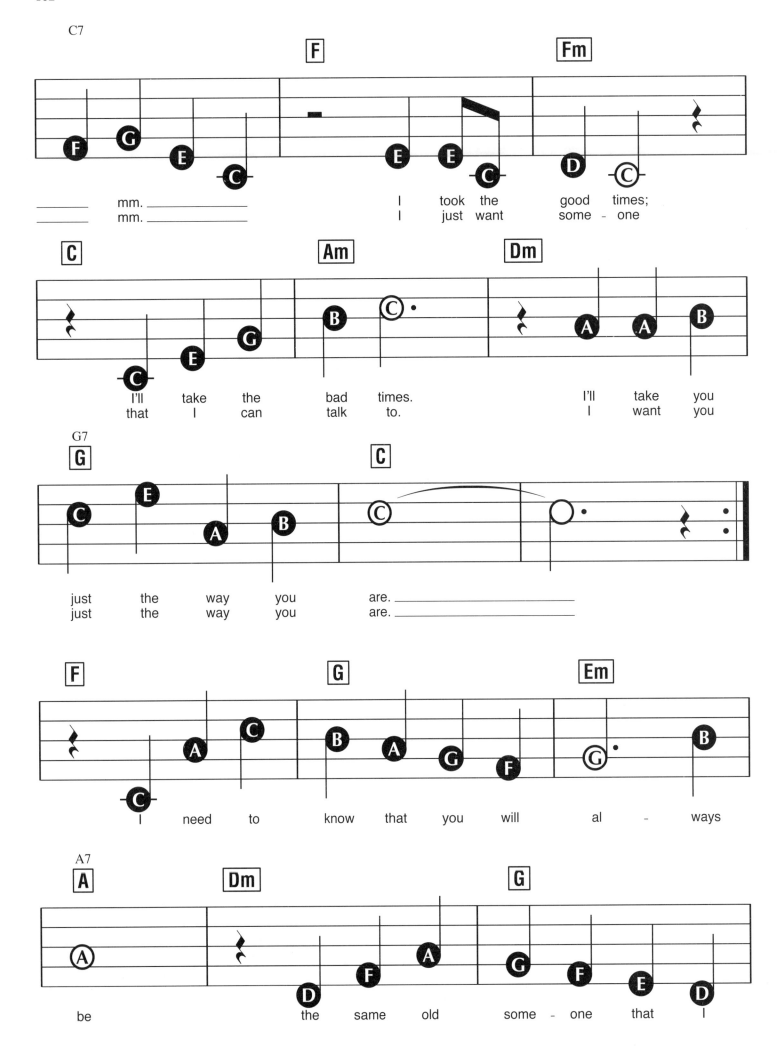

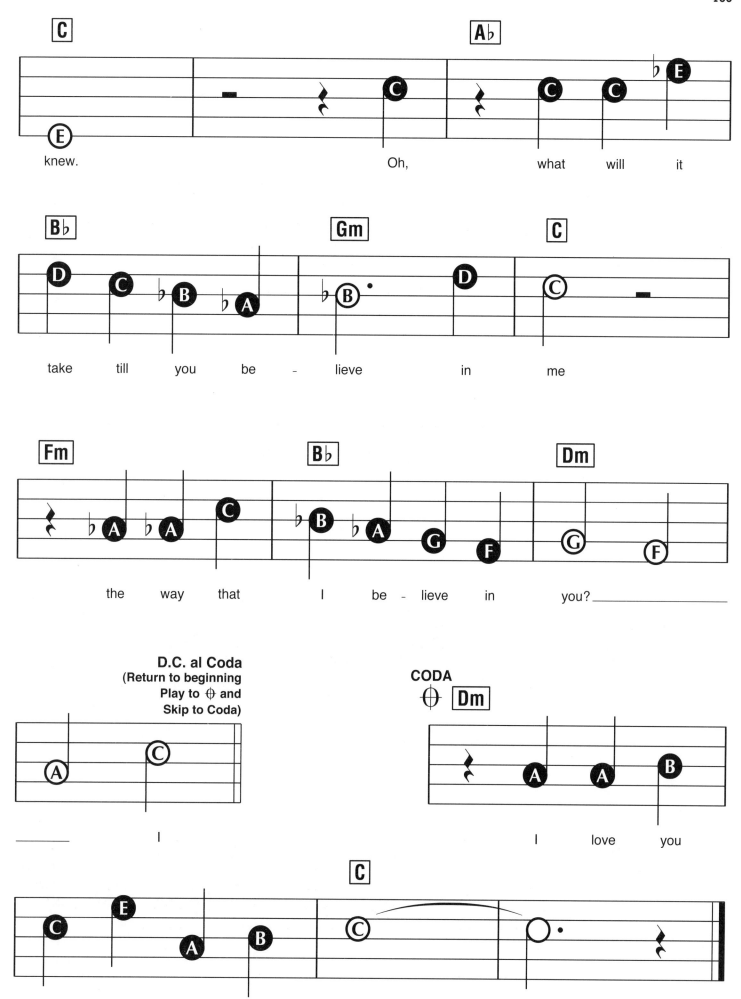

103

Killing Me Softly with His Song

Registration 2
Rhythm: Rock

Words by Norman Gimbel
Music by Charles Fox

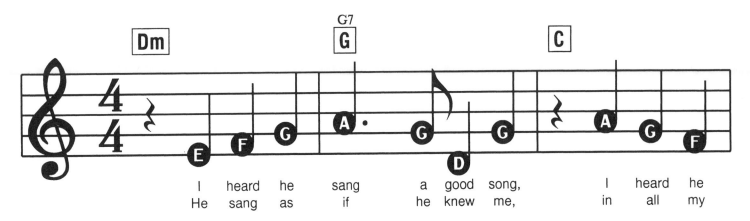

I heard he sang a good song, I heard he
He sang as if he knew me, in all my

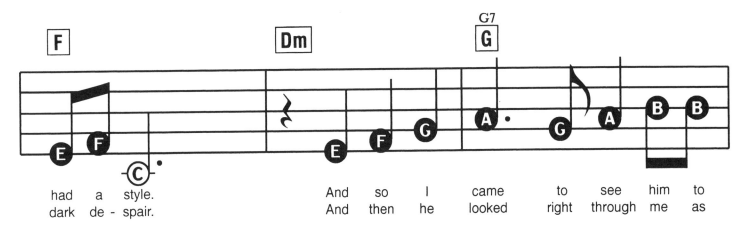

had a style. And so I came to see him to
dark de-spair. And then he looked right through me as

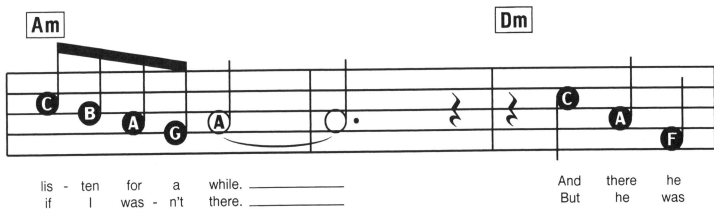

lis - ten for a while. _____
if I was-n't there. _____
And there he
But he was

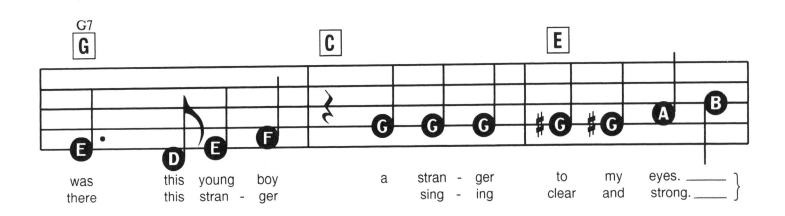

was this young boy a stran - ger to my eyes. _____
there this stran - ger sing - ing clear and strong. _____

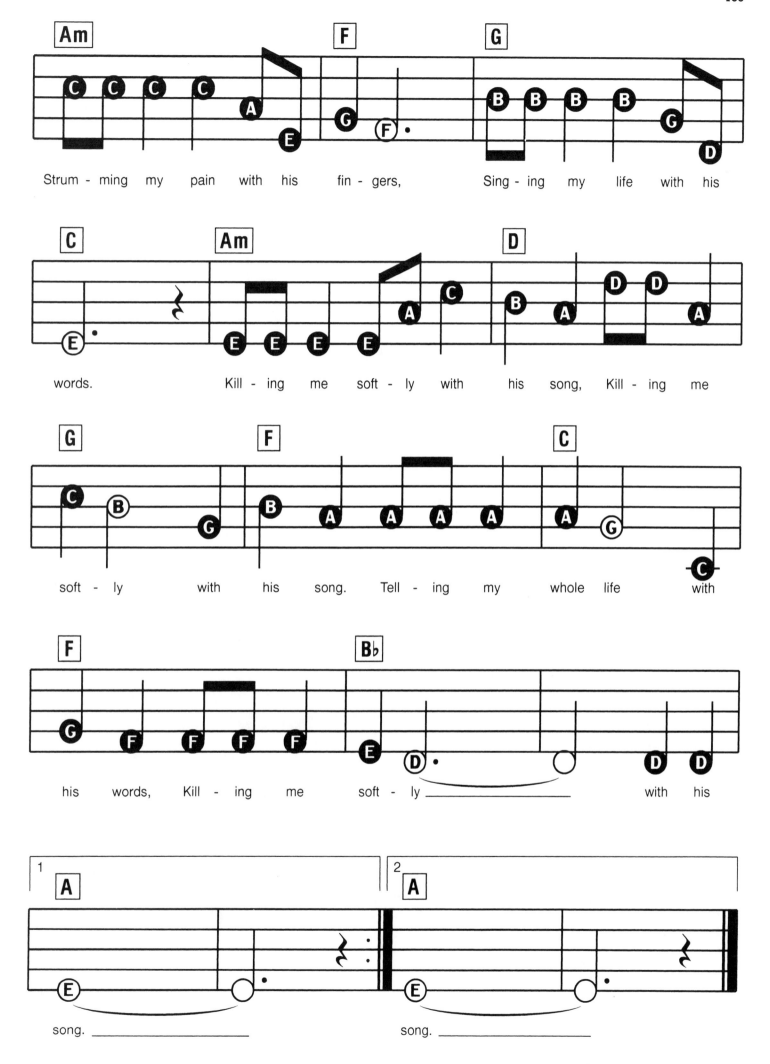

Longer

Registration 4
Rhythm: Ballad or Slow Rock

Words and Music by
Dan Fogelberg

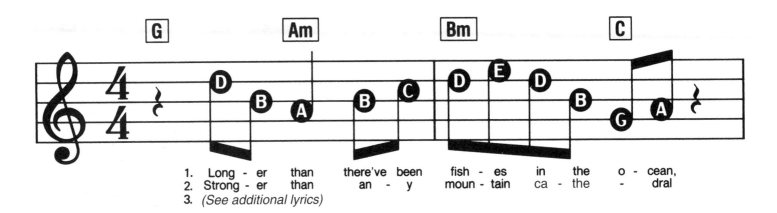

1. Long - er than there've been fish - es in the o - cean,
2. Strong - er than an - y moun - tain ca - the - dral
3. *(See additional lyrics)*

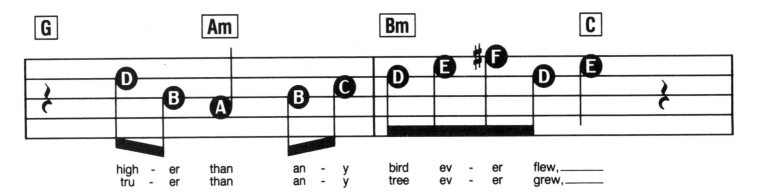

high - er than an - y bird ev - er flew,_____
tru - er than an - y tree ev - er grew,_____

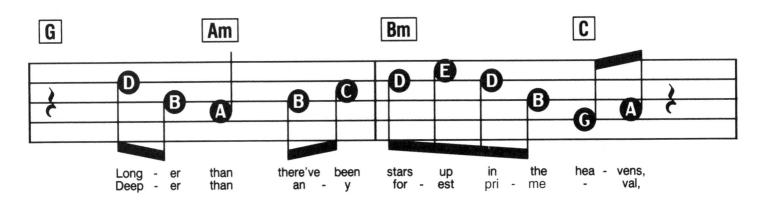

Long - er than there've been stars up in the hea - vens,
Deep - er than an - y for - est pri - me - val,

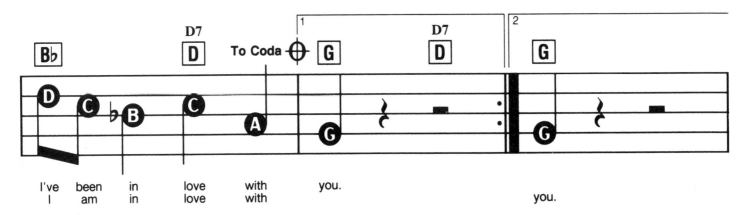

I've been in love with you.
I am in love with you.

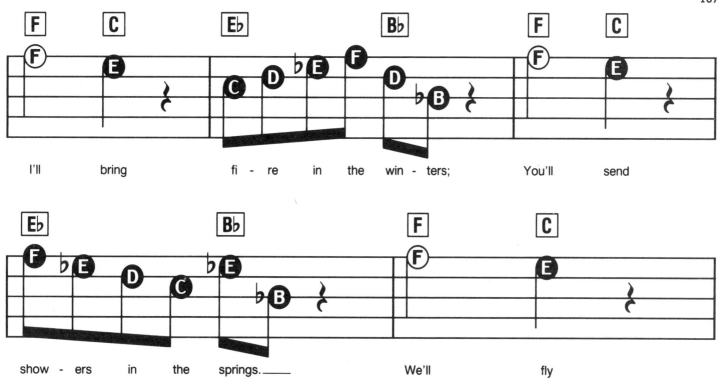

I'll   bring   fi - re   in   the   win - ters;   You'll   send

show - ers   in   the   springs.____   We'll   fly

D.C. al Coda
(Return to beginning. Play to ⊕
and skip to Coda)

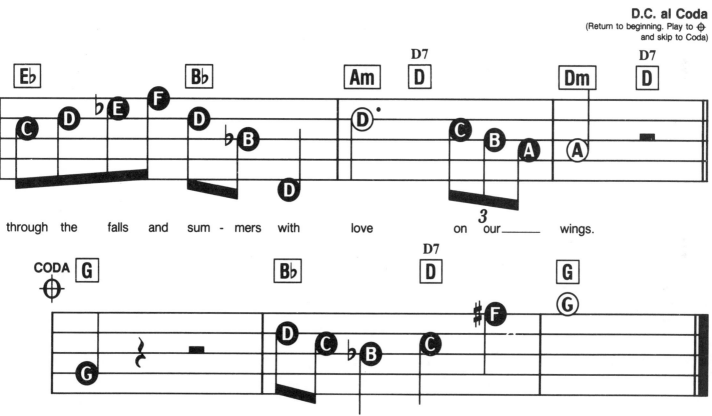

through   the   falls   and   sum - mers   with   love   on   our____   wings.

you.   I'll   be   in   love   with   you.

Additional Lyrics

3. Through the years as the fire starts to mellow,
   Burning lines in the book of our lives.
   Though the binding cracks and the pages start to yellow,
   I'll be in love with you.

Love Song

Registration 8
Rhythm: Rock or Dance

Words and Music by
Sara Bareilles

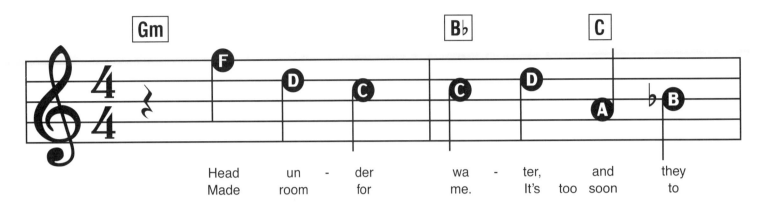

Head un - der wa - ter, and they
Made room for me. It's too soon to

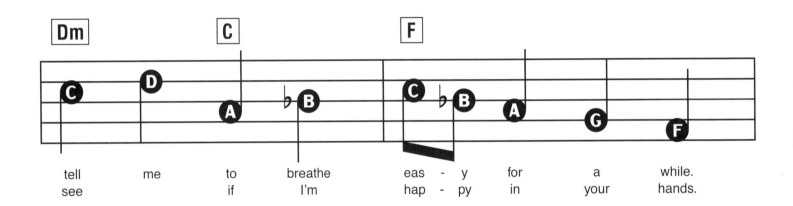

tell me to breathe eas - y for a while.
see if I'm hap - py in your hands.

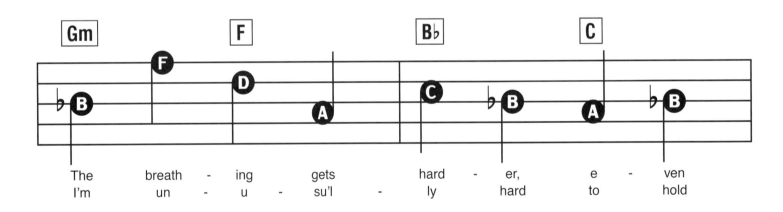

The breath - ing gets hard - er, e - ven
I'm un - u - su'l - ly hard to hold

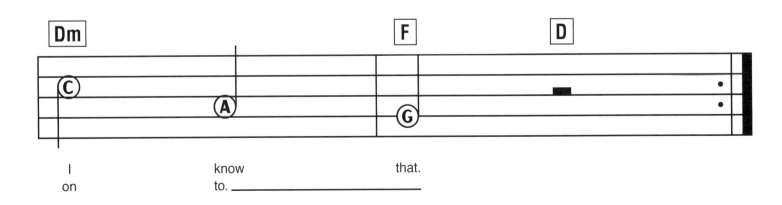

I know that.
on to. _____

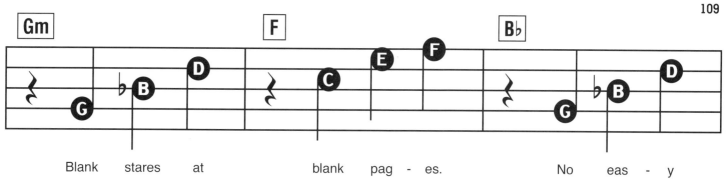

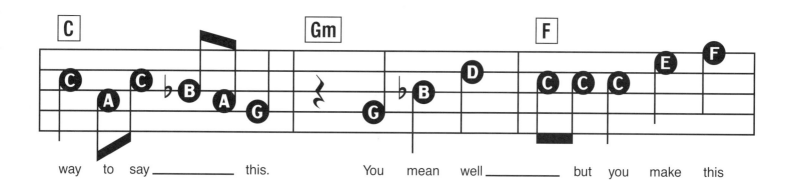

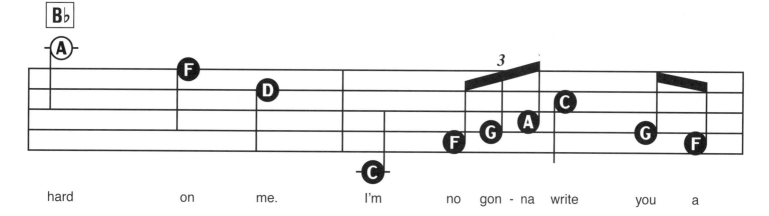

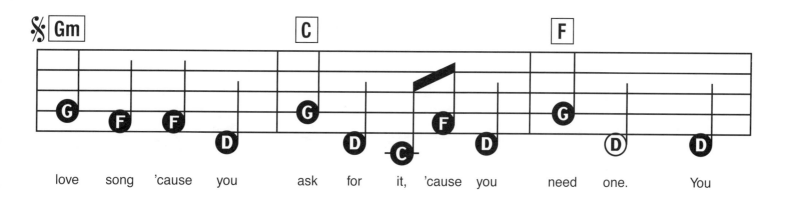

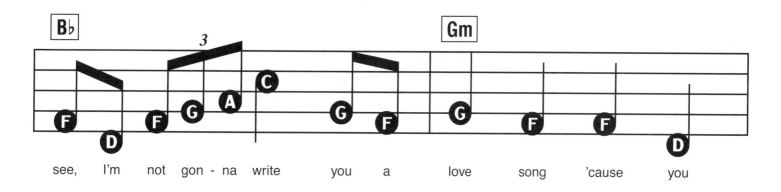

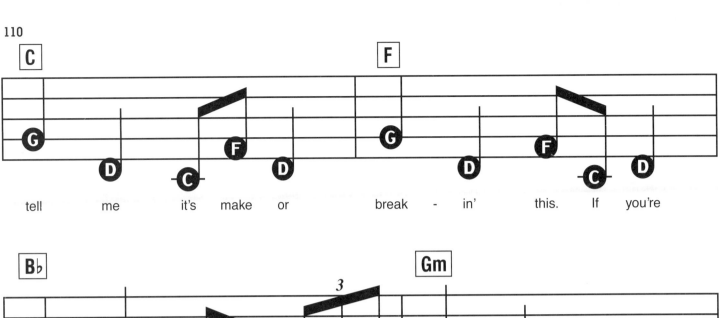

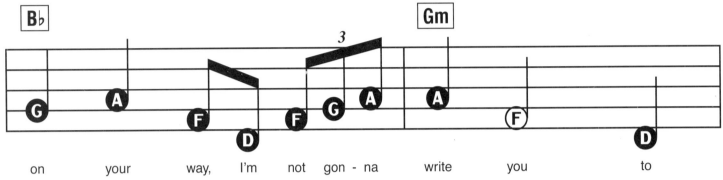

tell me it's make or break - in' this. If you're

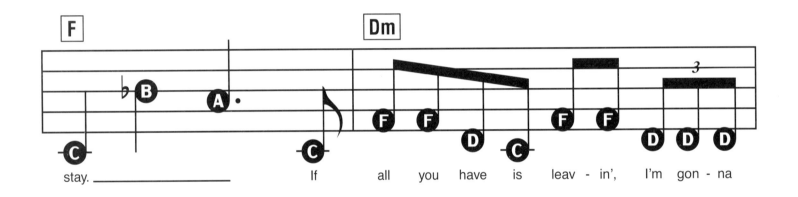

on your way, I'm not gon - na write you to

stay. _____ If all you have is leav - in', I'm gon - na

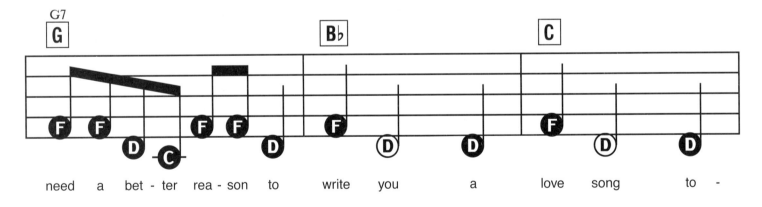

need a bet - ter rea - son to write you a love song to -

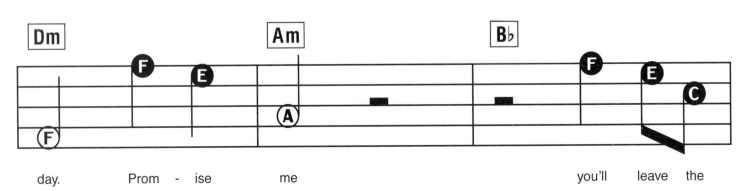

day. Prom - ise me you'll leave the

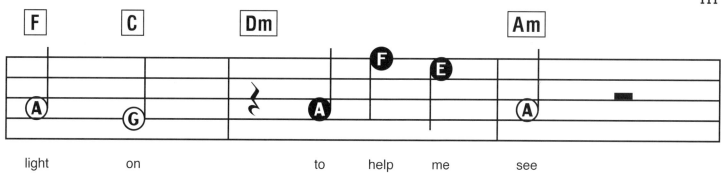

light   on   to   help   me   see

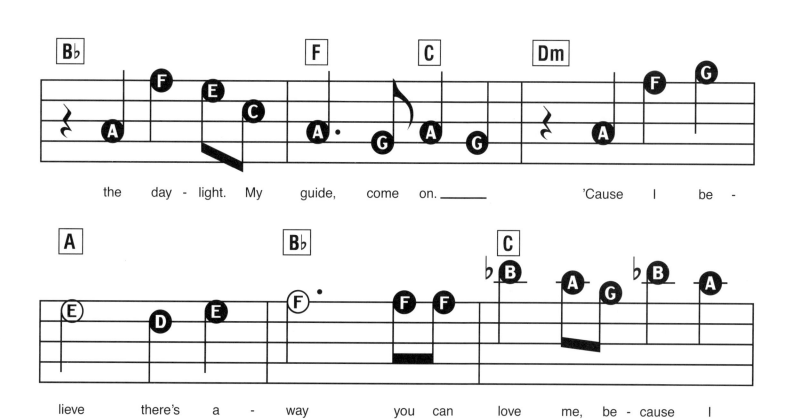

the   day - light.   My   guide,   come   on. _____   'Cause   I   be -

lieve   there's   a -   way   you   can   love   me,   be - cause   I

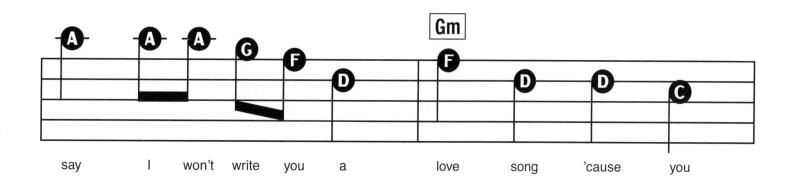

say   I   won't   write   you   a   love   song   'cause   you

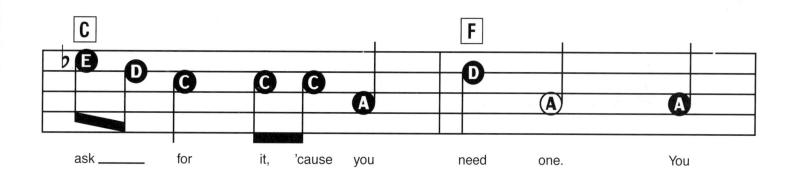

ask _____   for   it,   'cause   you   need   one.   You

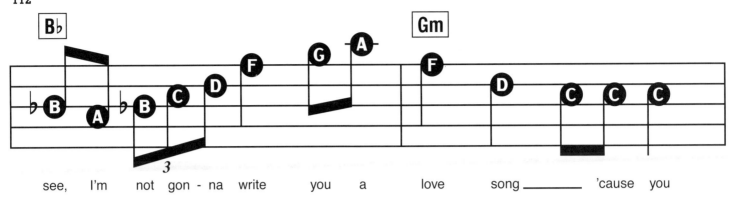

see, I'm not gon - na write you a love song _____ 'cause you

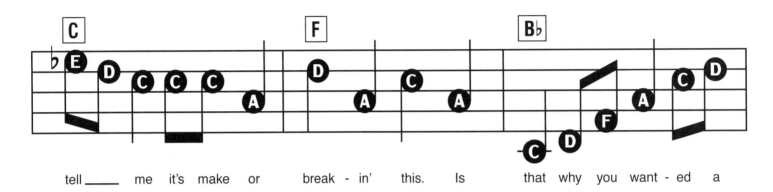

tell _____ me it's make or break - in' this. Is that why you want - ed a

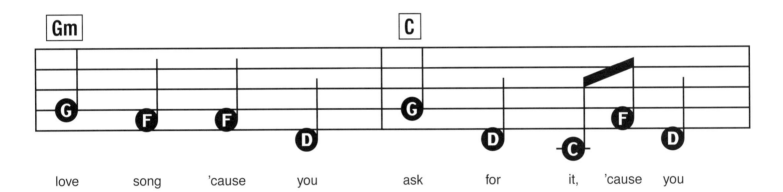

love song 'cause you ask for it, 'cause you

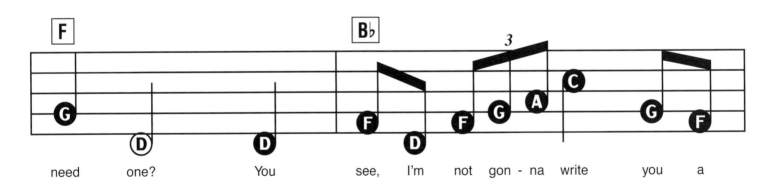

need one? You see, I'm not gon - na write you a

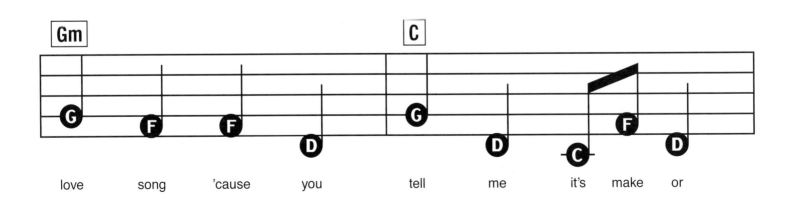

love song 'cause you tell me it's make or

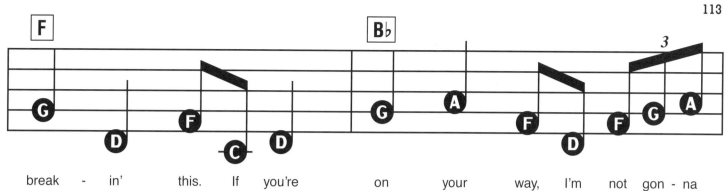

break - in' this. If you're on your way, I'm not gon - na

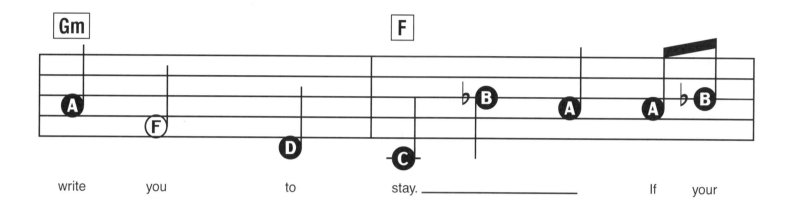

write you to stay. _____ If your

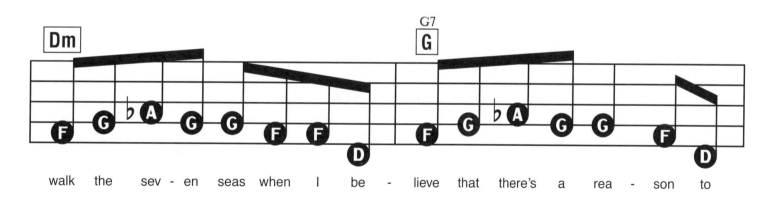

heart is no - where in it, I don't want it for a min - ute. Babe, I

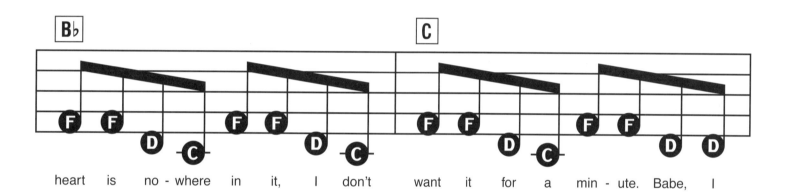

walk the sev - en seas when I be - lieve that there's a rea - son to

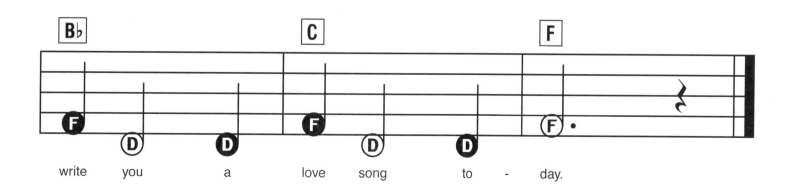

write you a love song to - day.

New Kid in Town

Registration 4
Rhythm: 8-Beat or Rock

Words and Music by John David Souther,
Don Henley and Glenn Frey

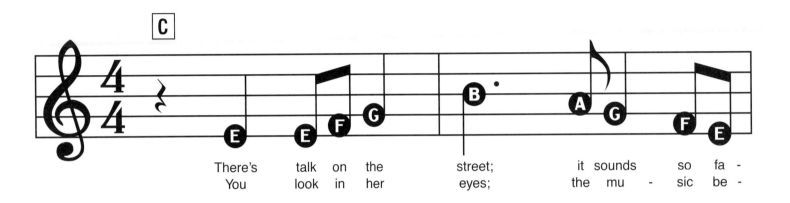

There's   talk   on   the   street;   it sounds   so   fa-
You   look   in   her   eyes;   the mu-sic   be-

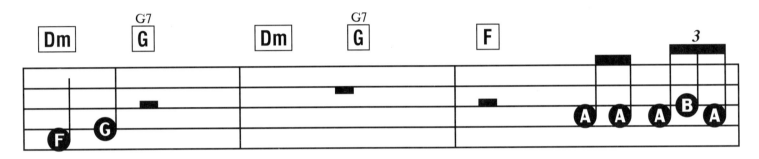

mil - iar.   Great ex - pec - ta -
gins to play.   Hope-less ro - man -

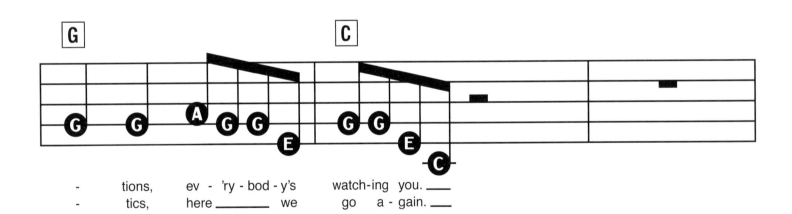

- tions,   ev - 'ry-bod-y's   watch-ing you. ___
- tics,   here _____ we   go   a - gain.

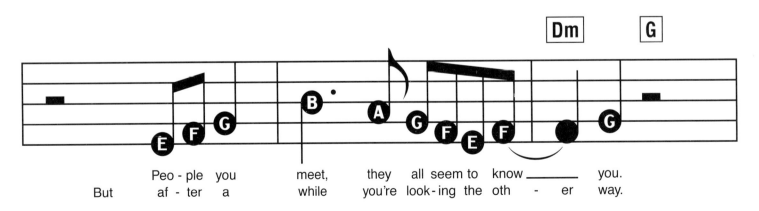

Peo - ple   you   meet,   they   all seem to   know _____ you.
But   af - ter   a   while   you're   look-ing the oth - er   way.

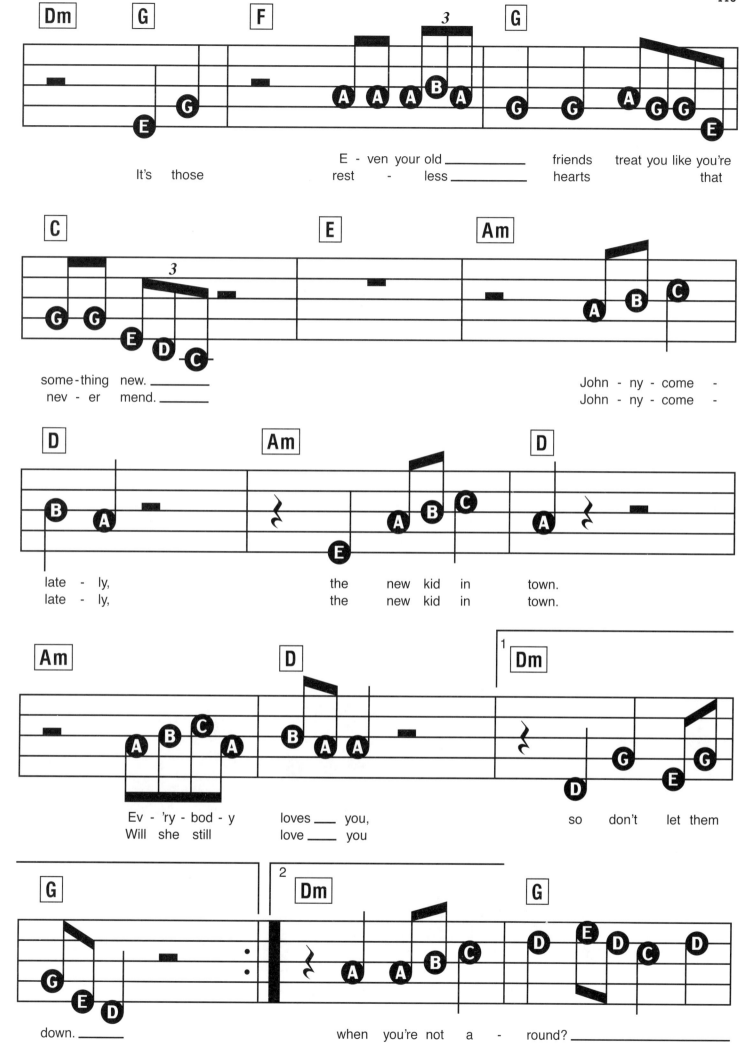

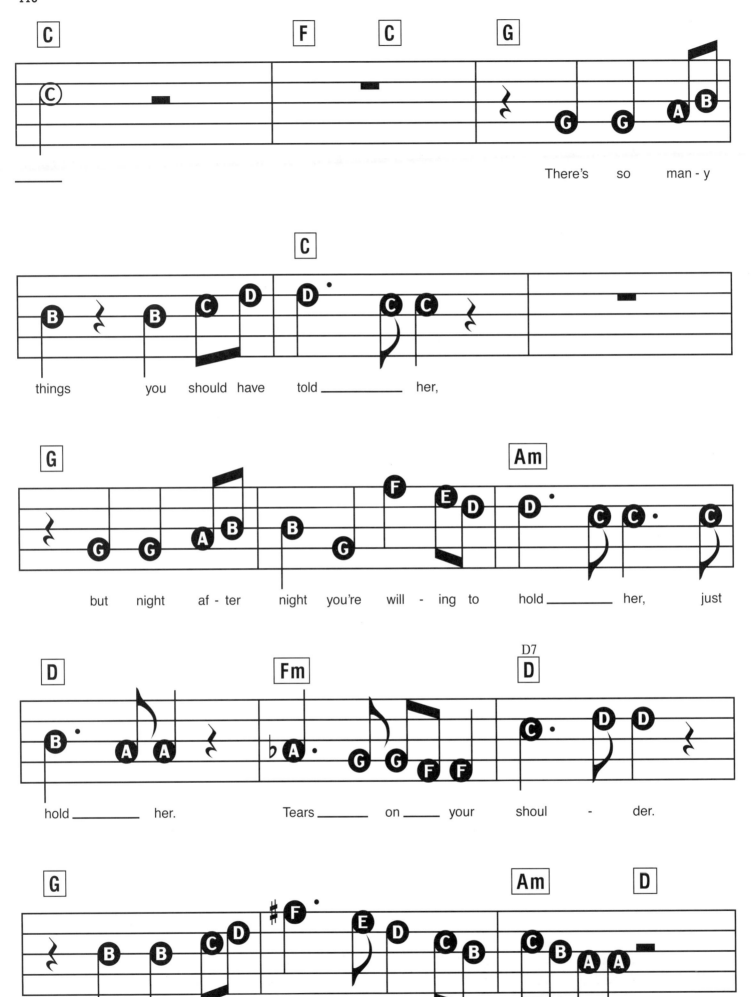

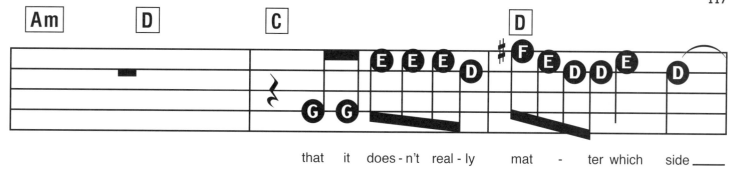

that it does-n't real-ly mat - ter which side ____

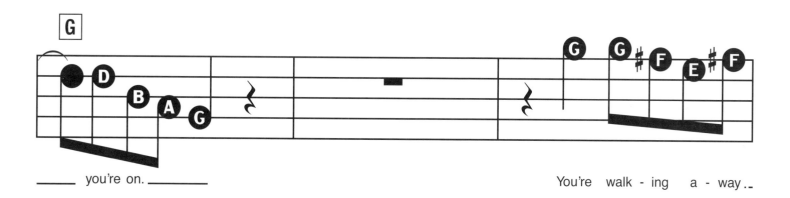

____ you're on. _____   You're walk-ing a-way...

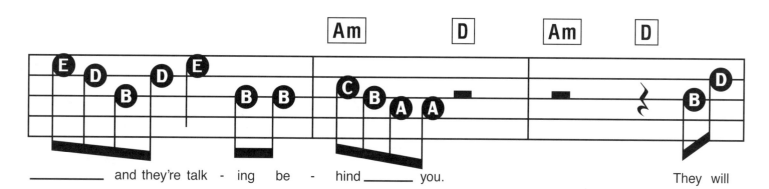

_____ and they're talk - ing be - hind _____ you.   They will

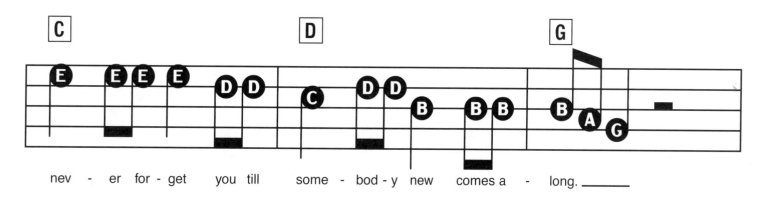

nev - er for-get you till some - bod-y new comes a - long. _____

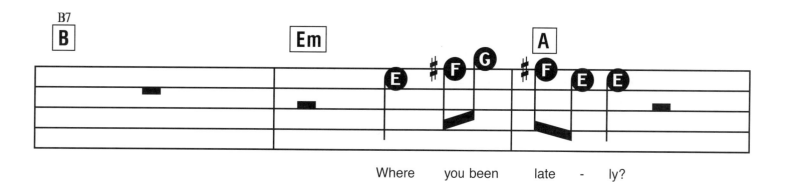

Where you been late - ly?

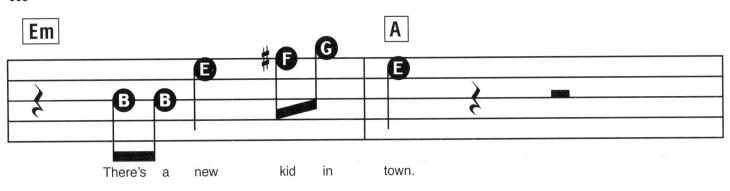

There's a new kid in town.

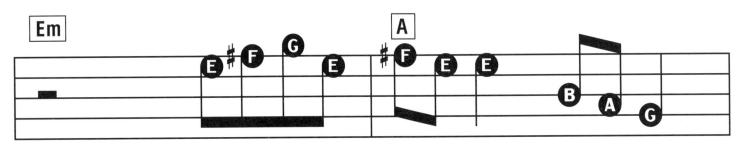

Ev - 'ry - bod - y loves _____ him, don't _____

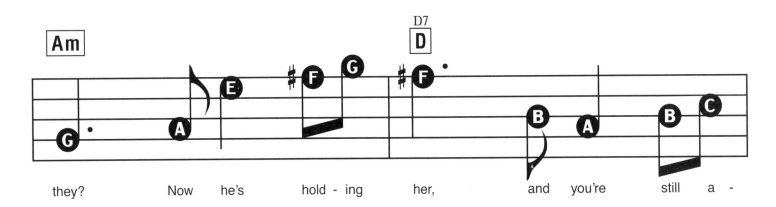

they? Now he's hold - ing her, and you're still a -

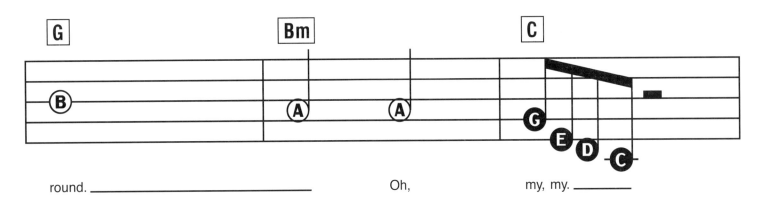

round. _____ Oh, my, my. _____

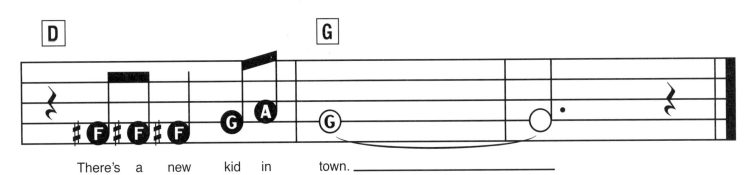

There's a new kid in town. _____

Nights in White Satin

Registration 6
Rhythm: Waltz

Words and Music by
Justin Hayward

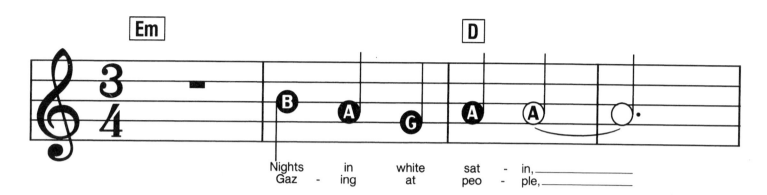

Nights in white sat - in,_____
Gaz - ing at peo - ple,_____

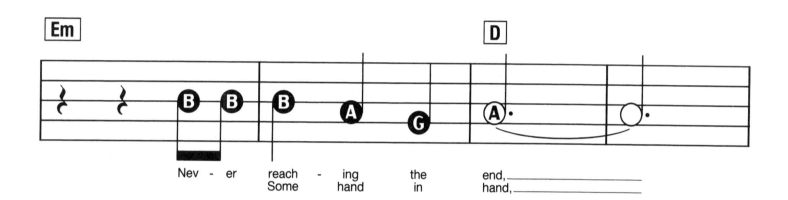

Nev - er reach - ing the end,_____
Some hand in hand,_____

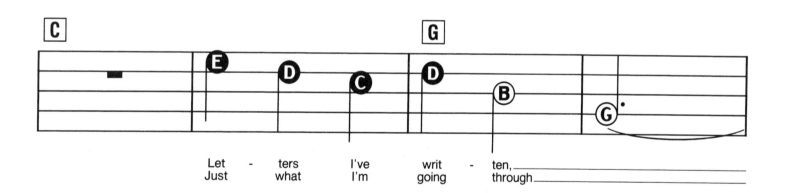

Let - ters I've writ - ten,_____
Just what I'm going through_____

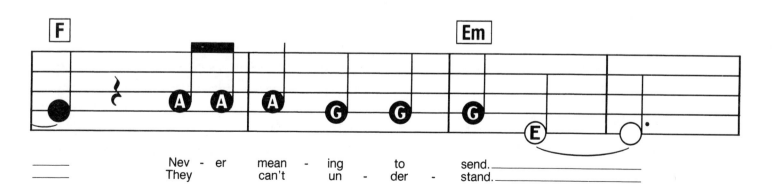

Nev - er mean - ing to send._____
They can't un - der - stand._____

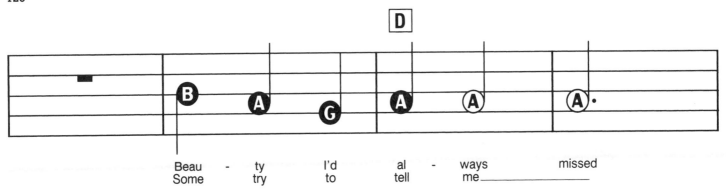

Beau - ty I'd al - ways missed
Some try to tell me

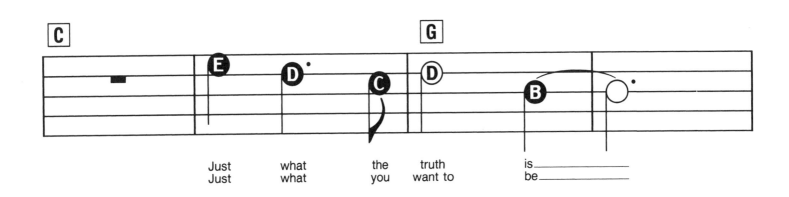

with these eyes be - fore,
Thoughts they can - not de - fend,

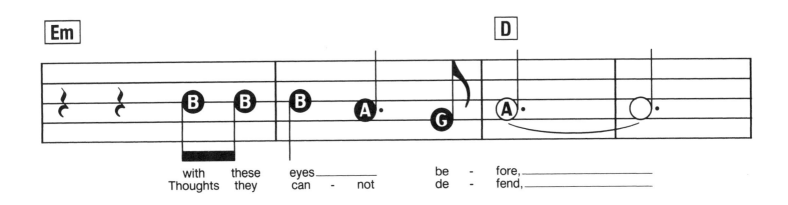

Just what the truth is
Just what you want to be

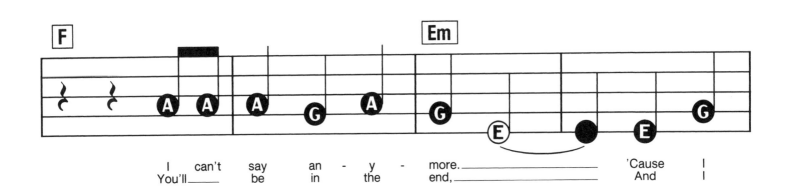

I can't say an - y - more. 'Cause I
You'll be in the end, And I

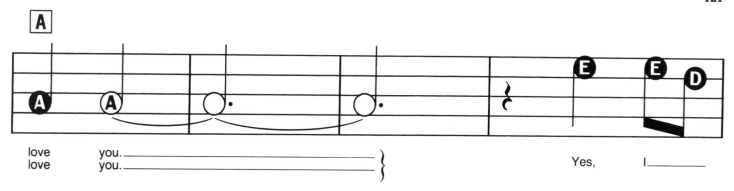

love you.
love you.   Yes,   I

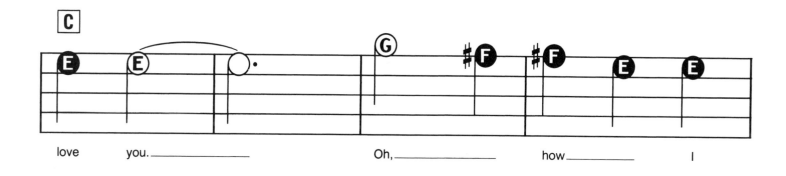

love   you.   Oh,   how   I

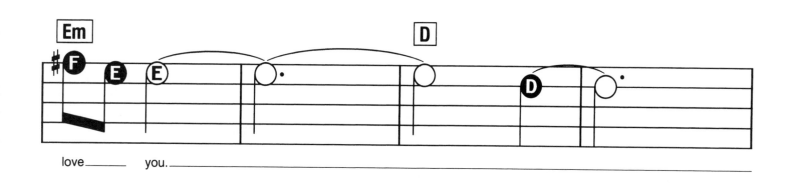

love   you.

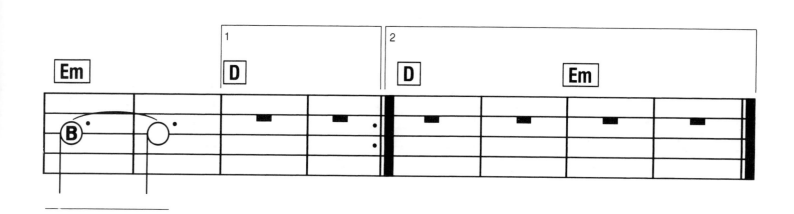

Pure Imagination
from WILLY WONKA AND THE CHOCOLATE FACTORY

Registration 9
Rhythm: Ballad

Words and Music by Leslie Bricusse
and Anthony Newley

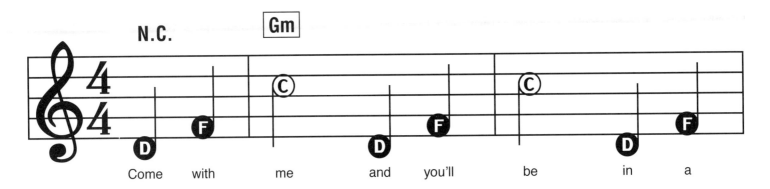

Come with me and you'll be in a

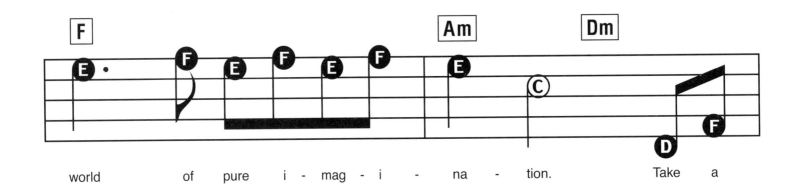

world of pure i - mag - i - na - tion. Take a

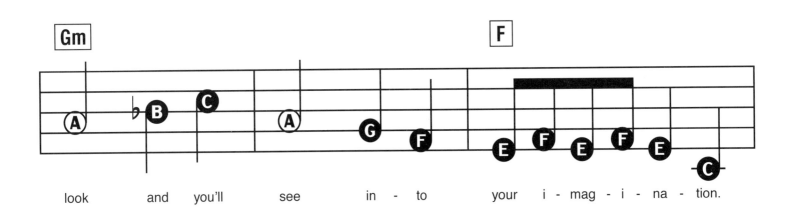

look and you'll see in - to your i - mag - i - na - tion.

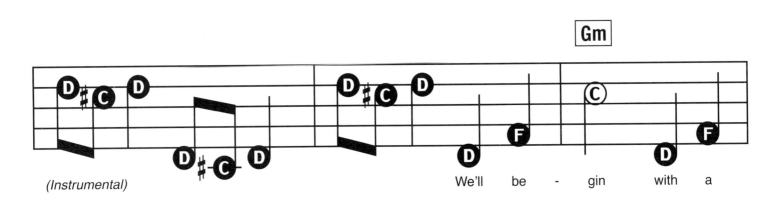

(Instrumental)

We'll be - gin with a

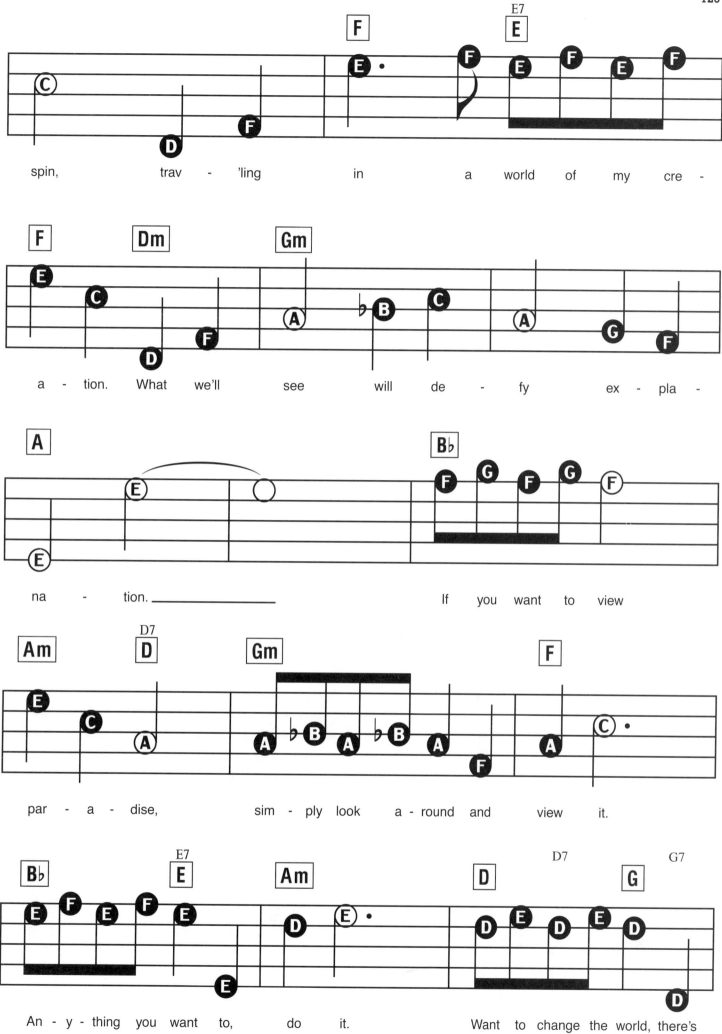

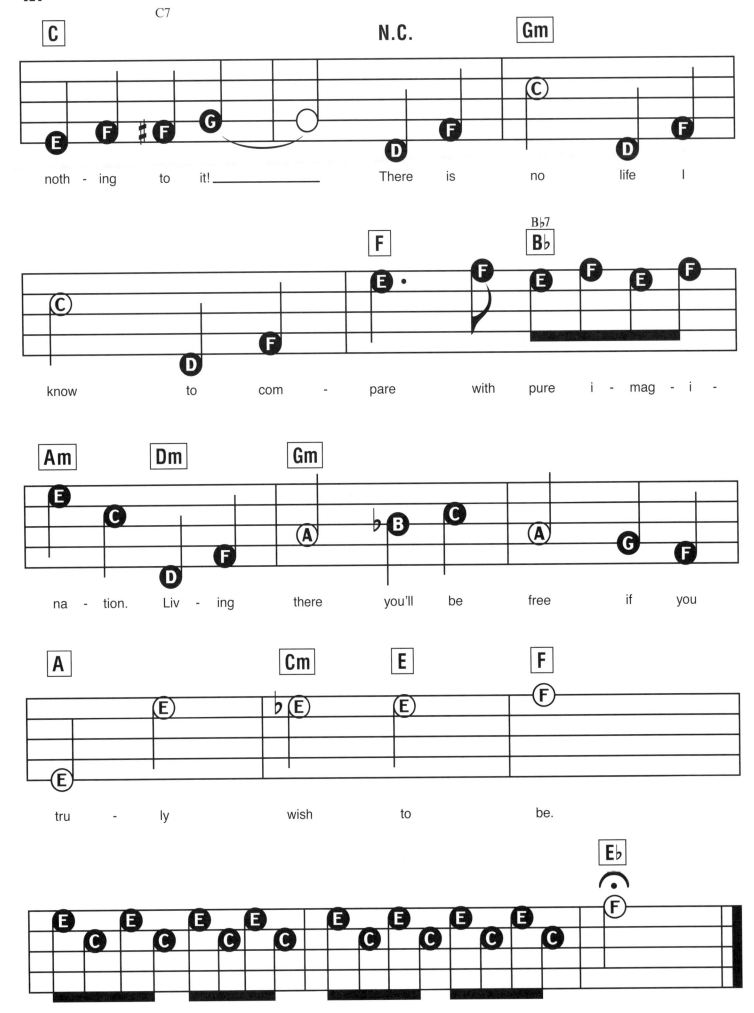

(Instrumental)

Strawberry Fields Forever

Registration 2
Rhythm: Rock

Words and Music by John Lennon
and Paul McCartney

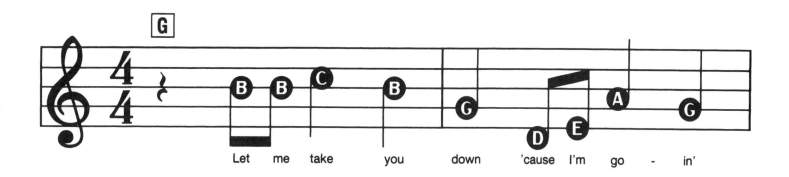

Let me take you down 'cause I'm go - in'

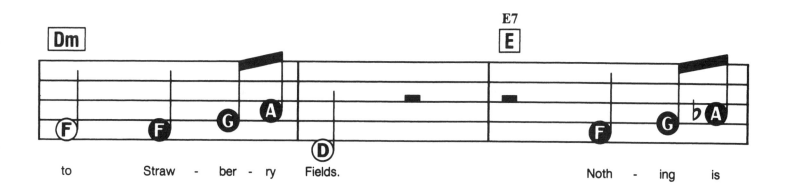

to Straw - ber - ry Fields. Noth - ing is

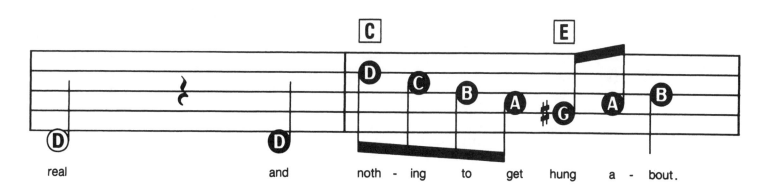

real and noth - ing to get hung a - bout.

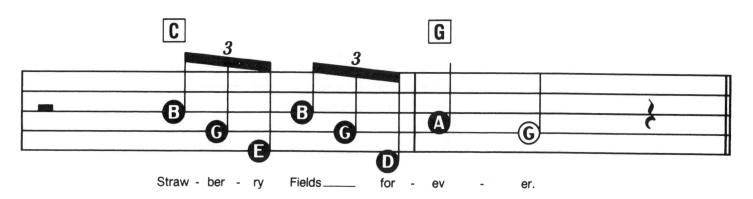

Straw - ber - ry Fields_____ for - ev - er.

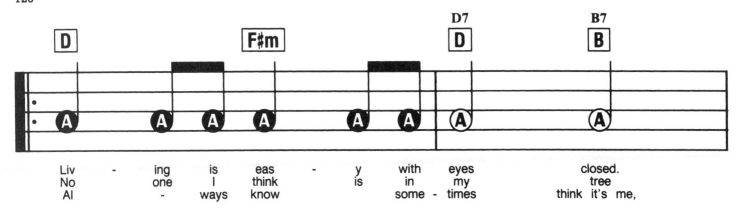

Liv - ing is eas - y with eyes closed.
No one I think is in my tree
Al - ways know some - times think it's me,

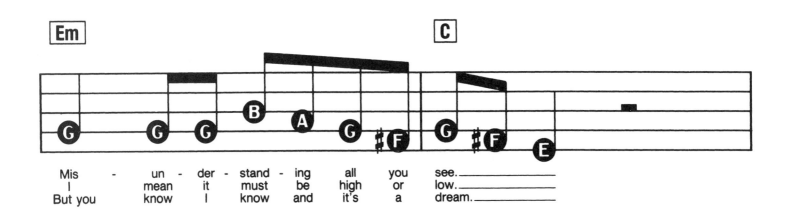

Mis - un - der - stand - ing all you see._____
I mean it must be all high or low._____
But you know I know and it's a dream._____

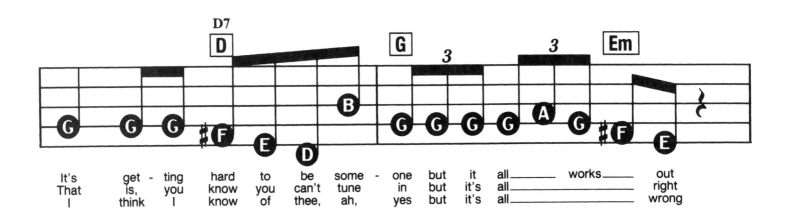

It's get - ting hard to be some - one but it all_____ works_____ out
That is, you know you can't tune in but it's all_____ right
I think I know of thee, ah, yes but it's all_____ wrong

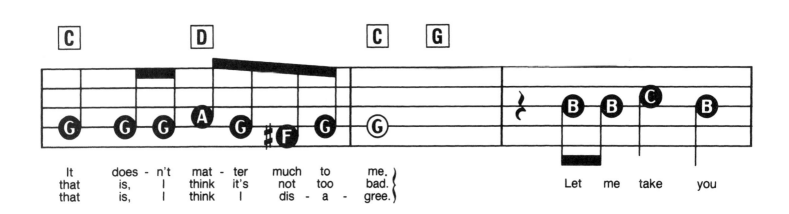

It does - n't mat - ter much to me.
that is, I think it's not too bad.
that is, I think I dis - a - gree.

Let me take you

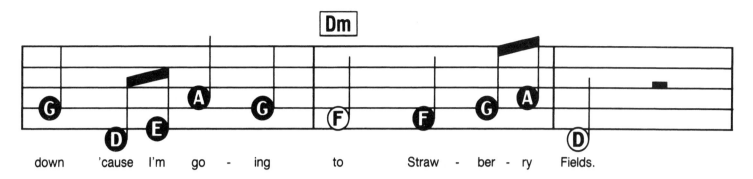

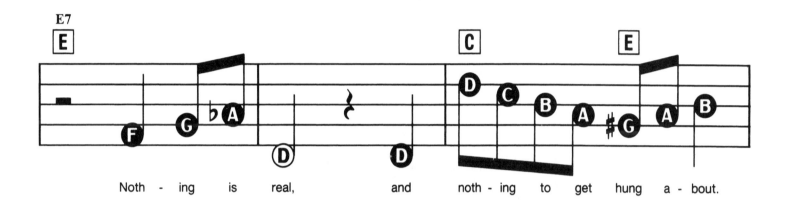

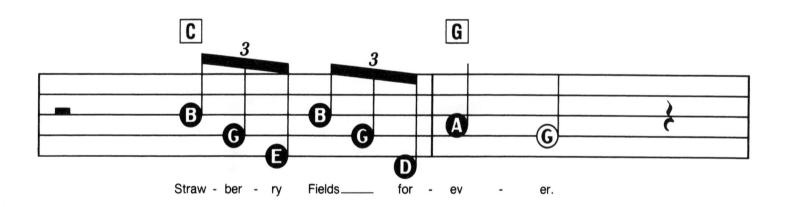

Repeat and Fade

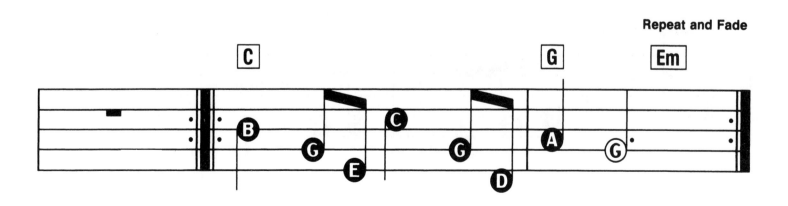

Rolling in the Deep

Registration 4
Rhythm: Rock or Pop

Words and Music by Adele Adkins
and Paul Epworth

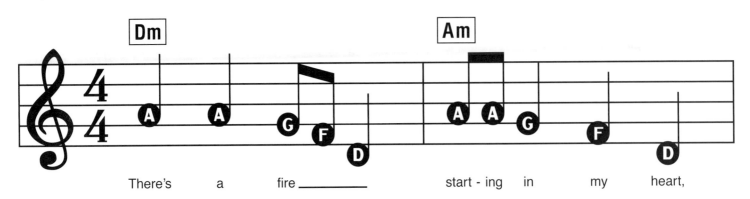

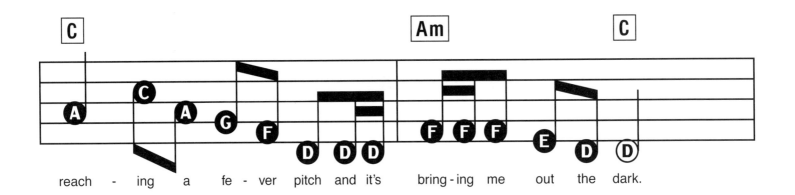

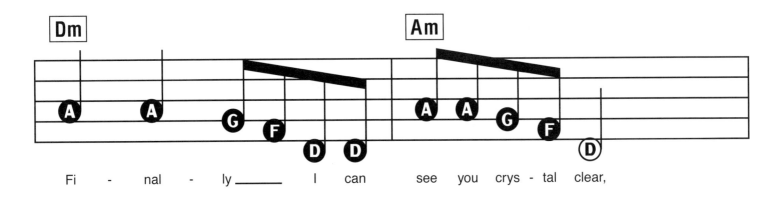

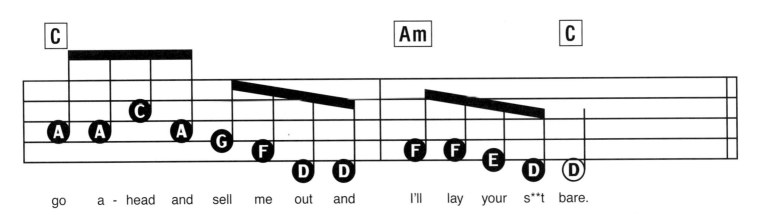

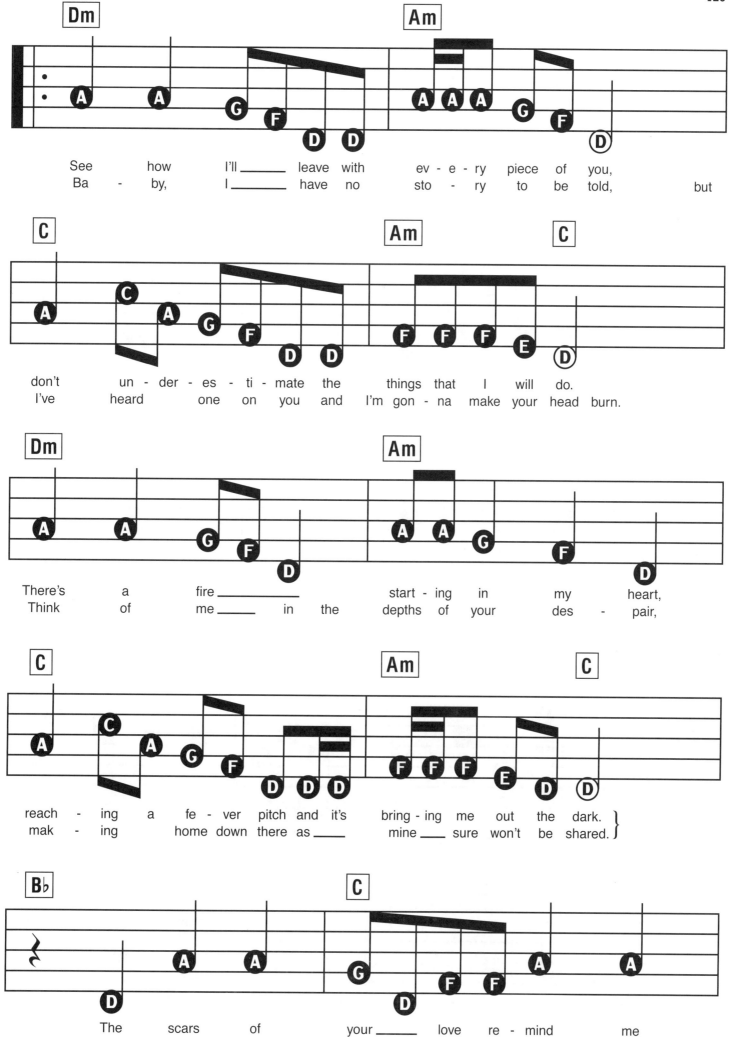

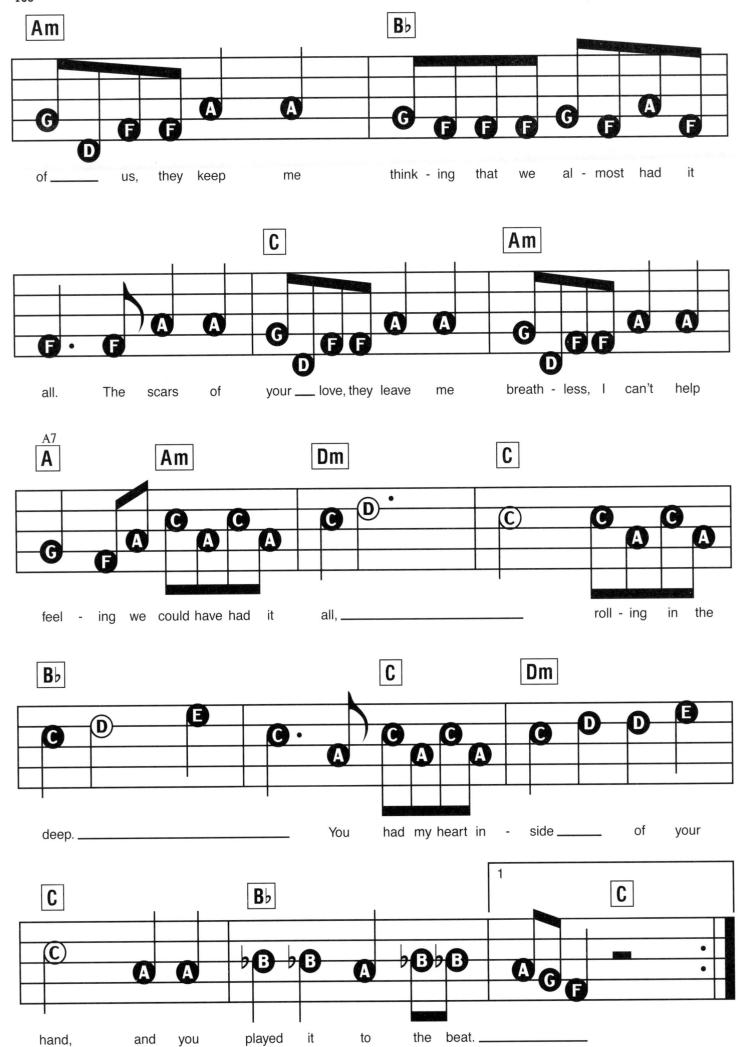

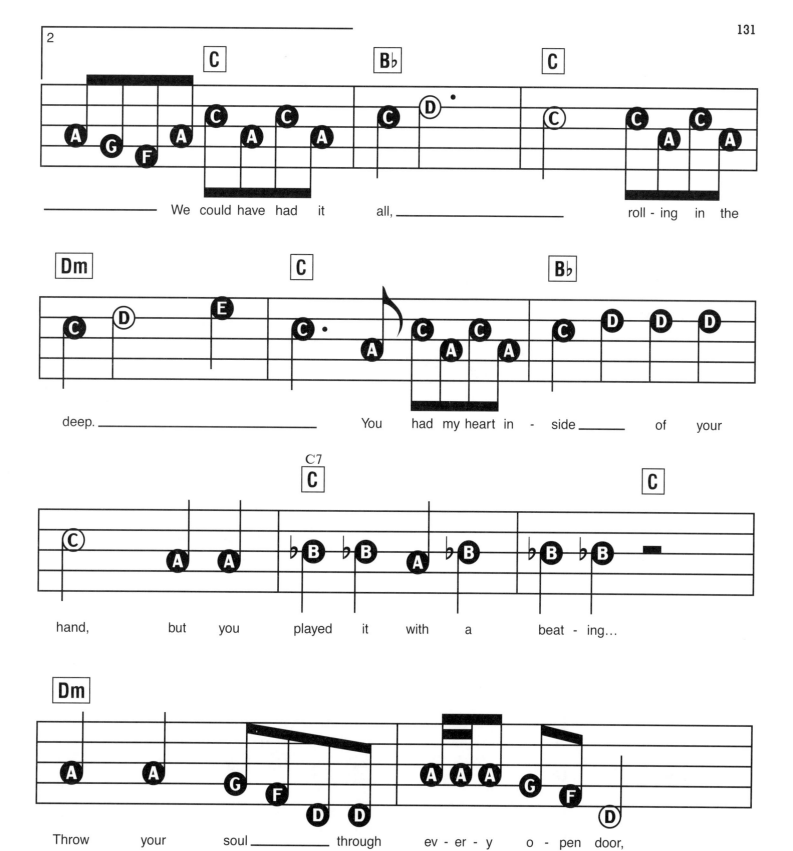

We could have had it all, _____ roll - ing in the

deep. _____ You had my heart in - side _____ of your

hand, but you played it with a beat - ing...

Throw your soul _____ through ev - er - y o - pen door,

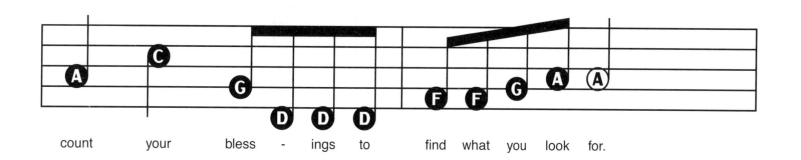

count your bless - ings to find what you look for.

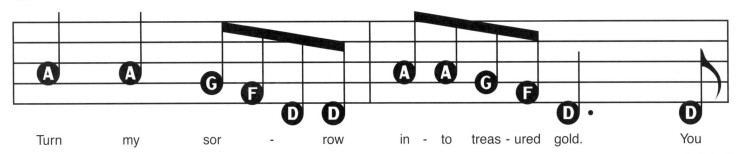

Turn my sor - row in - to treas - ured gold. You

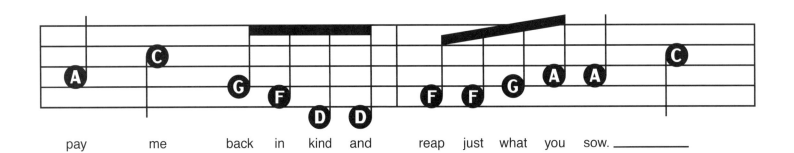

pay me back in kind and reap just what you sow. ____

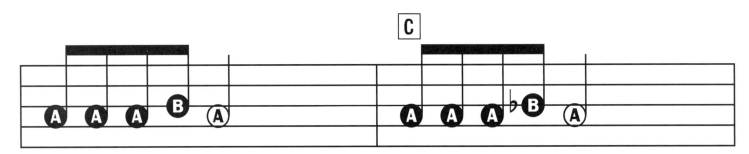

You're gon - na wish you nev - er had met me,

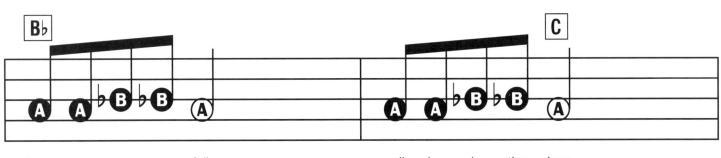

tears are gon - na fall, roll - ing in the deep.

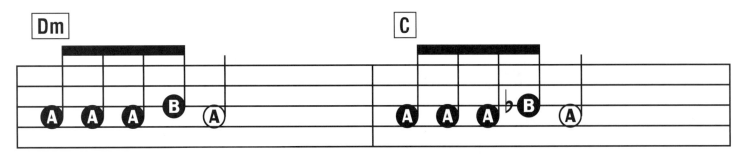

You're gon - na wish you nev - er had met me,

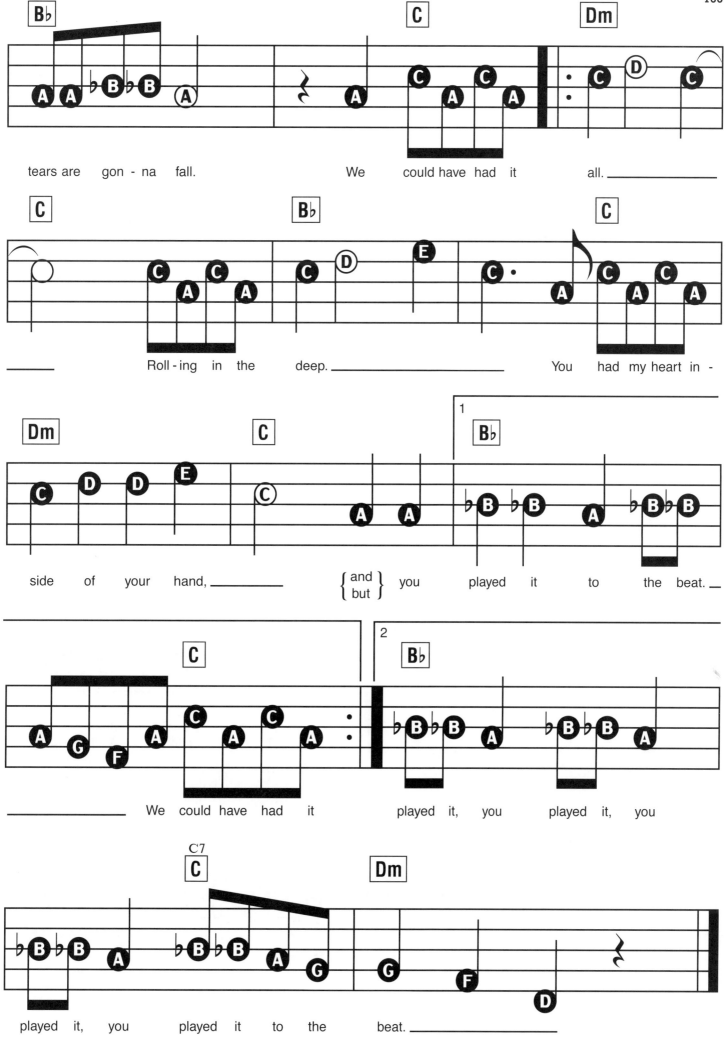

Rosanna

Registration 4
Rhythm: Rock

Words and Music by
David Paich

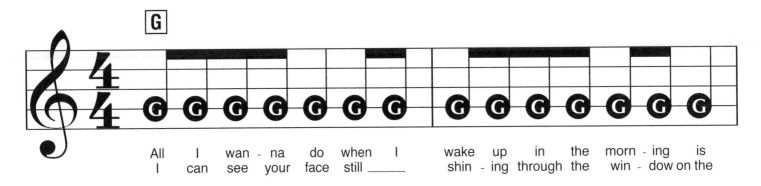

All I wan - na do when I wake up in the morn - ing is
I can see your face still _____ shin - ing through the win - dow on the

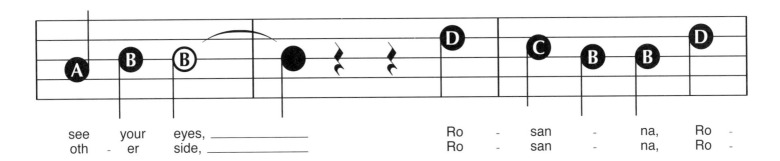

see your eyes, _____ Ro - san - na, Ro -
oth - er side, _____ Ro - san - na, Ro -

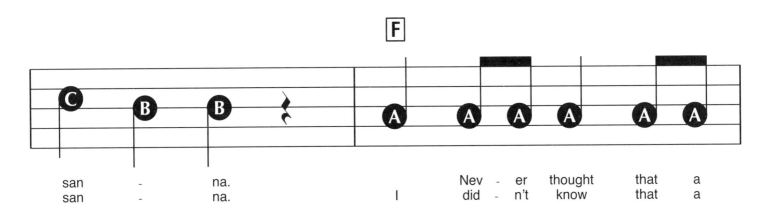

san - na. Nev - er thought that a
san - na. I did - n't know that a

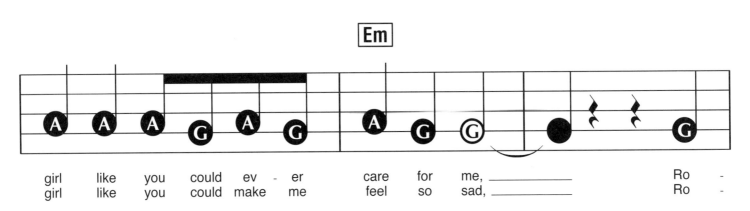

girl like you could ev - er care for me, _____ Ro -
girl like you could make me feel so sad, _____ Ro

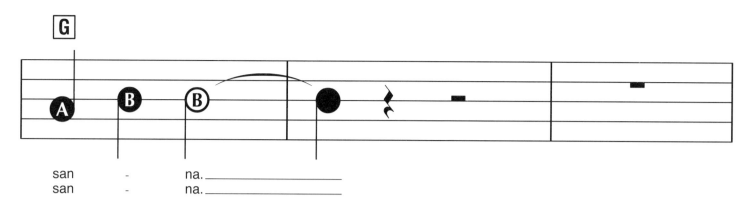

san - na._____
san - na._____

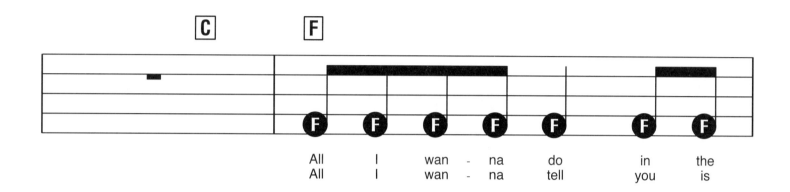

All   I   wan - na   do   in   the
All   I   wan - na   tell   you   is

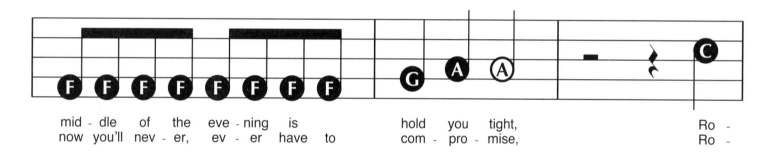

mid - dle   of   the   eve - ning   is   hold   you   tight,   Ro -
now   you'll   nev - er,   ev - er   have   to   com - pro - mise,   Ro -

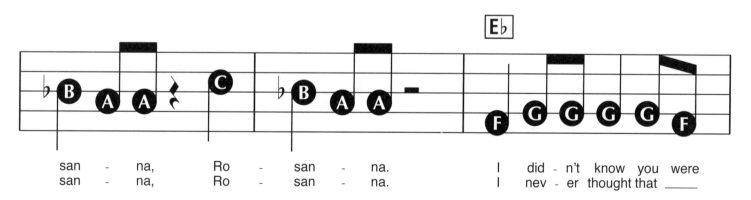

san - na,   Ro - san - na.   I   did - n't   know   you   were
san - na,   Ro - san - na.   I   nev - er   thought   that ____

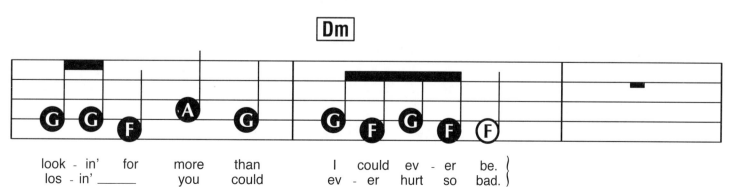

look - in'   for   more   than   I   could   ev - er   be.
los - in' ____   you   could   ev - er   hurt   so   bad.

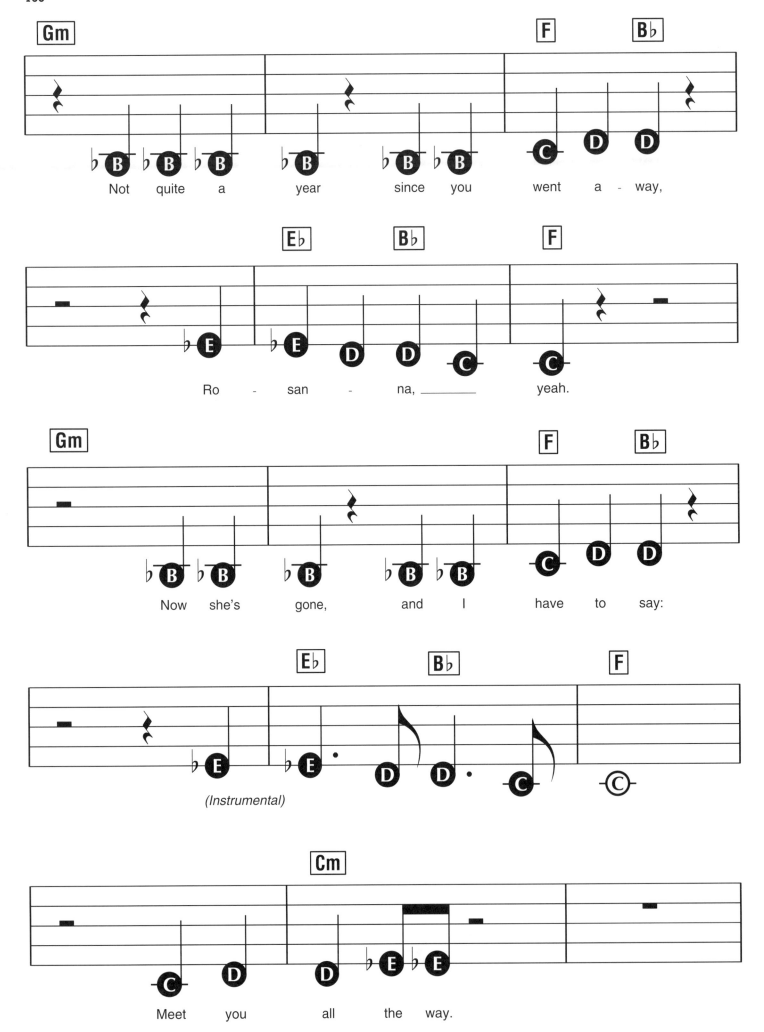

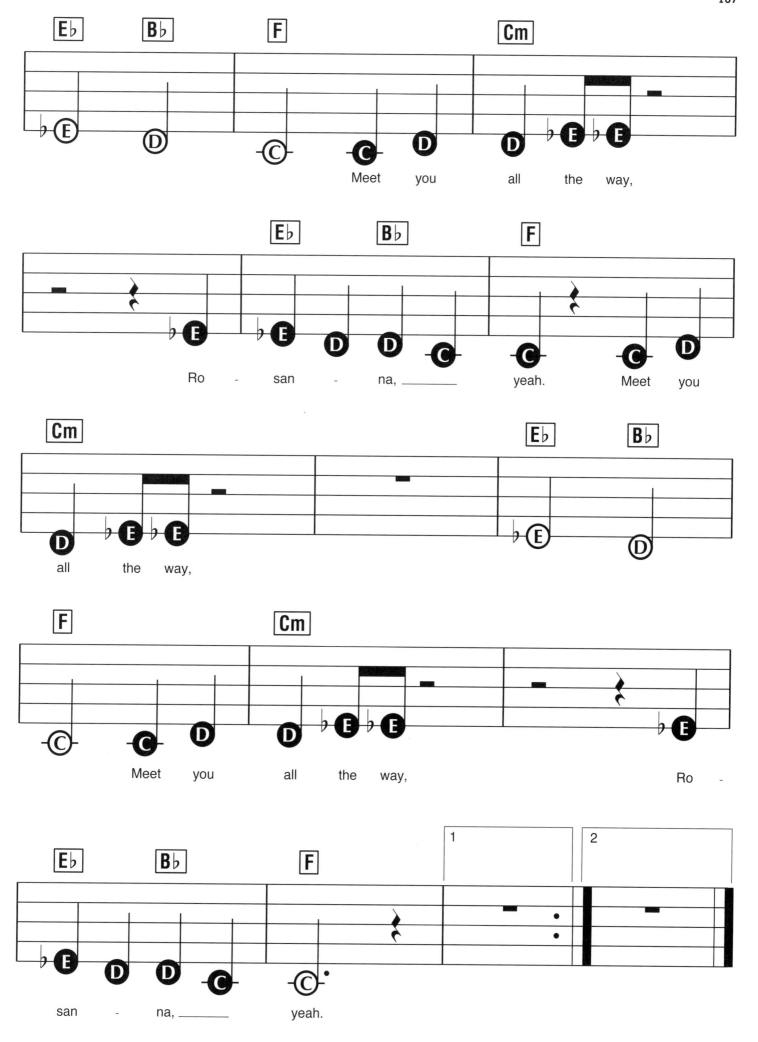

Still Crazy After All These Years

Registration 1
Rhythm: Waltz

Words and Music by
Paul Simon

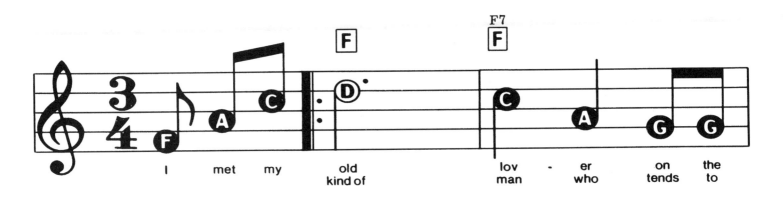

I met my old
kind of

lov - er who on the
man tends to

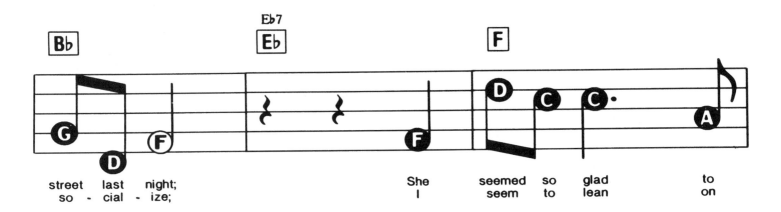

street last night;
so - cial - ize;

She
I

seemed so glad
seem to lean

to
on

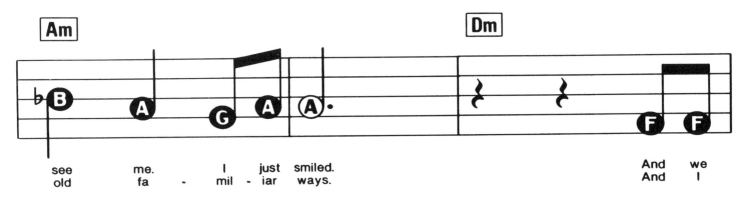

see me.
old fa - mil - iar

I just smiled.
ways.

And we
And I

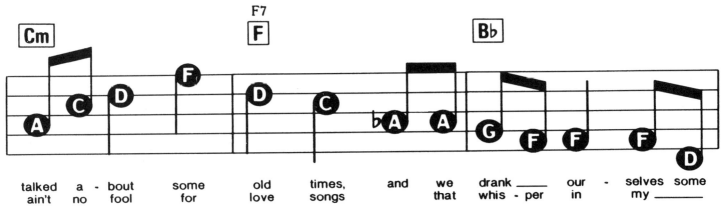

talked a - bout some old
ain't no fool for

times, and we drank
love songs that whis - per in

our - selves some
my _____

139

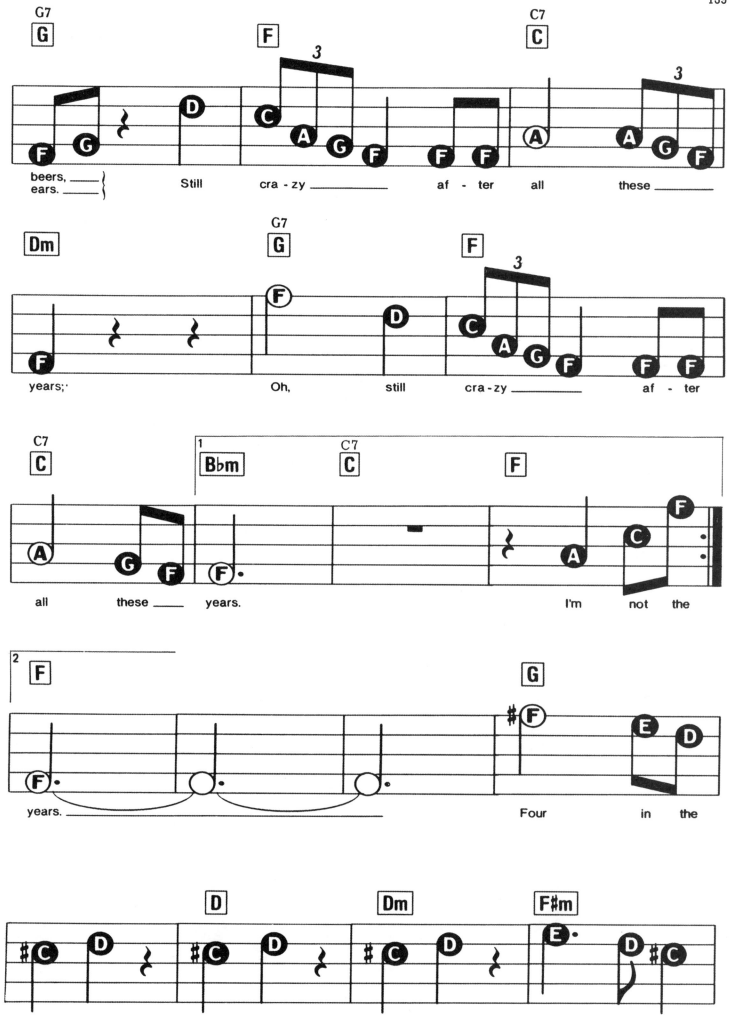

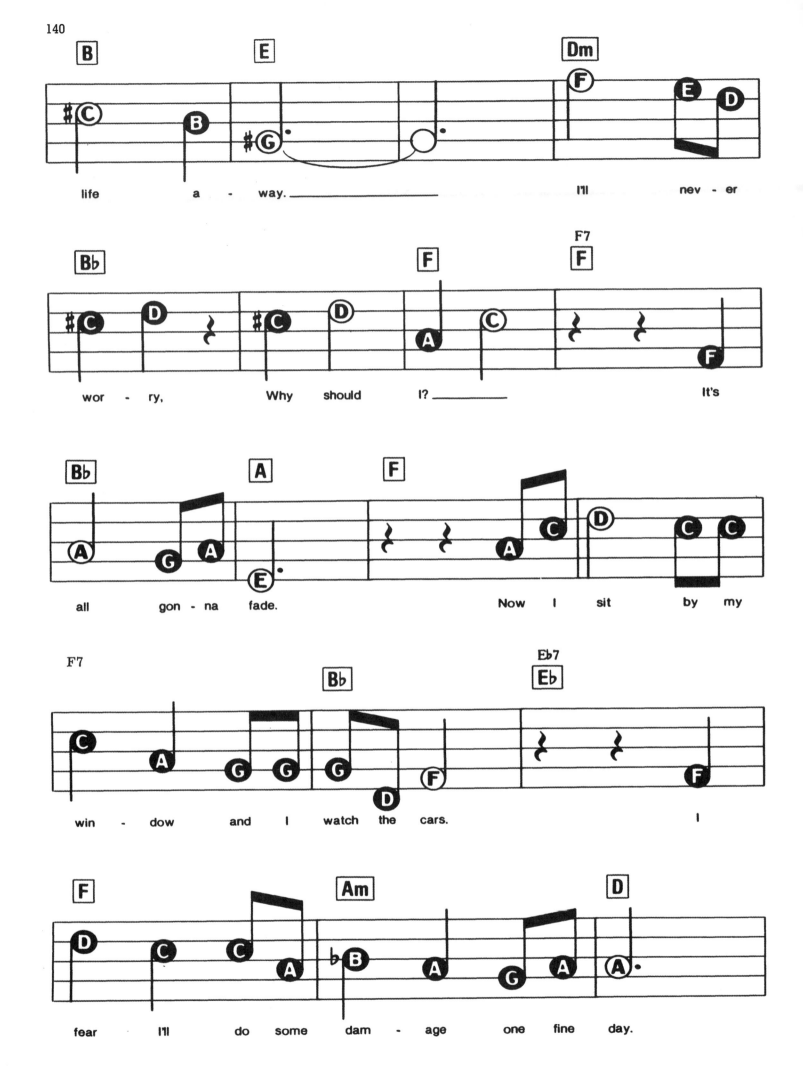

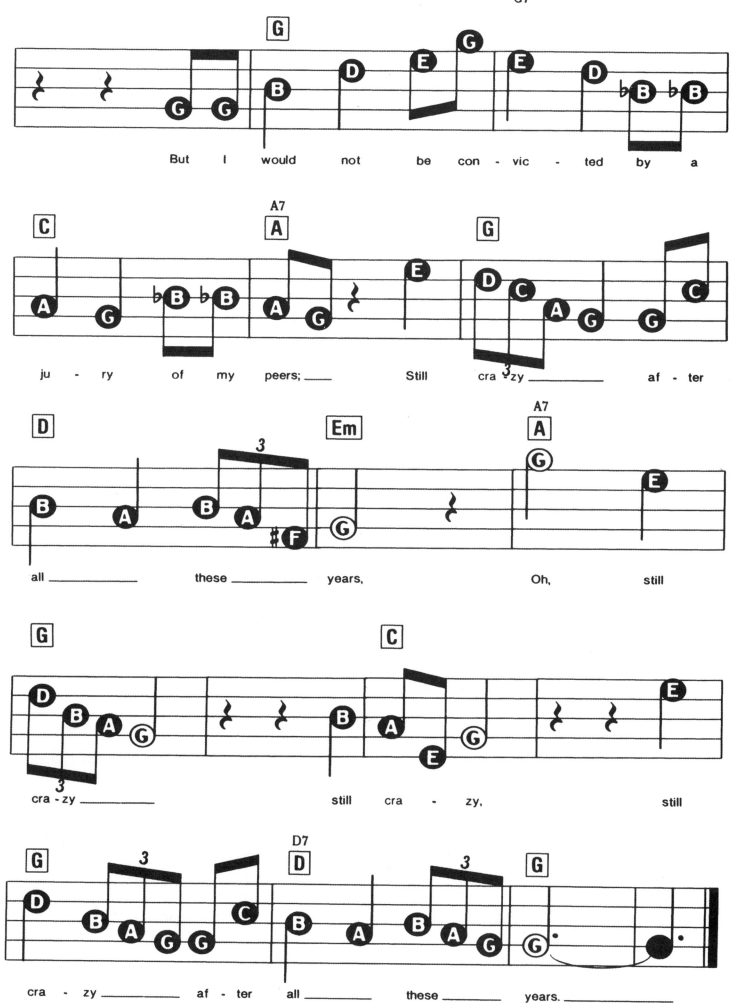

Superman
(It's Not Easy)

Registration 8
Rhythm: Pop or Rock

Words and Music by
John Ondrasik

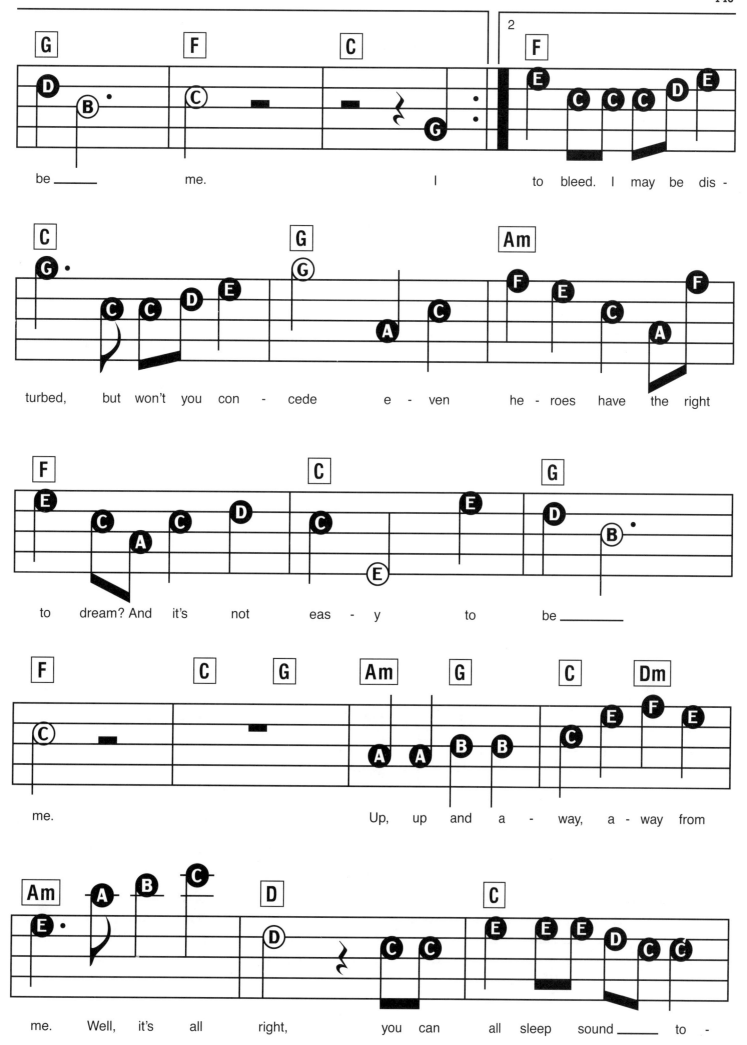

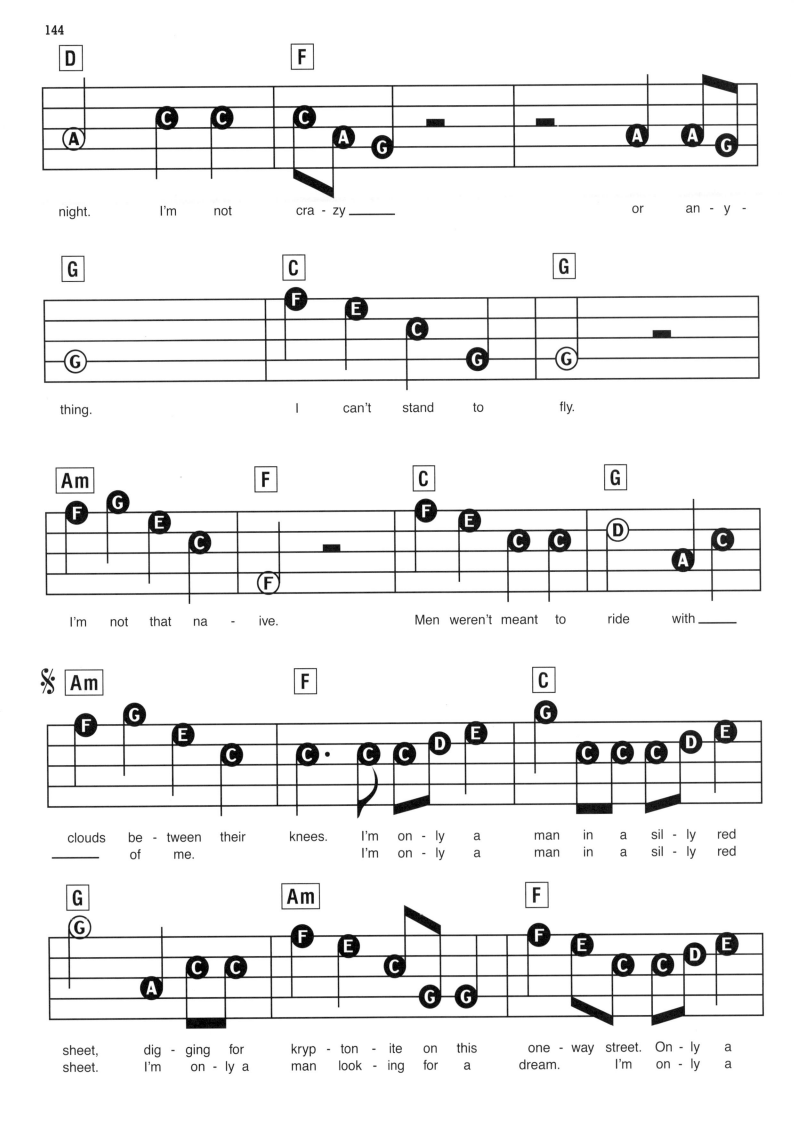

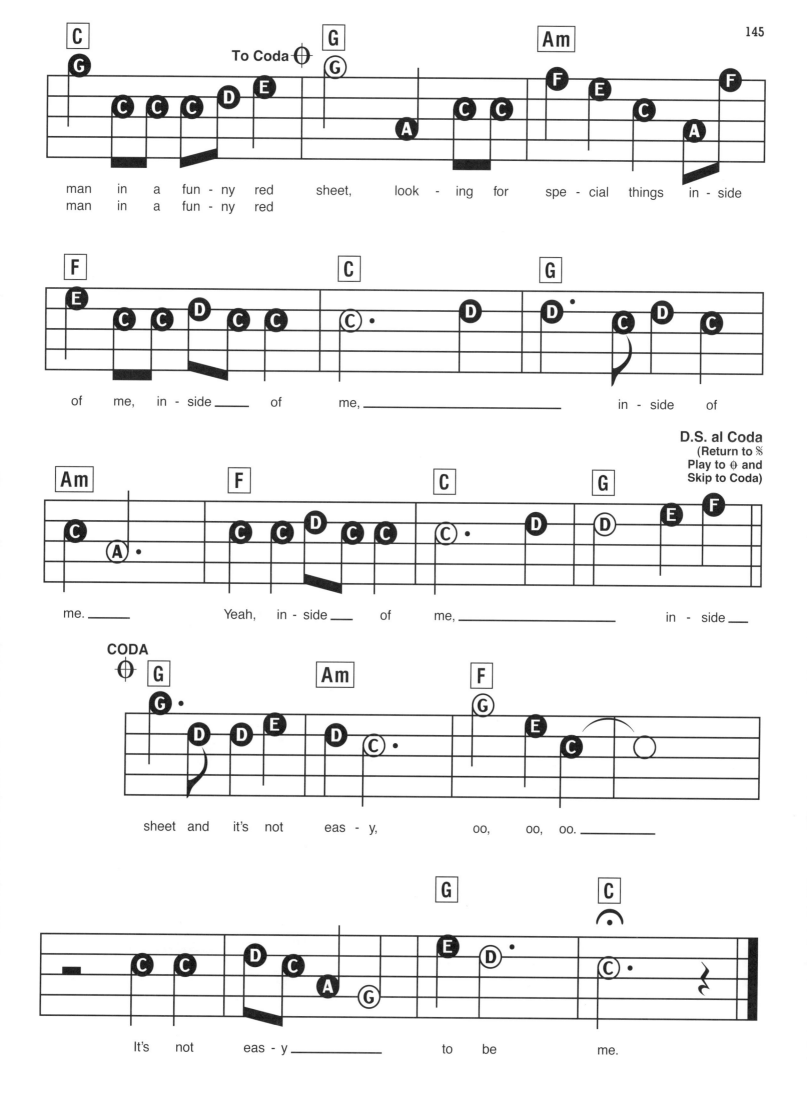

Sweet Dreams
(Are Made of This)

Registration 3
Rhythm: Pops

Words and Music by Annie Lennox
and David Stewart

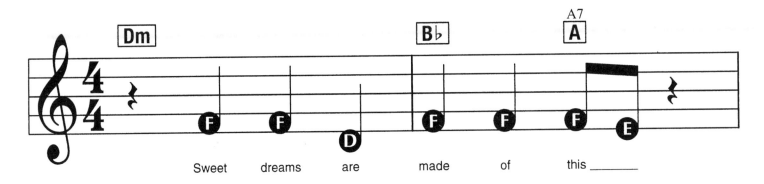

Sweet dreams are made of this _____

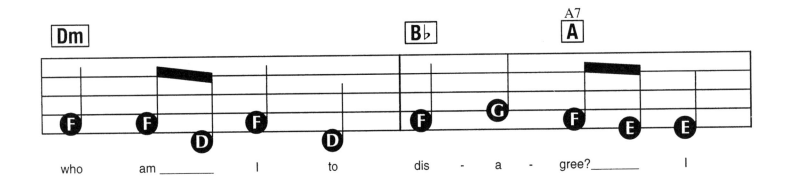

who am _____ I to dis - a - gree? _____ I

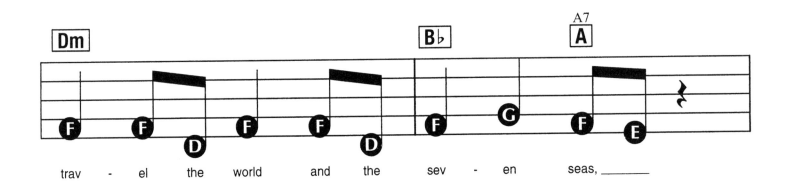

trav - el the world and the sev - en seas, _____

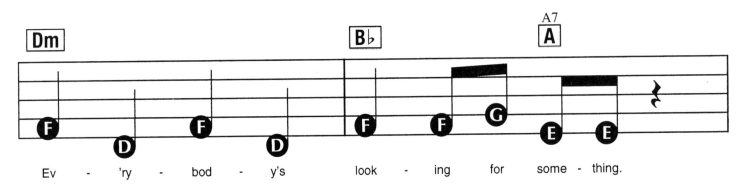

Ev - 'ry - bod - y's look - ing for some - thing.

147

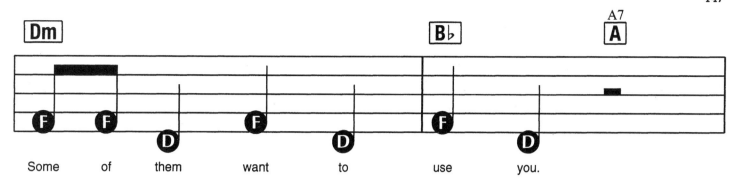

Some of them want to use you.

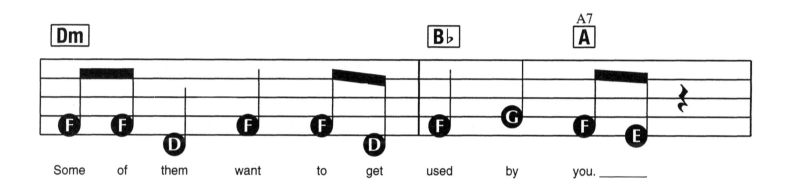

Some of them want to get used by you. _____

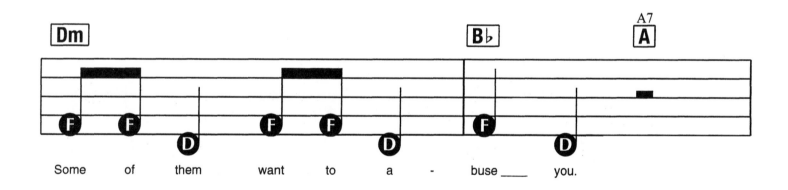

Some of them want to a - buse ____ you.

To Coda ⊕

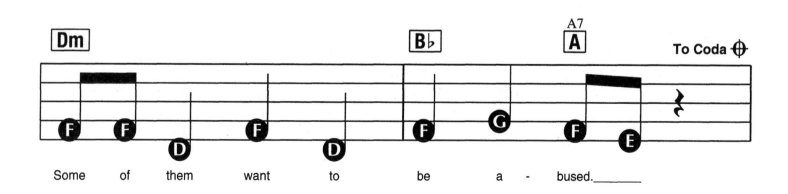

Some of them want to be a - bused._____

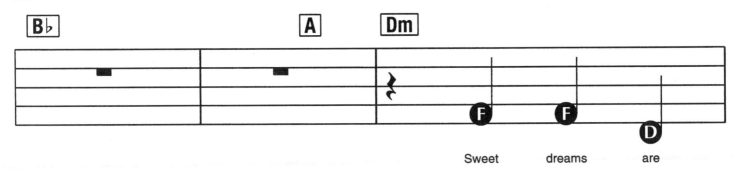

Sweet dreams are

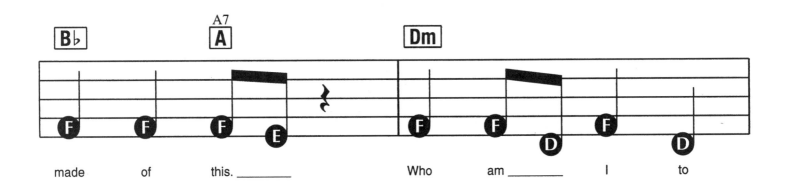

made of this. _____ Who am _____ I to

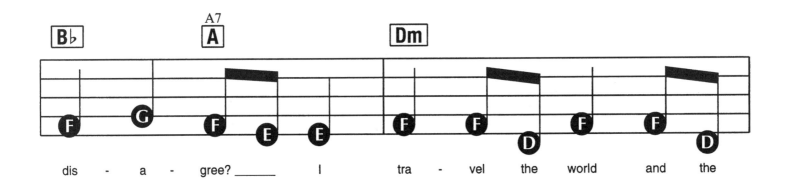

dis - a - gree? _____ I tra - vel the world and the

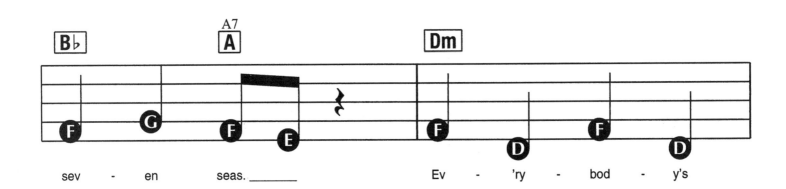

sev - en seas. _____ Ev - 'ry - bod - y's

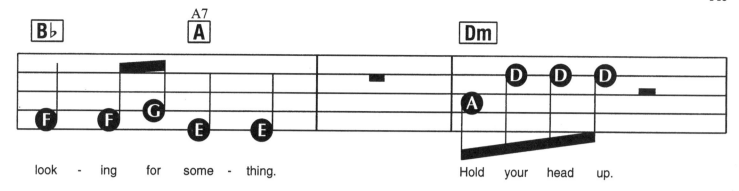

look - ing for some - thing.　　Hold your head up.

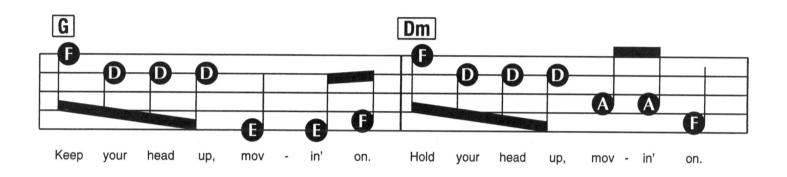

Keep your head up, mov - in' on. Hold your head up, mov - in' on.

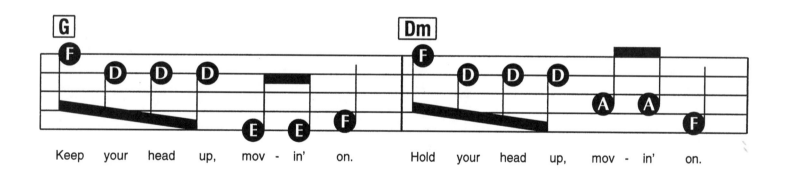

Keep your head up, mov - in' on. Hold your head up, mov - in' on.

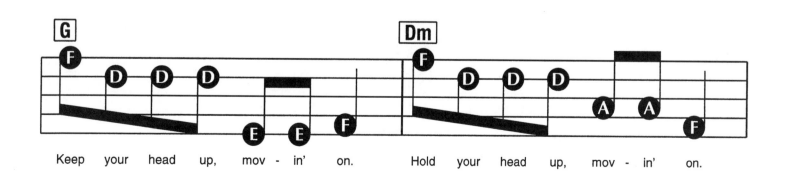

Keep your head up, mov - in' on. Hold your head up, mov - in' on.

D.C. al Coda
(Return to beginning
Play to ⊕ and
Skip to Coda)

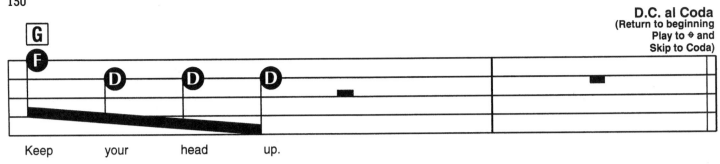

Keep your head up.

CODA

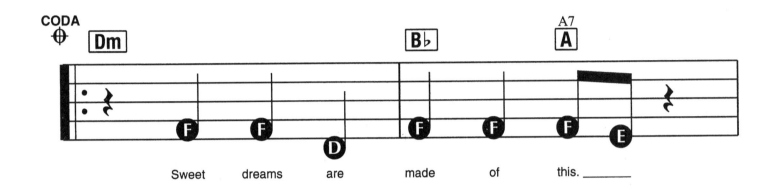

Sweet dreams are made of this. _____

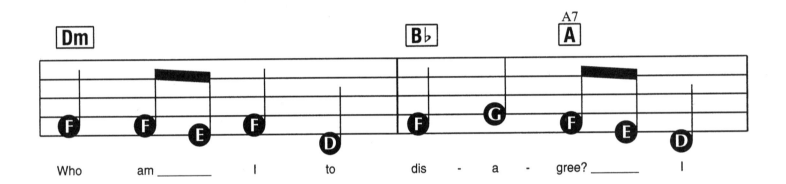

Who am _____ I to dis - a - gree? _____ I

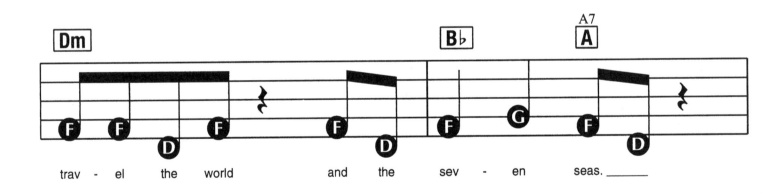

trav - el the world and the sev - en seas. _____

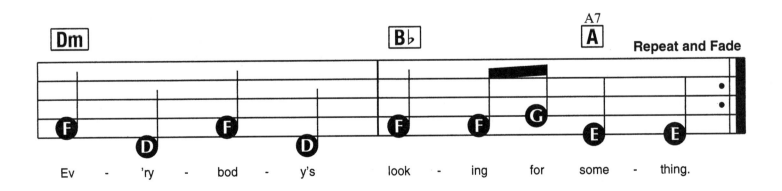

Repeat and Fade

Ev - 'ry - bod - y's look - ing for some - thing.

Sweet Caroline

Registration 2
Rhythm: Swing or Fox Trot

Words and Music by
Neil Diamond

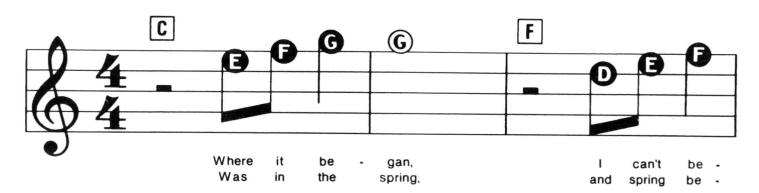

Where it be - gan,   I can't be -
Was in the spring,   and spring be -

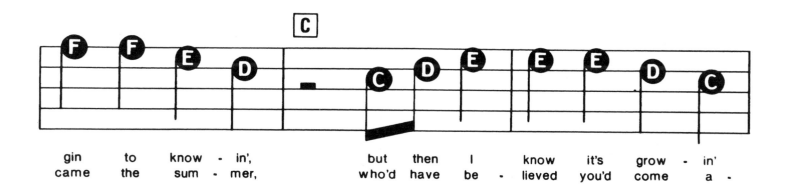

gin to know - in',   but then I know it's grow - in'
came the sum - mer,   who'd have be - lieved you'd come a -

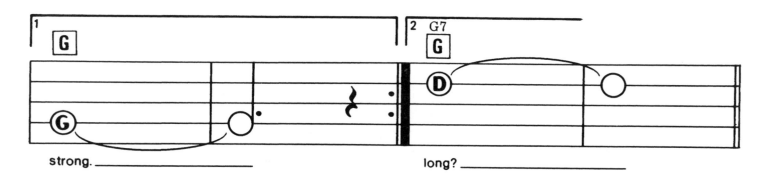

strong. _____   long? _____

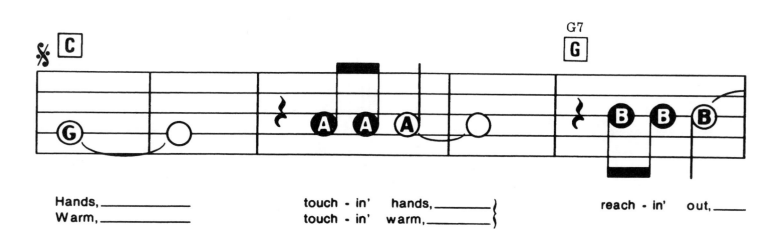

Hands, _____   touch - in' hands, _____ }   reach - in' out, _____
Warm, _____   touch - in' warm, _____ }

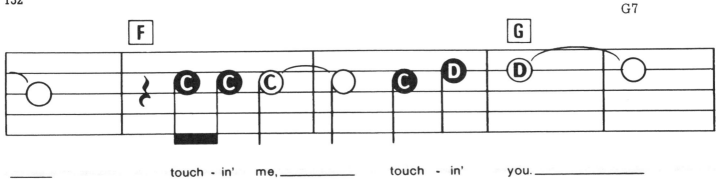

touch - in' me,_____ touch - in' you._____

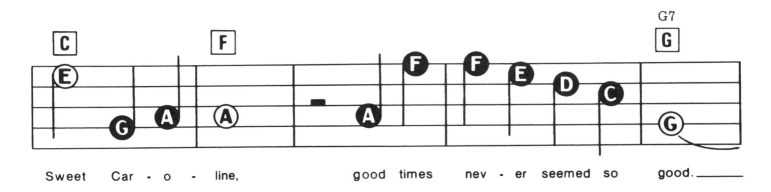

Sweet Car - o - line, good times nev - er seemed so good._____

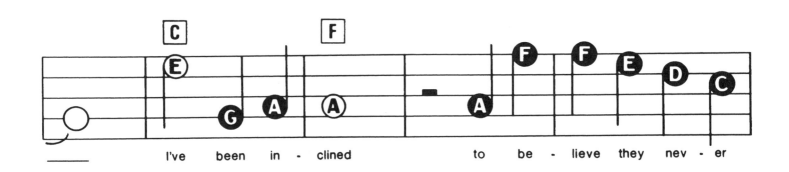

_____ I've been in - clined to be - lieve they nev - er

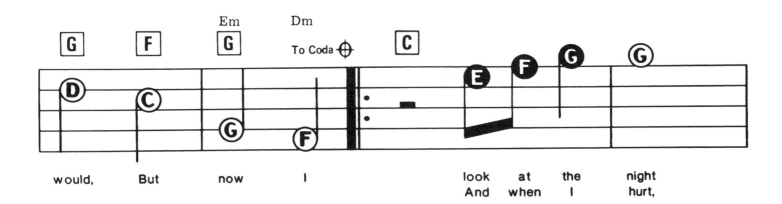

would, But now I look at the night
And when I hurt,

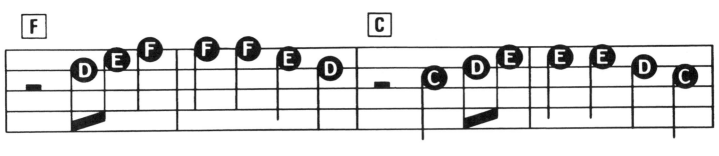

and it don't seem so lone - ly, we fill it up with on - ly
hurt - in' runs off my shoul - der. How can I hurt when hold - in'

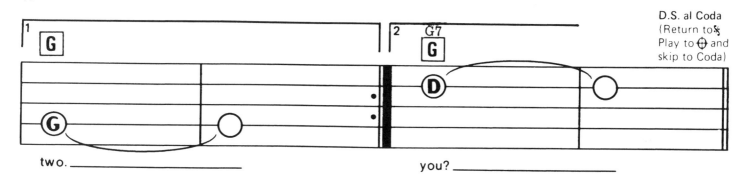

D.S. al Coda
(Return to %
Play to ⊕ and
skip to Coda)

two. _____ you? _____

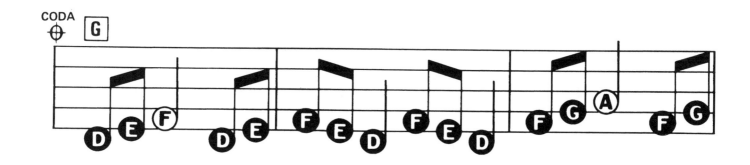

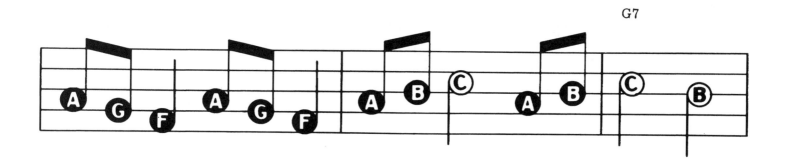

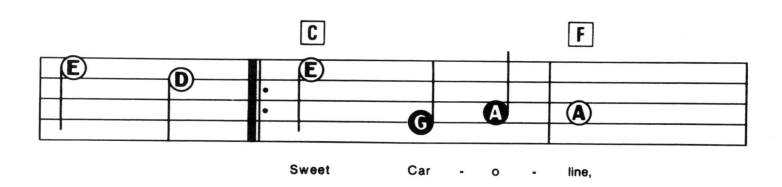

Sweet Car - o - line,

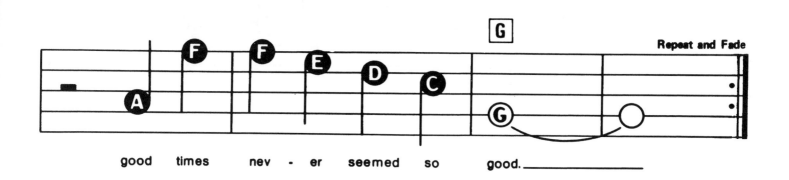

good times nev - er seemed so good. _____

Repeat and Fade

That's What Friends Are For

Registration 1
Rhythm: Rock or Pops

Music by Burt Bacharach
Words by Carole Bayer Sager

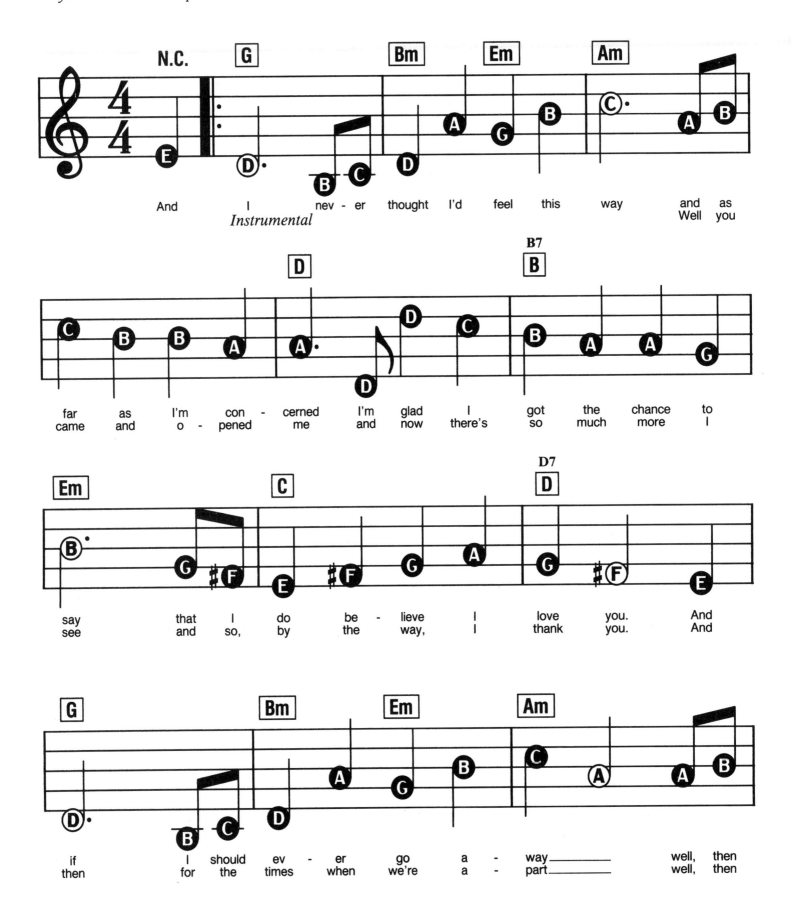

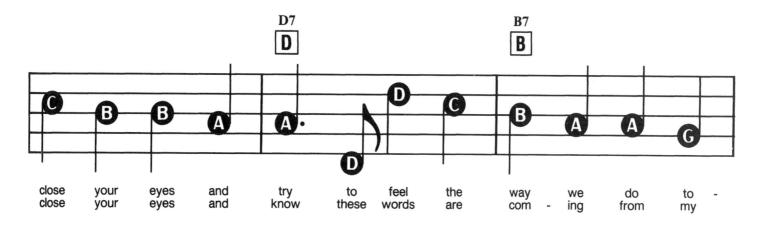

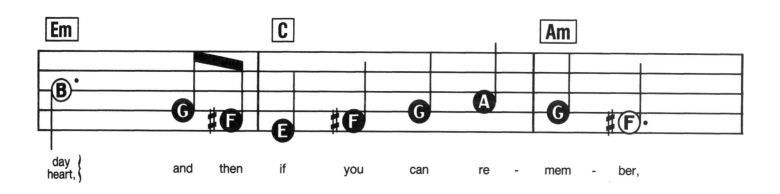

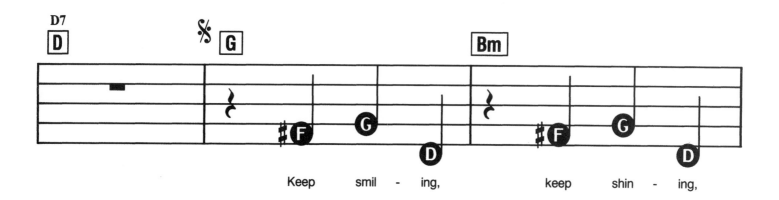

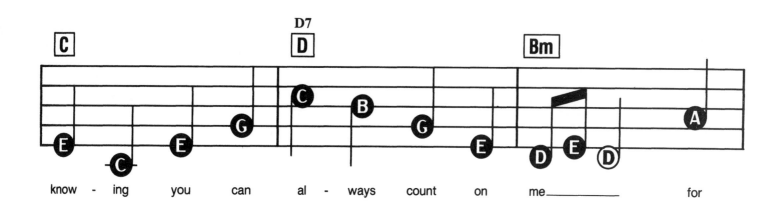

156

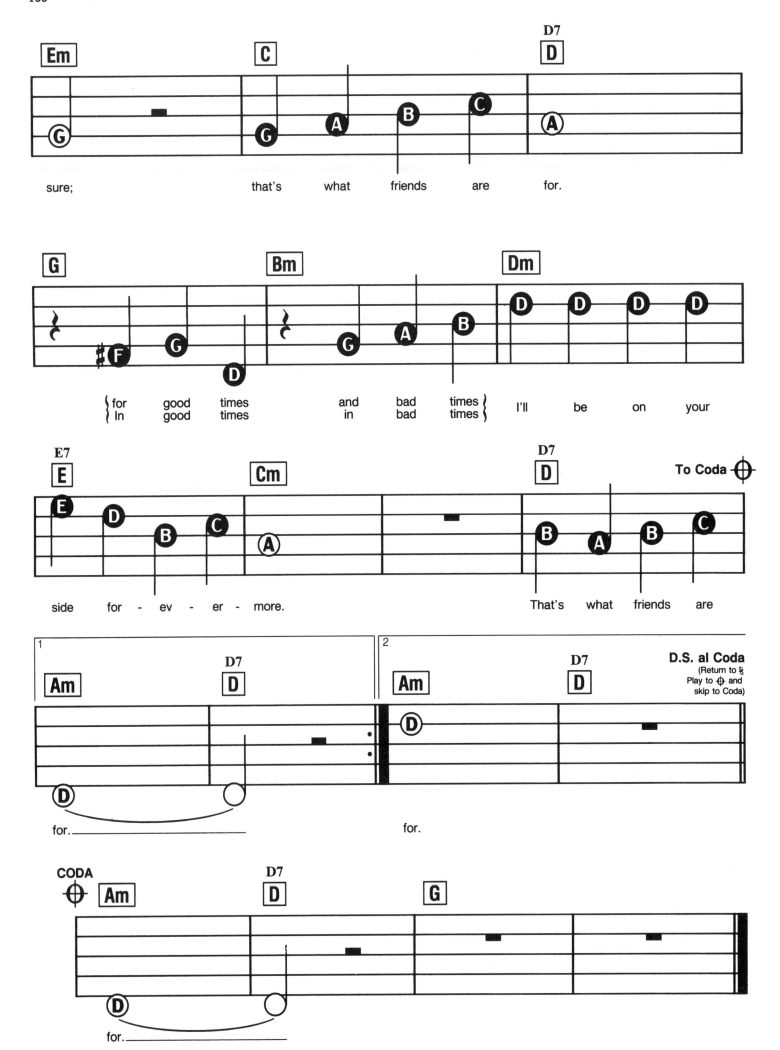

A Thousand Miles

Registration 4
Rhythm: Rock or Dance

Words and Music by
Vanessa Carlton

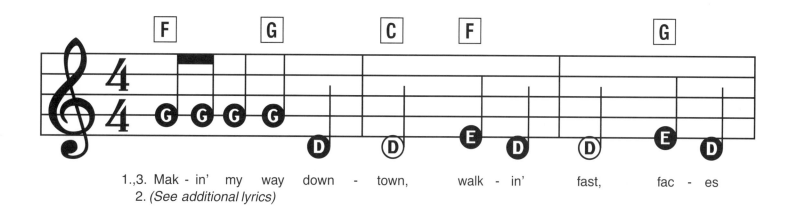

1.,3. Mak - in' my way down - town, walk - in' fast, fac - es
2. (See additional lyrics)

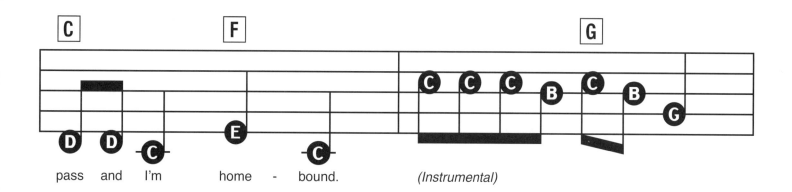

pass and I'm home - bound. (Instrumental)

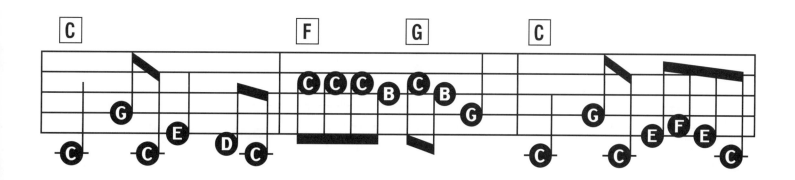

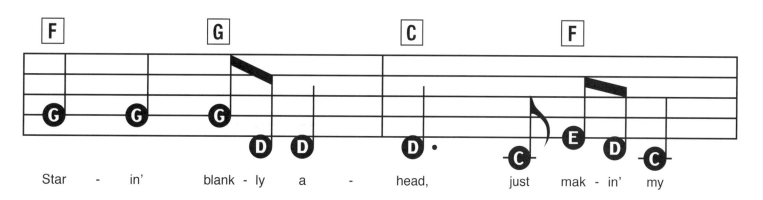

Star - in' blank - ly a - head, just mak - in' my

way,   mak - in'   a   way &underline;   through the crowd.

(Instrumental)

And   I   need   you, &underline;

and   I   miss   you,

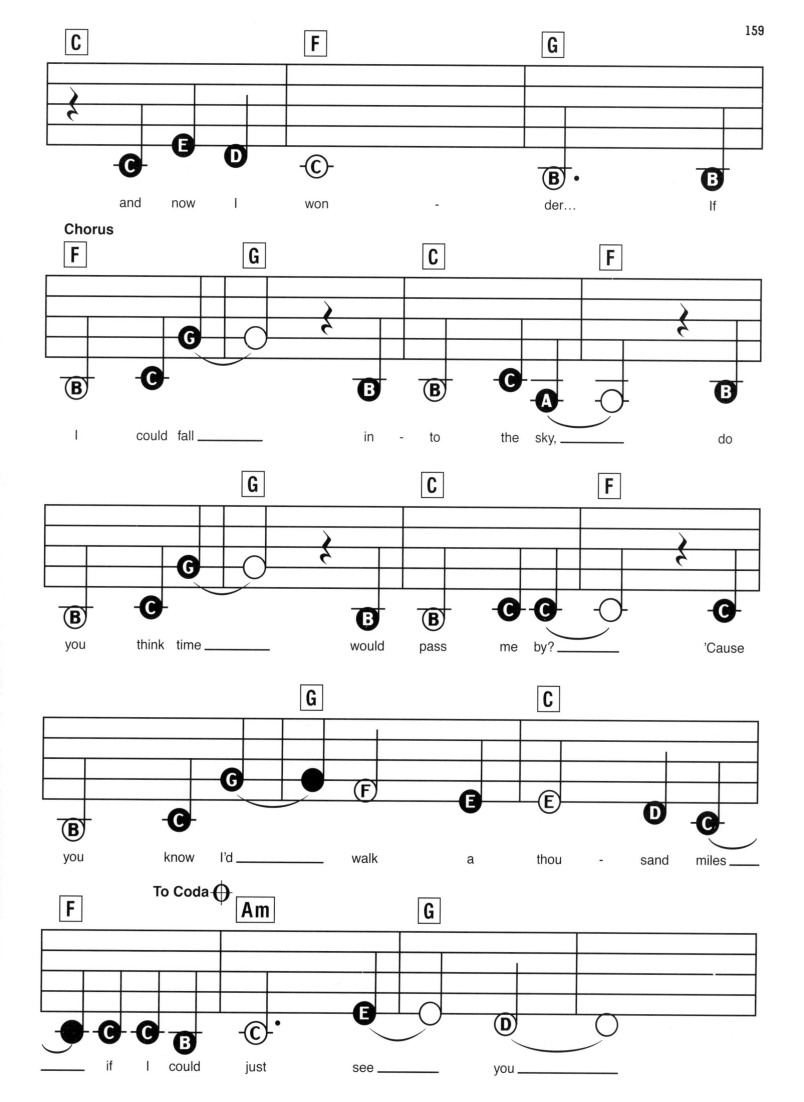

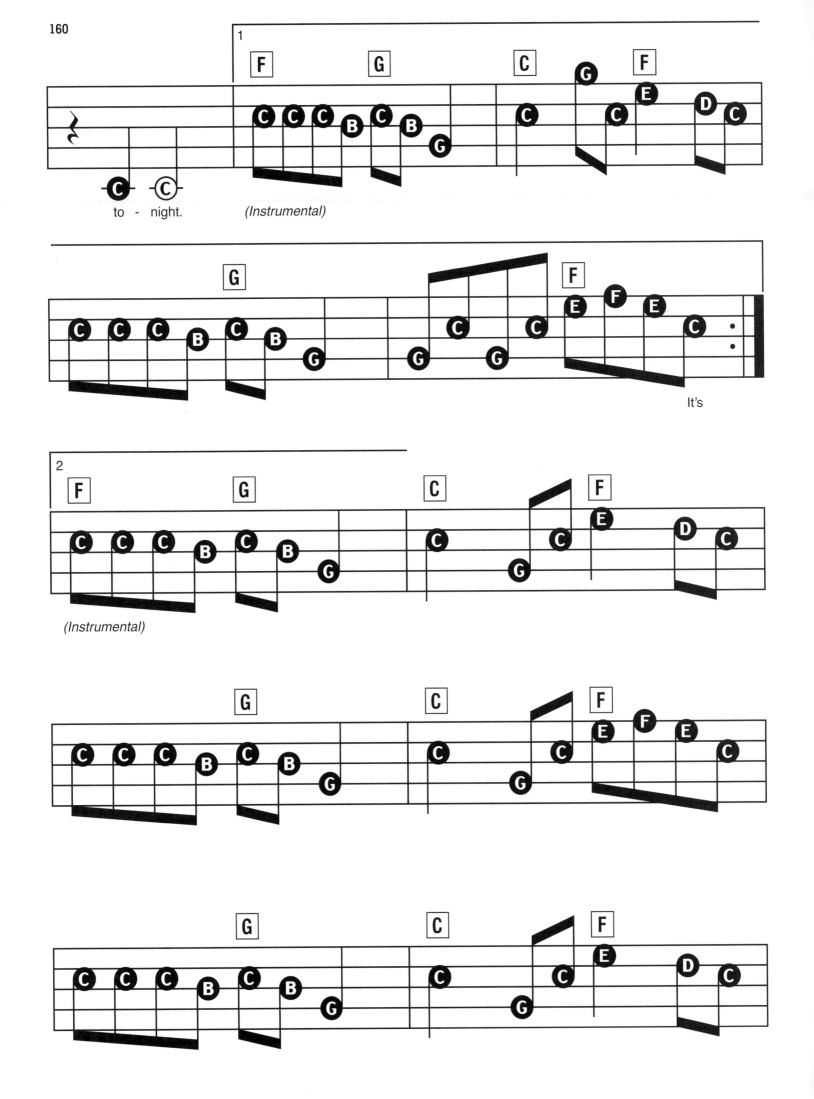

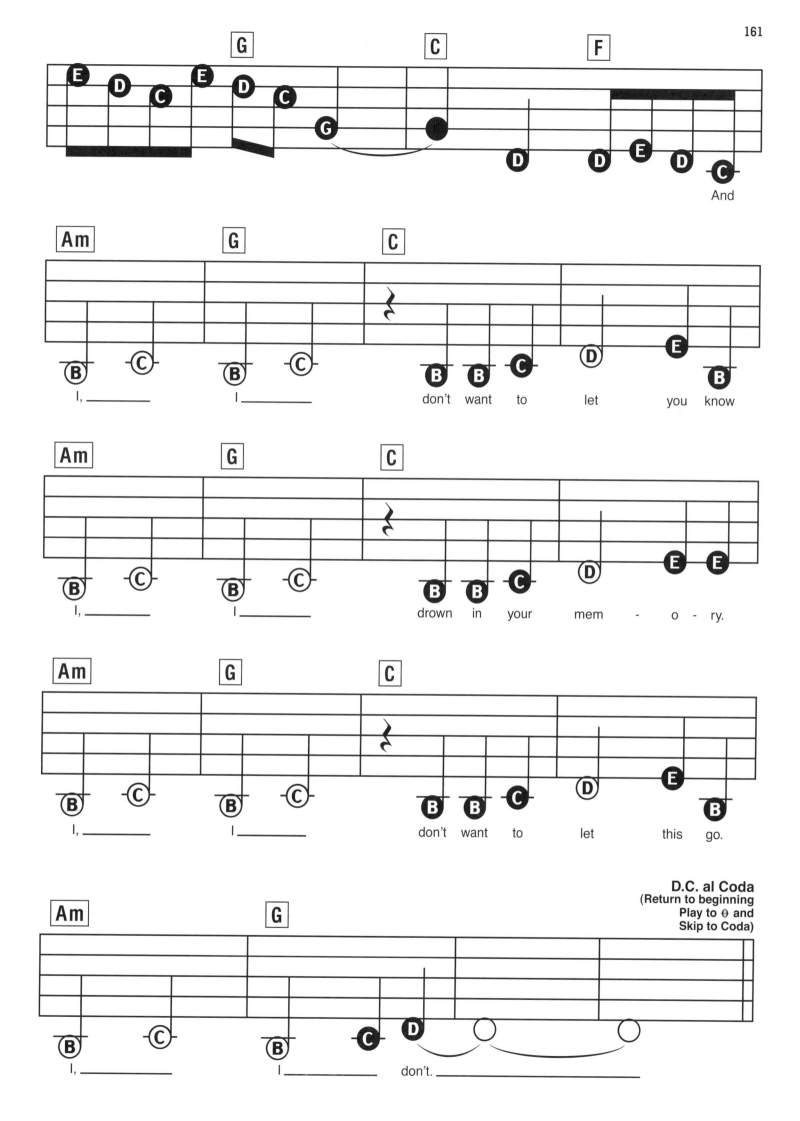

D.C. al Coda
(Return to beginning
Play to ⊕ and
Skip to Coda)

162

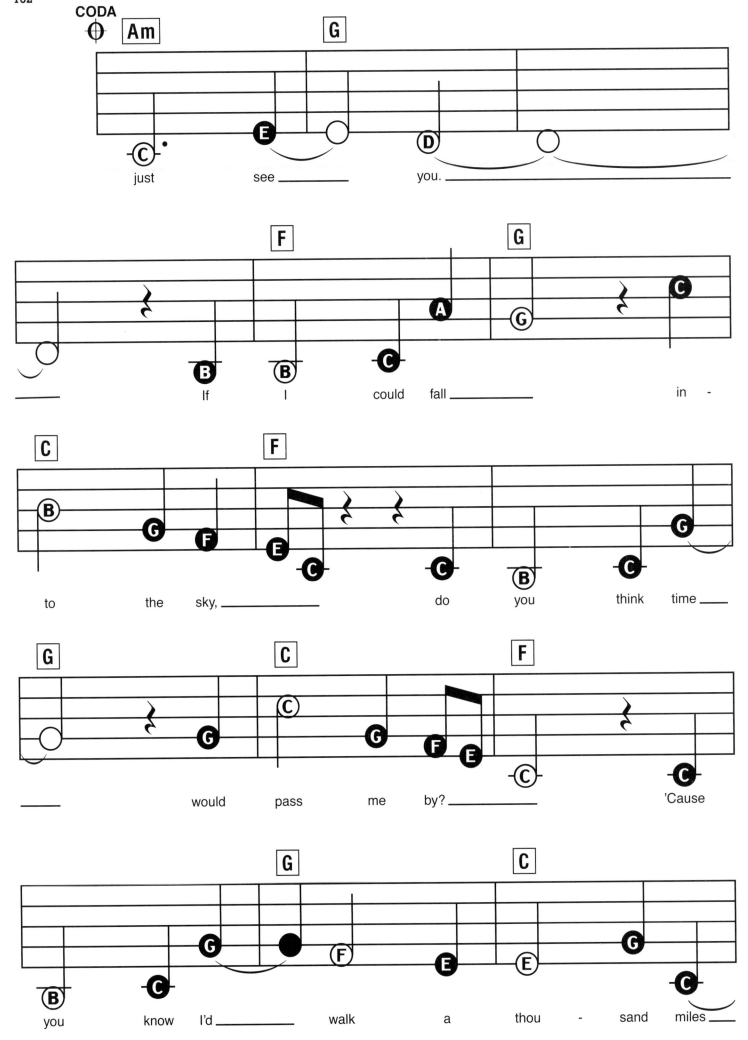

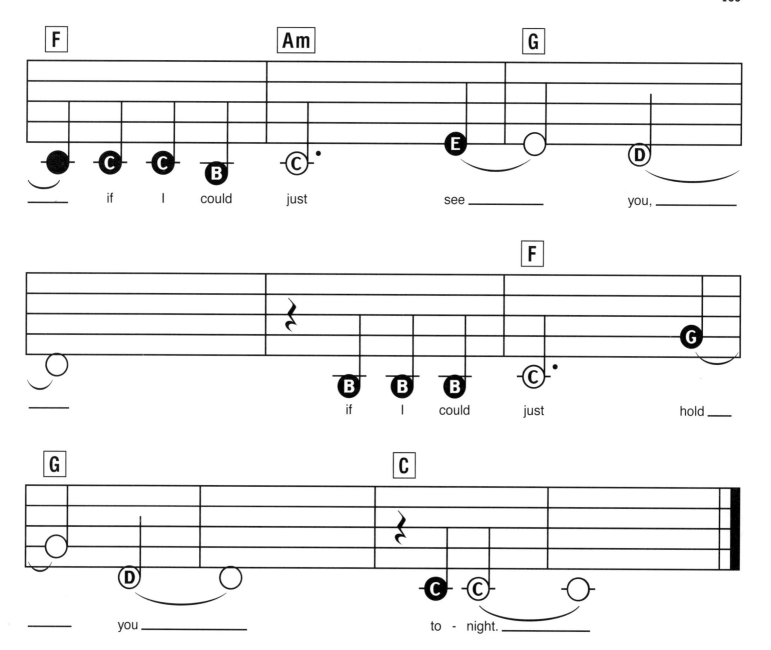

Additional Lyrics

2. It's always times like these when I think of you
And wonder if you ever think of me.
'Cause everything's so wrong and I don't belong
Livin' in your precious memory.
'Cause I need you,
And I miss you,
And I wonder...
Chorus

Wave

Registration 8
Rhythm: Bossa Nova or Latin

Words and Music by
Antonio Carlos Jobim

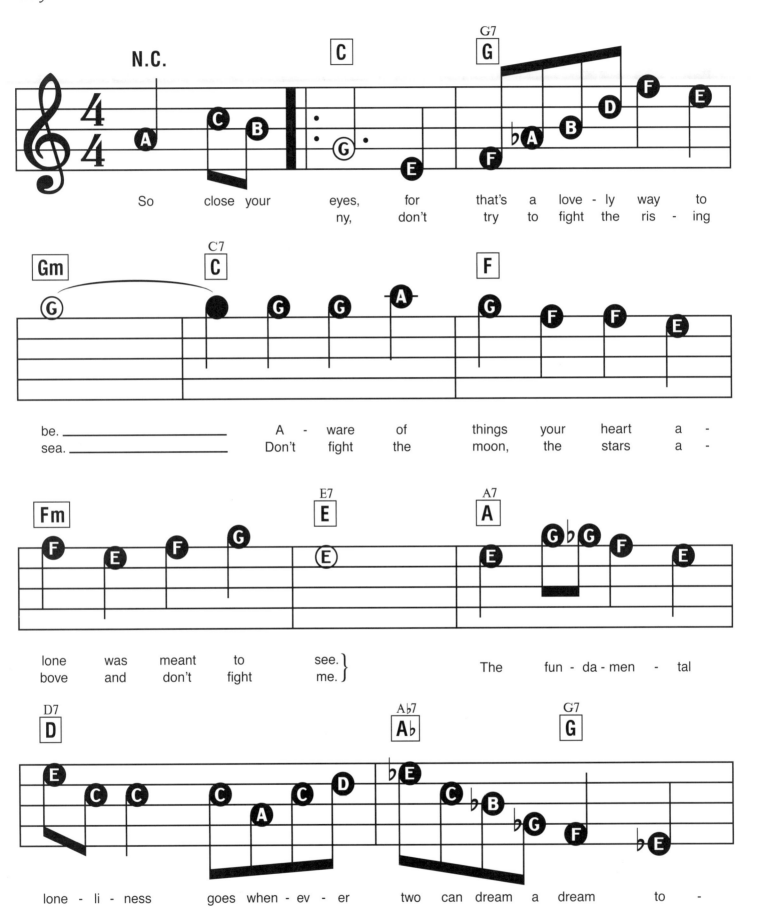

165

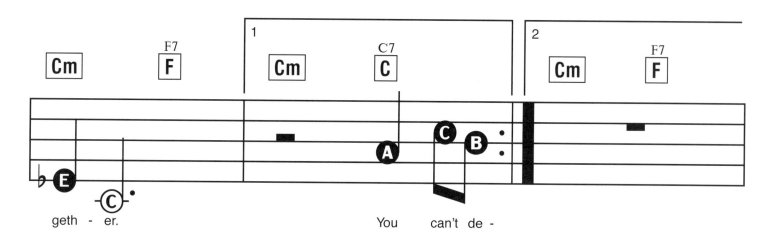

geth - er.   You   can't de -

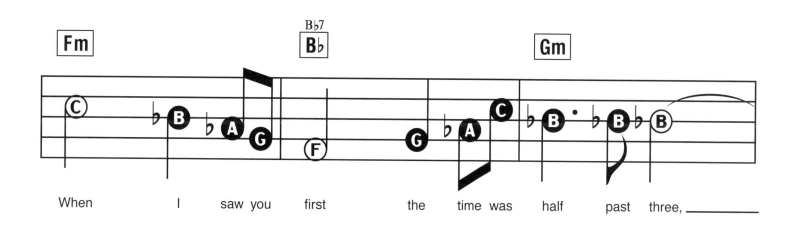

When   I   saw you   first   the   time was   half   past   three, _____

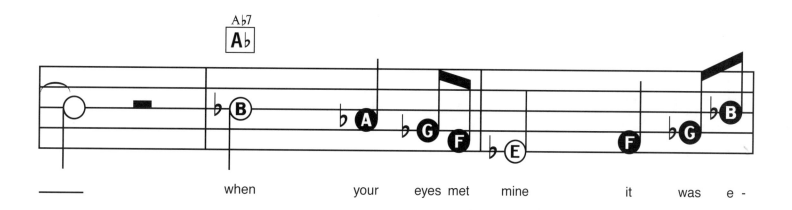

_____   when   your   eyes met   mine   it   was   e -

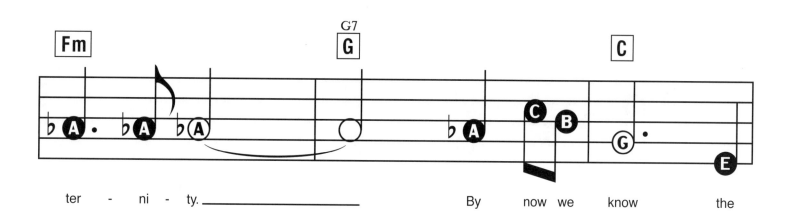

ter - ni - ty. _____   By   now we   know   the

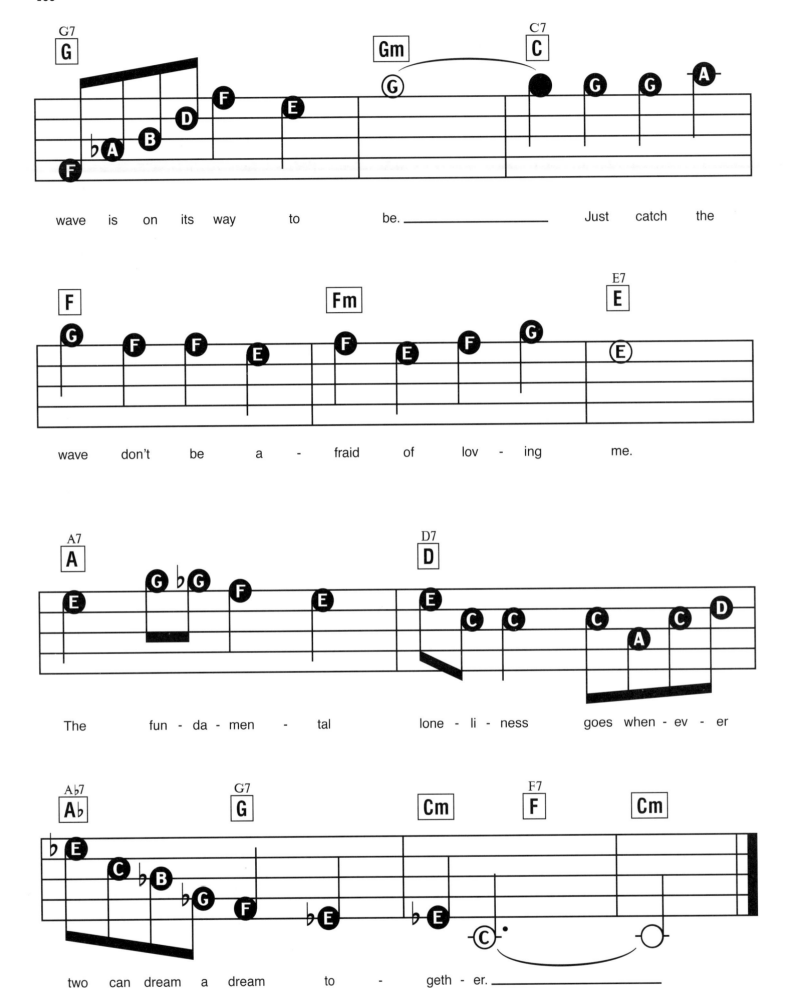

wave is on its way to be. _____ Just catch the

wave don't be a - fraid of lov - ing me.

The fun - da - men - tal lone - li - ness goes when - ev - er

two can dream a dream to - geth - er. _____

Time After Time

Registration 3
Rhythm: Rock or Jazz Rock

Words and Music by Cyndi Lauper
and Rob Hyman

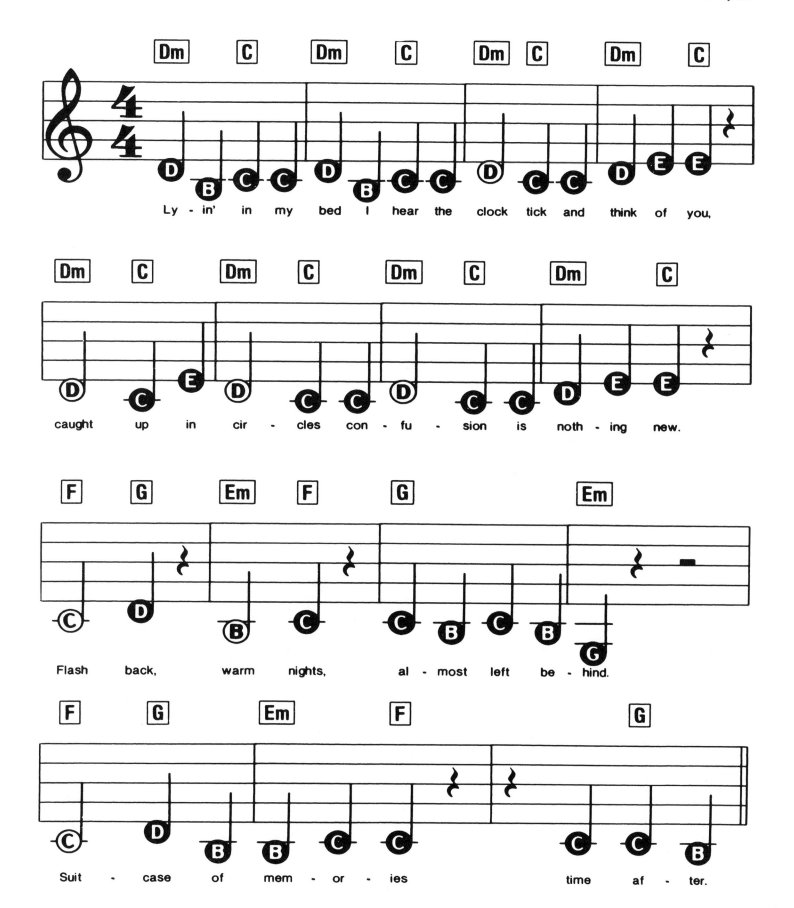

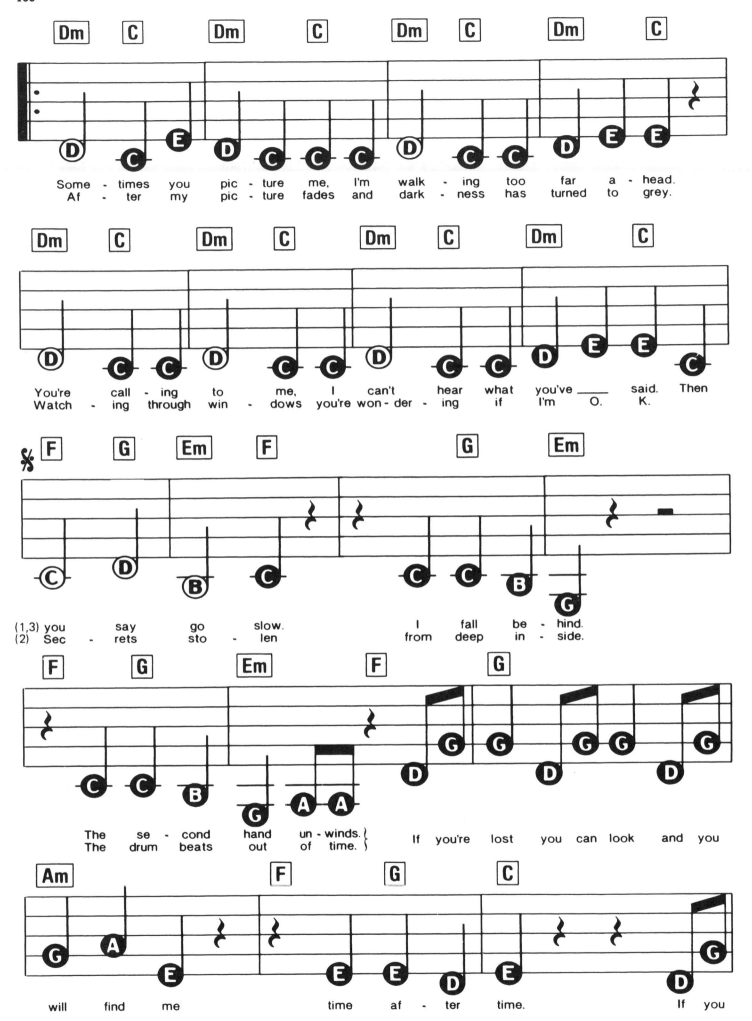

169

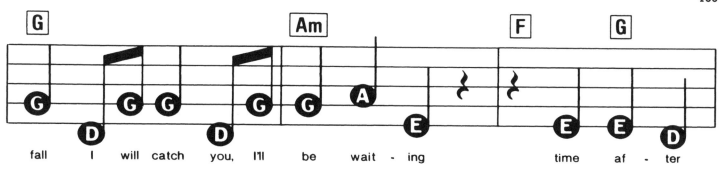

fall   I   will   catch   you,   I'll   be   wait - ing   time   af - ter

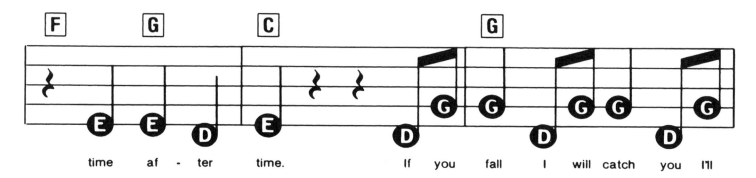

time.   { If   you're   lost   you   can   look   and   you   will   find   me
        { (Instrumental)

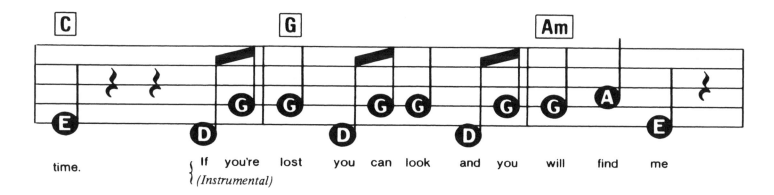

time   af - ter   time.   If   you   fall   I   will   catch   you   I'll

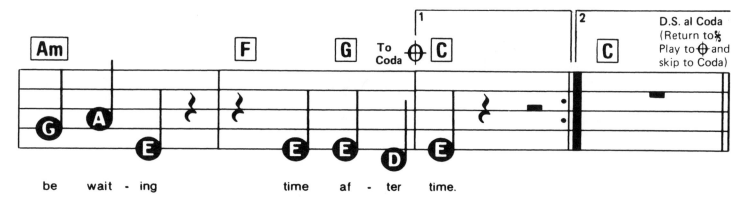

be   wait - ing   time   af - ter   time.

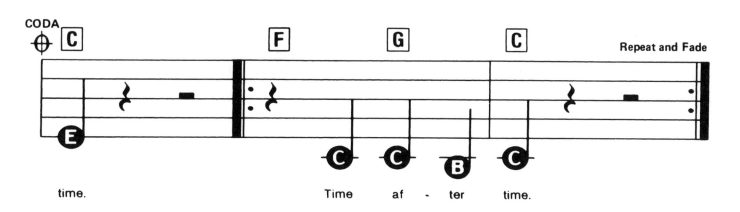

time.   Time   af - ter   time.

You Are the Sunshine of My Life

Registration 7
Rhythm: 8-Beat or Bossa Nova

Words and Music by
Stevie Wonder

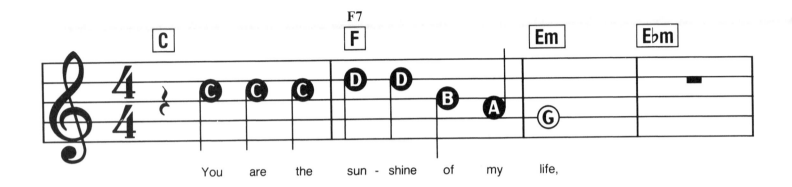

You are the sun - shine of my life,

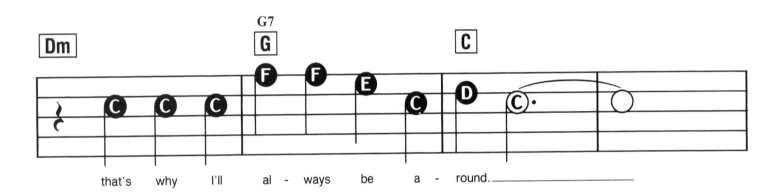

that's why I'll al - ways be a - round._____

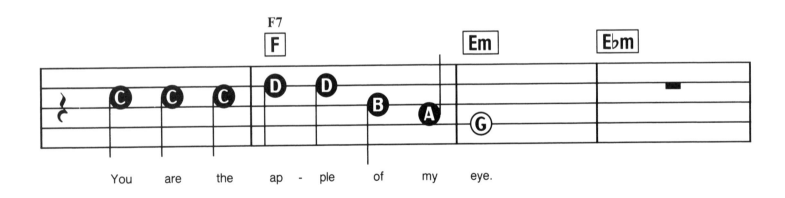

You are the ap - ple of my eye.

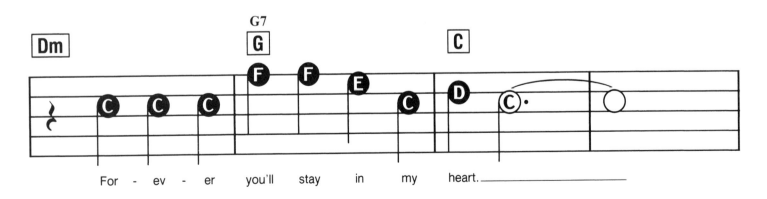

For - ev - er you'll stay in my heart._____

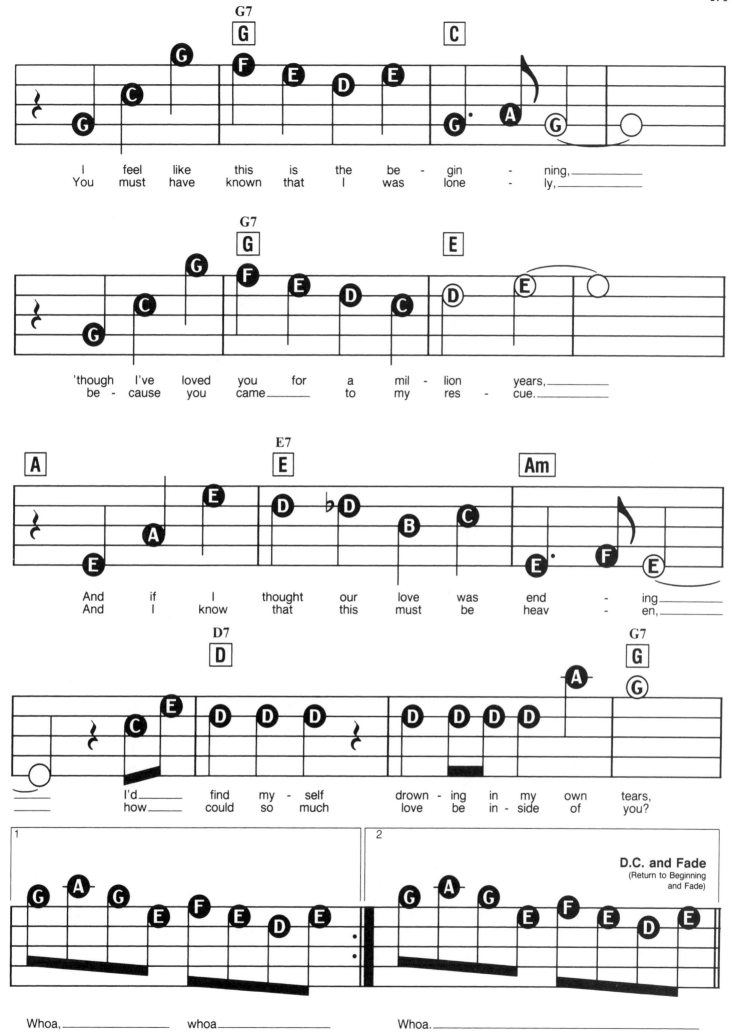

You Belong to Me

Registration 5
Rhythm: Disco or 16-Beat

Words by Carly Simon
Music by Michael McDonald

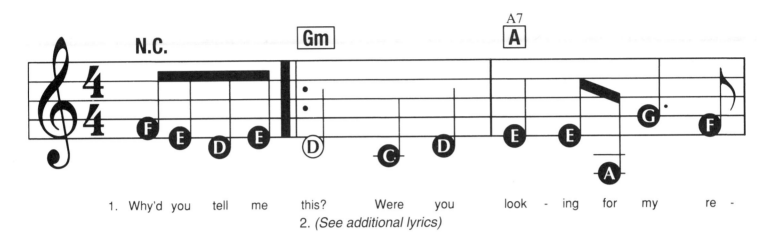

1. Why'd you tell me this? Were you look - ing for my re -
2. *(See additional lyrics)*

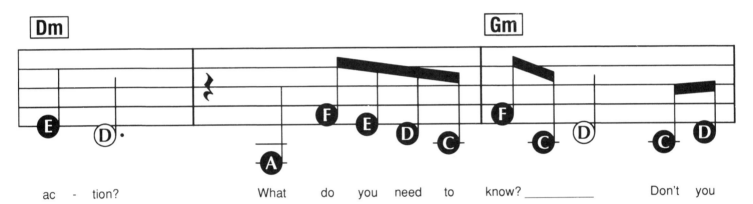

ac - tion?   What do you need to know? _____ Don't you

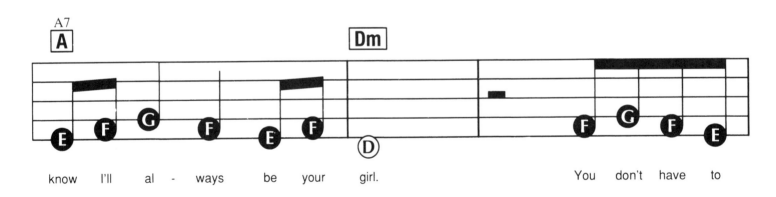

know I'll al - ways be your girl.   You don't have to

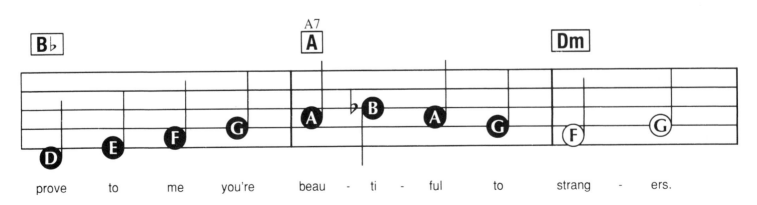

prove to me you're beau - ti - ful to strang - ers.

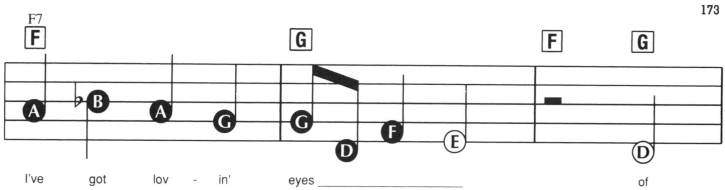

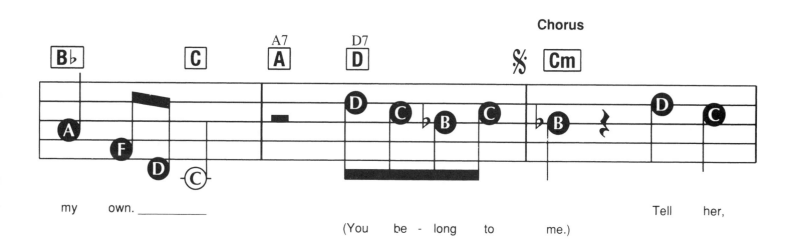

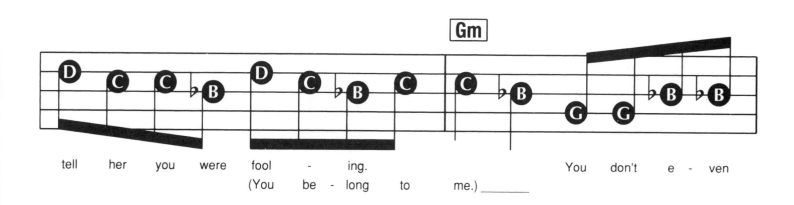

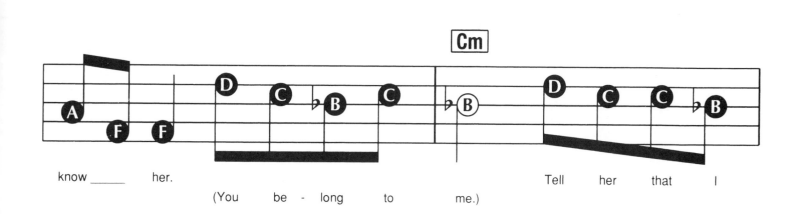

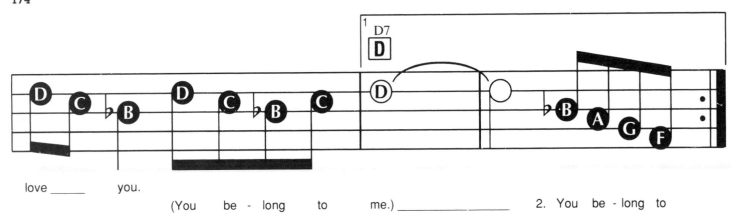

love _____ you. you. (You be - long to me.) _____ 2. You be - long to

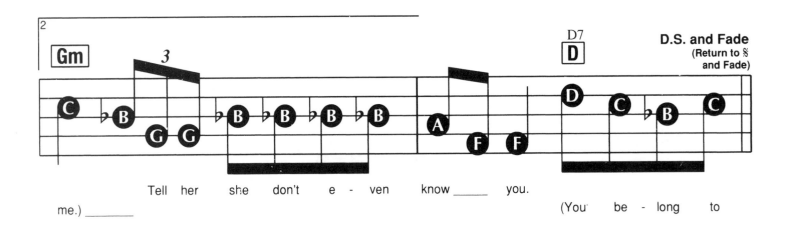

D.S. and Fade
(Return to %
and Fade)

me.) _____ Tell her she don't e - ven know _____ you. (You be - long to

Additional Lyrics

2. You belong to me. Can it be that you're not sure?
   You belong to me. Thought we'd closed the book, locked the door.
   You don't have to prove to me that you're beautiful to strangers.
   Well, I've got loving eyes of my own, and I can tell . . .

Chorus 2:
You belong to me. Can it be that you're not sure?
You belong to me. Thought we'd closed the book, locked the door.
You don't have to prove to me that you're beautiful to strangers.
Well, I've got loving eyes of my own, and I can tell . . .

You're My Best Friend

Registration 4
Rhythm: Rock or Shuffle

Words and Music by
John Deacon

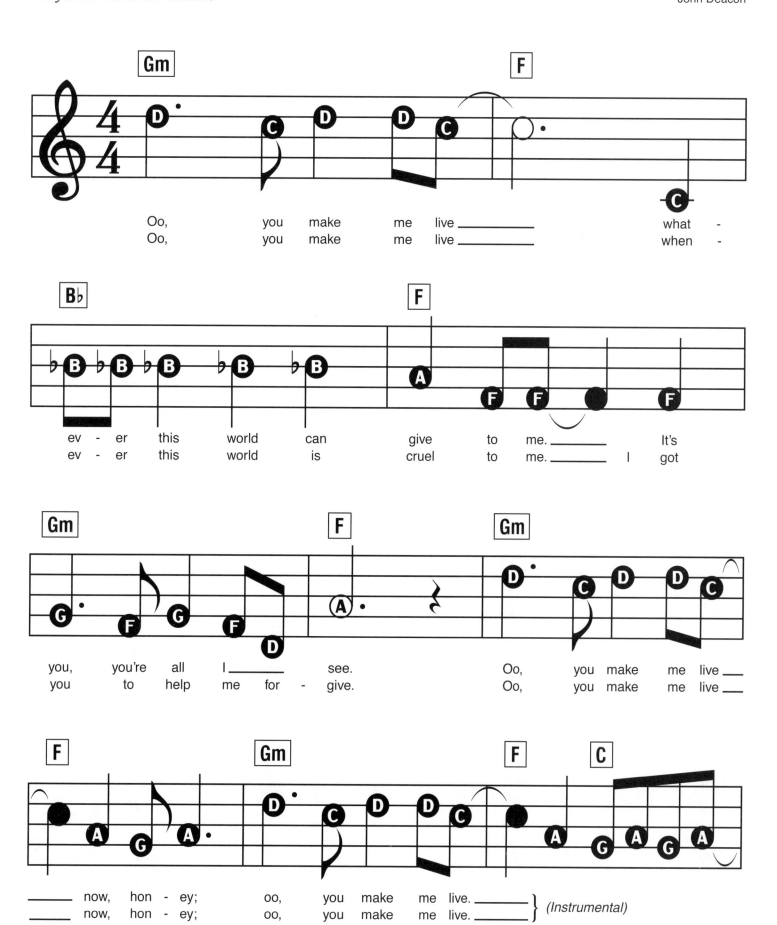

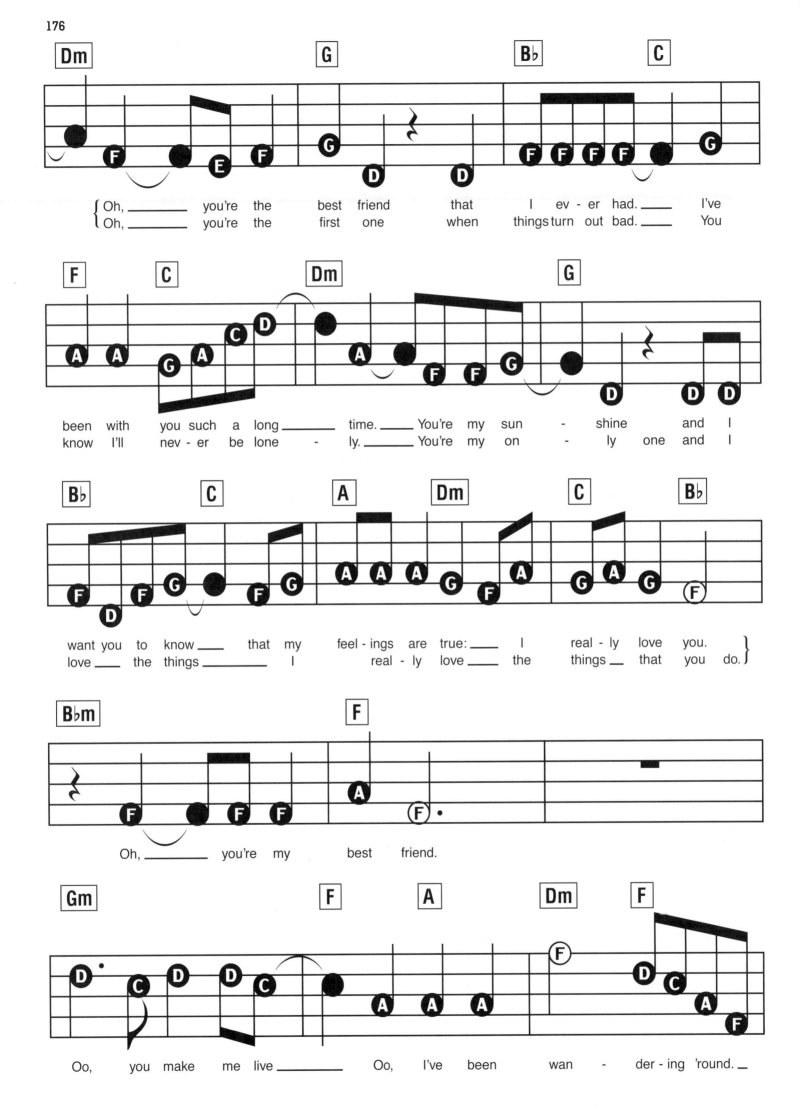

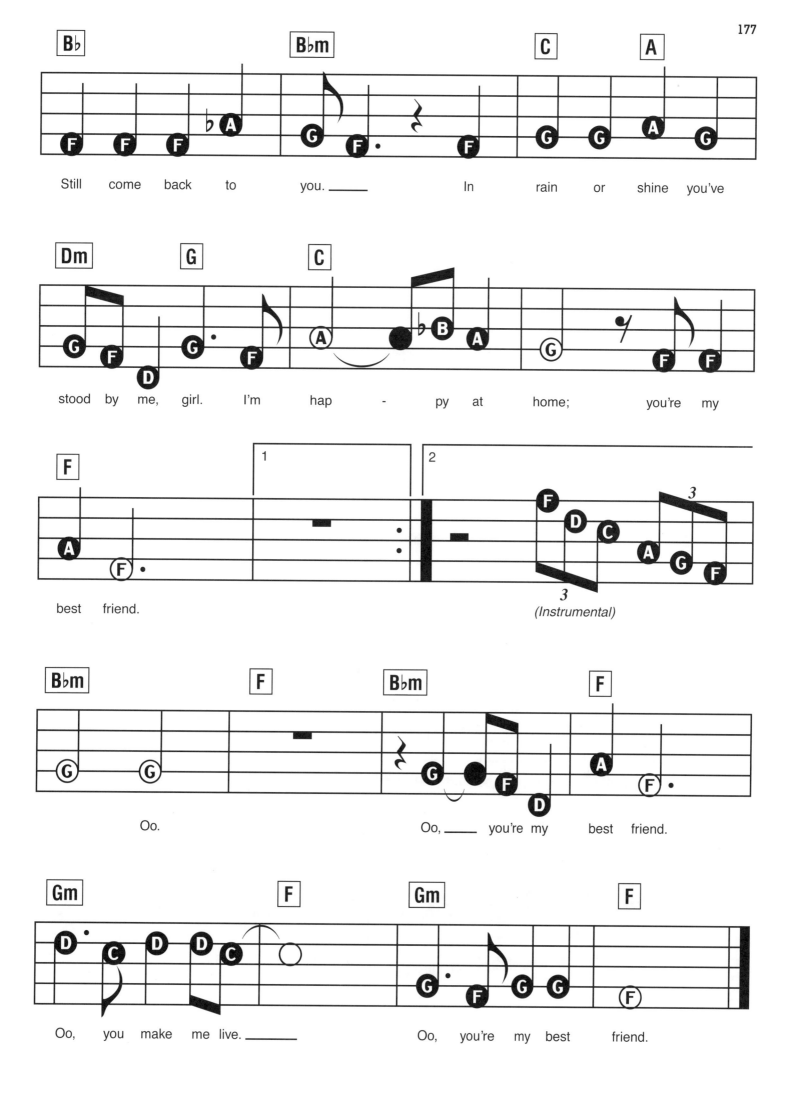

You're the Inspiration

Registration 1
Rhythm: Slow Rock

Words and Music by Peter Cetera
and David Foster

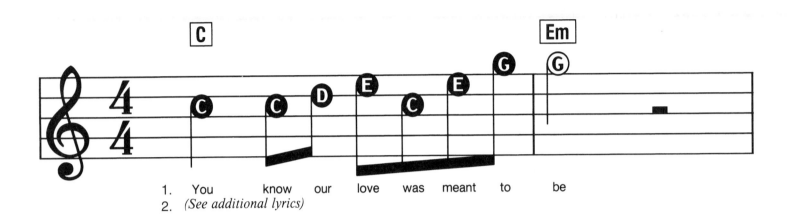

1. You know our love was meant to be
2. *(See additional lyrics)*

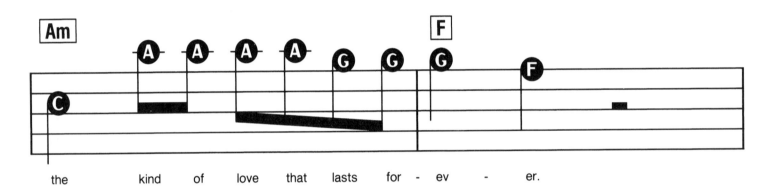

the kind of love that lasts for - ev - er.

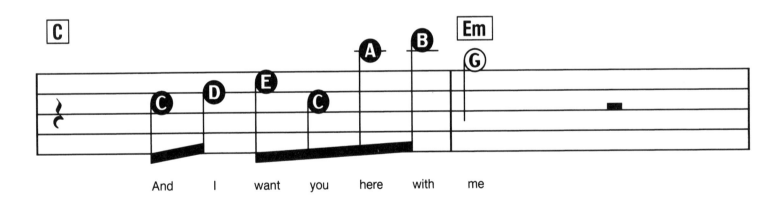

And I want you here with me

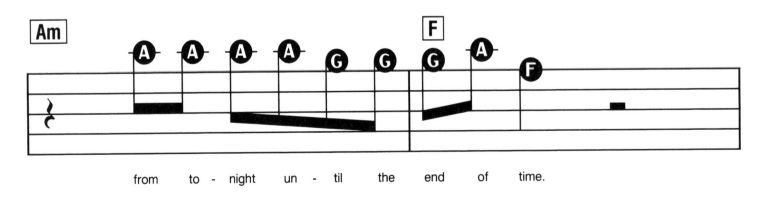

from to - night un - til the end of time.

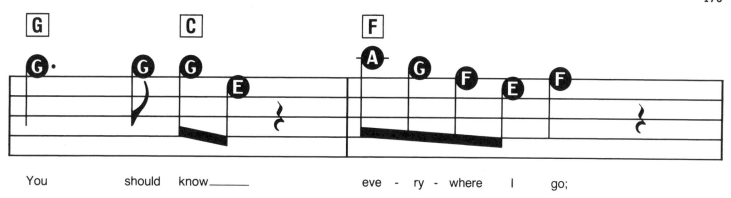

You should know____ eve - ry - where I go;

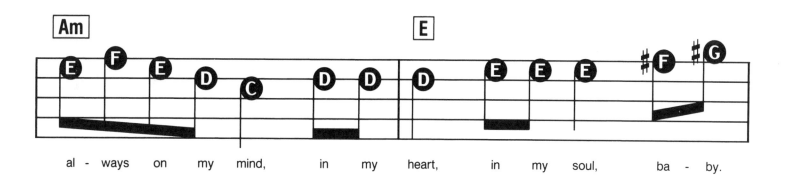

al - ways on my mind, in my heart, in my soul, ba - by.

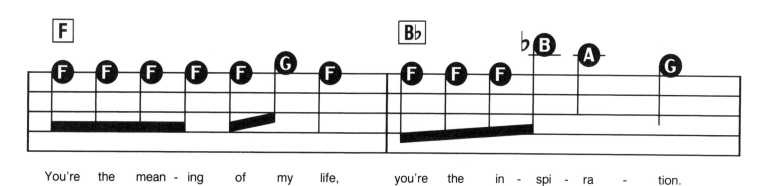

You're the mean - ing of my life, you're the in - spi - ra - tion.

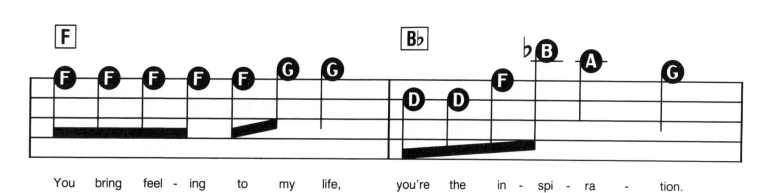

You bring feel - ing to my life, you're the in - spi - ra - tion.

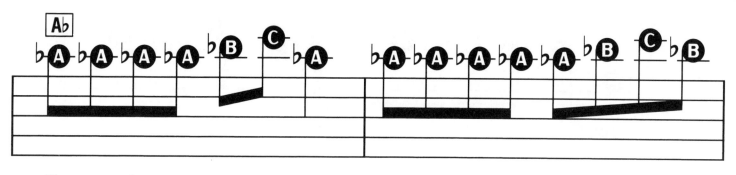

Wan - na have you near me, I wan - na have you near me say - ing

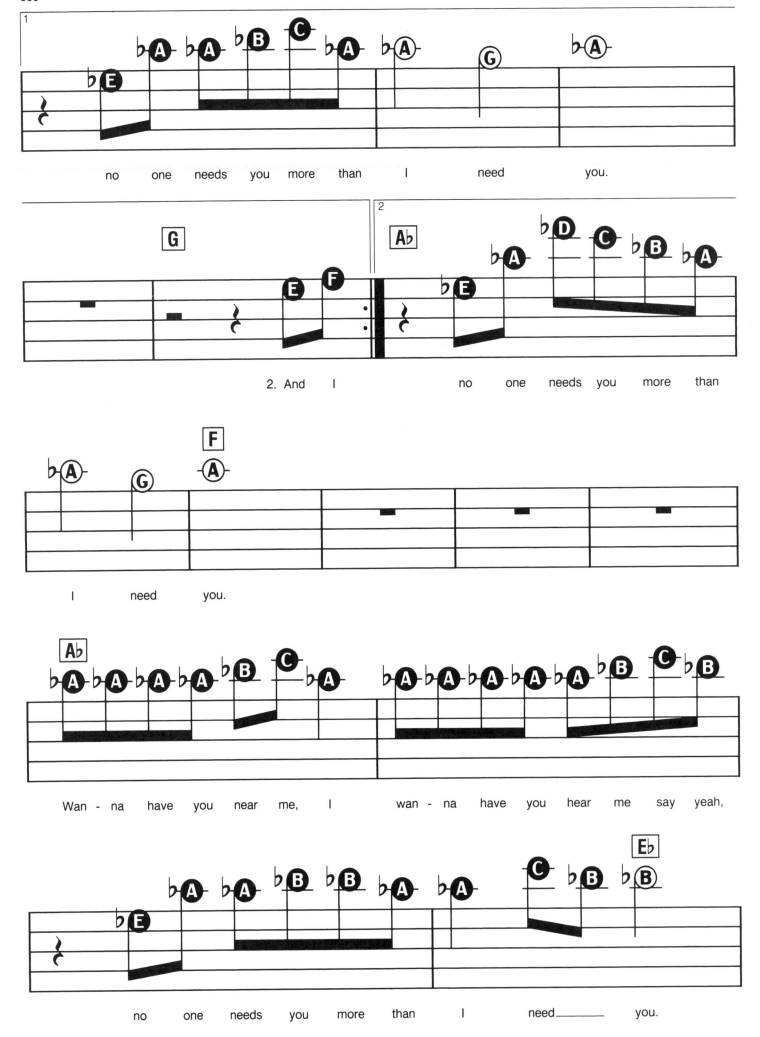

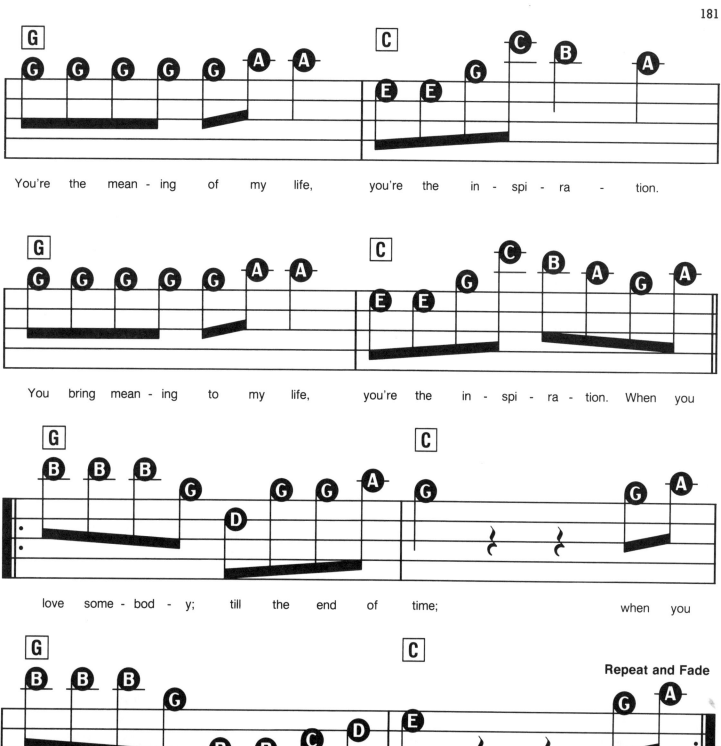

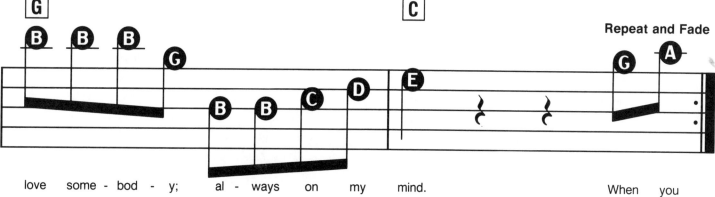

Additional Lyrics

2. And I know (yes, I know)
That it's plain to see
We're so in love when we're together.
Now I know (now I know)
That I need you here with me
From tonight until the end of time.
You should know everywhere I go;
Always on my mind, you're in my heart, in my soul.

 # Registration Guide

- Match the Registration number on the song to the corresponding numbered category below. Select and activate an instrumental sound available on your instrument.

- Choose an automatic rhythm appropriate to the mood and style of the song. (Consult your Owner's Guide for proper operation of automatic rhythm features.)

- Adjust the tempo and volume controls to comfortable settings.

Registration

1	Mellow	Flutes, Clarinet, Oboe, Flugel Horn, Trombone, French Horn, Organ Flutes
2	Ensemble	Brass Section, Sax Section, Wind Ensemble, Full Organ, Theater Organ
3	Strings	Violin, Viola, Cello, Fiddle, String Ensemble, Pizzicato, Organ Strings
4	Guitars	Acoustic/Electric Guitars, Banjo, Mandolin, Dulcimer, Ukulele, Hawaiian Guitar
5	Mallets	Vibraphone, Marimba, Xylophone, Steel Drums, Bells, Celesta, Chimes
6	Liturgical	Pipe Organ, Hand Bells, Vocal Ensemble, Choir, Organ Flutes
7	Bright	Saxophones, Trumpet, Mute Trumpet, Synth Leads, Jazz/Gospel Organs
8	Piano	Piano, Electric Piano, Honky Tonk Piano, Harpsichord, Clavi
9	Novelty	Melodic Percussion, Wah Trumpet, Synth, Whistle, Kazoo, Perc. Organ
10	Bellows	Accordion, French Accordion, Mussette, Harmonica, Pump Organ, Bagpipes